Surviving Life And Covid-19

Sharol Mason

CITIOFBOOKS, INC.
3736 Eubank NE Suite A1
Albuquerque, NM 87111-3579
www.citiofbooks.com
Hotline: 1 (877) 389-2759
Fax: 1 (505) 930-7244

Ordering Information:
Quantity sales. Special discounts are available on quantity purchases by corporations, associations, and others. For details, contact the publisher at the address above.

Printed in the United States of America.
ISBN-13:   Paperback   979-8-89391-306-4
              eBook   979-8-89391-307-1

Library of Congress Control Number: 2024919058

CONTENTS

To my loving family
Mom and Dad
Alice, Tim, Ted, Theresa, Paul, Evelyn, and Audrey
My children—Joey, Amy, and Ryan
Their dad, Ralph
All my grandkids and great-grandkids
All our foster children and extended family
Rick, my husband, soulmate, and best friend
You will all be in my heart forever
God bless you all.

INTRODUCTION

I finally begin my life story. My name is Sharol Mason. I live on a farm outside of Verndale, Minnesota. I am sixty-six years old at present, five feet two inches tall, and of medium frame. I have bright-blue eyes and light- brown hair on its way to whitish gray. My mom had pure white hair, and I'm so hoping mine turns like hers. It was so beautiful, just like she was.

I have worked from age fifteen until sixty-five years, at which time I retired. I now can begin our bucket list. I am married to Rick, my soulmate, and we have crossed a few things off our list already.

I have been a caregiver throughout my entire life. I've had the privilege of being a sister, auntie, wife, mother, grandmother, great-grandma, respite provider, foster parent, CNA, and a certified paraprofessional for many years. I have worn many hats quite proudly. My life has been the best it could be, and I wouldn't change a thing. My memories have been gathered over the many years, and I plan to share with family, friends, and avid readers in my book.

COVID BEGINS

Why now? Well, we are right smack-dab in the middle of a pandemic. It is the summer of 2020, and we became aware in March that COVID-19 is here. A pandemic, according to Google, refers to an epidemic that has spread over several countries and continents. It also affects a large number of people getting very sick or dying. It is also a noun meaning "a pandemic disease."

On March 11, 2020, the CDC officially declared the COVID-19 outbreak, a pandemic due to the global spread and severity of this disease. The difference between an epidemic and pandemic is this. If a disease is spreading like wildfire, it's an epidemic. If it's already spread like fire and is currently massive in its reach and impact, it's a pandemic. Good to know! News reports are saying it's a coronavirus that started with bats that were infecting animals at an open market in China. It then spread to the people there. In July 2020, in China, the numbers are 83,184 cases and already over five thousand deaths. This is current statistics we know of now. In the United States, specifically New York, they have 416,000 cases with a death toll already of 32,285. Florida is reporting 415,000 cases with over six thousand deaths. California has some but not sure of their numbers. It looks like the shore lines and outer edges of the US are where it's starting to spread.

With this kind of outbreak, hospitals and medical equipment are not available for so many cases. Many companies are already starting to make equipment and masks to come to the rescue. Ventilators are one of the most needed to give people oxygen along with PP (personal protection) like masks to protect the health-care staff and patients.

The funeral homes cannot take the influx of the dead bodies. They are being piled in freezer trucks stacked to the top. None of us can even fathom the devastating effects of this terrible virus.

The last pandemic was in 1918. That was called the Spanish flu. It was estimated that 500 million people or a third of the world population became infected with this virus. The death toll was estimated at least 50 million worldwide with 6,754,000 deaths in the US. It was known as the H1N1 influenza (flu) pandemic.

Our technology and sciences have come a lot further since then. We are hopeful that they will find a vaccine and antibodies sooner to fight this one. The longer this drags on, the more it feels like our families, neighbors, and friends died. It's lonely to not see them. It feels like a plague. It's definitely not normal, and the unknowns are very scary. No one panicked at first as we live in a rural community on a large farm. We have fresh air and sunshine, which is supposed to be good for this. In the 1918 pandemic, the soldiers and people on ships and boats were found to survive at a much higher rate if they were brought up from below and put on the deck. The sunshine saved some of them.

We have three steps that have been laid out for us to follow. Step one is to wash our hands for thirty seconds or more and try not to touch your mouth and face. It spreads through droplets from our mouth, nose, and bodily fluids. Step two is to social-distance, which means to stay six feet apart everywhere you go. Step three is to disinfect any area that collects germs or poses the transfer of germs while also wearing a mask over your nose and mouth. Many people are sewing their own masks, and some are donating them also.

Governor Walz, within two weeks, has mandated a stay-at-home order. Now it's feeling quite scary and real. It's all we hear on the news about COVID-19. That has been great, so we know how serious it has become.

The schools have started closing all around us, so the students went to distant learning. They each got a tablet computer and can connect to Zoom to get and do their assignments. I had retired after thirty-four years from working as a paraprofessional a year ago, so I did not experience this chaos. I watched my grandkids and neighbors go through this. It was devastating to be without your friends and teachers. There was no social life to be had. At first it was like a vacation, but a few weeks into it, they felt so lost. Parents had to step up and be their children's teachers and see that homework and projects got done and turned in.

This was among some of them losing their jobs because of shutdowns. The restaurants, cafés, coffee shops, hair salons all closed, many in a day's notice. We also had theaters, bars, and all athletic sports shut down. It was happening during basketball tournaments, and those couldn't even get played. So now there would be no spring sports like tennis, track, baseball, or camps for kids. Churches had to close until further notice. We had ours in Hope Chapel parking lot with the cars running to keep warm. Of course,

April and May were colder than normal, so there's very little to do. What a change for all of us. Rick, my husband, handled it way better than me. I was used to going to clean the Pioneer Journal three hours a week, but I got laid off because of the pandemic. I also had been going out to eat with the ladies once per week. Also our retirees got together the second Tuesday of every month. It all stopped abruptly.

Rick had retired several years before me due to health issues. He wore his back out doing construction for forty years. So he was becoming a homebody. Not me, it was very hard to have nothing to do. So of course, you did the next best thing and start cleaning every corner you can find in our house. I started with the cupboards, then closet, and did each room in the house.

Then I got all caught up on my scrapbooking for the grandkids. We have nineteen altogether and one great-grandson, Henry. I made a memory album for each of them from birth until they graduated, and they get them on their high school graduation. It is a very relaxing and positive hobby to see pictures as they grow. I feel it's way better than just having a picture on a cell phone. Not that I'm against cell phones, but there's a place and time for them. Currently I am working on ten of them.

Now it is getting warmer out, so we are doing projects outside. So far, I have painted the doghouse for Ace and the cathouse for the five cats— Hewey, Lewey, Medium, Harley, and Tom. They are scaredy cats except for Tom. He loves to be petted. The others run if you look at them. The mama cat has her babies in the woods and teaches them to hunt even though they know where the cat food is by the back door.

I also stained the picnic table and put stain on our house. It has to be done on cedar every five to seven years. Rick and our son Vernon tackled the shop cleaning, which was way overdue. You now can walk in there.

Vernon and his partner, Amber, moved here in March to stay on the farm with us. She worked in a hair salon by the cities, and he is a machinist. He was planning on moving back as he didn't like the rat race. Neither did she. So when she lost her job due to the pandemic, they bought a camper and parked it here with all the hookups, water, sewer, and heat and air. March, April, and May were colder than usual, so they went through a lot of propane. They were glad when summer came.

It lifted Rick up with all his pain from back issues to have Vernon home. He had two back surgeries this last two months, so he is still recovering. It was a blessing to have the extra help from Vernon and Amber. Rick helped them right back by putting a new kitchen floor in their camper and sturdy steps for the kids to get in and out of the camper. He also built Amber a cubby shelf to put her hair colors in for the salon. She started work at salon in June, and so did Vernon at a machining business. Now they are saving to buy a house in the fall. It is so nice when we can help one another out.

We have a camper, but Rick has not felt like going yet. Hopefully yet this summer we will get some trips that we had planned in retirement. At the moment we are so hoping to camp. Time will tell. We just got the camper back from a guy that put some mountain murals on it. When we bought it, they were sun weathered. I did the lettering on the camper, which took me a couple days, and it turned out great.

Rick and I keep busy with a big garden. We do a lot of green beans, onions, tomatoes, and cucumbers along with cabbage, broccoli, carrots, and squash. I have several flower beds to take care of also. I love fresh vegetables, and so does Rick.

We also have a lot of grass to mow, so as you see, we keep pretty busy but so wish we could venture out and take some trips. Hopefully soon!

The economy is in pretty bad shape. Many restaurants couldn't reopen even at 25 to 50 percent, so they closed. If you do go out to eat, the menus are not like before. They are limited as money is tight for these business so they cut down on supply. The government did come through for people on unemployment, so from March to end of July, they gave anyone on unemployment that weekly amount plus $600 more every week to help pay bills, rent, and food. It is now August 1, 2020, and there is no more $600 stimulus cheeks. A lot of people are mad because of this. Others were mad that essential workers didn't get it also for their exposure to this virus. It also created a trend of "why work?" attitudes as they made more sitting at home drawing a lot of money. Now some will have to find a job. We also got $4,200 per person from the government to help stimulate the economy. There is talk that more may be coming. Time will tell.

As of August 2020 now, we have to wear masks in public places, social- distance, and wash hands regularly. Also, resist large groups. Most places also take your temperature. So for birthday, retirements, parties, and graduations, many have a drive-by celebration by driving by their residence and honking, dropping cards off, decorating vehicles, balloons, etc. The graduation took place with social distances and in their cars in the parking lot to get diplomas. It works but is so very different.

Some places have opened up with tables set farther apart and masks required until you eat. Each state has kinda their own rules. In North Dakota, it's more lax. We do a lot of drive-through if we eat out as that is the safest. We also noticed there is mostly reruns on TV as they can't do live shows right now. There is not much for sports either.

Another impact of this is the medical field. They are doing a lot over the phone or telecommunications, FaceTime, and video chats and only what's necessary. I went in for a medical visit, and there was only a few people in the waiting room. That's been the case for Rick, who has seen several specialists for his yearly checkups.

Where we live here in Verndale and surrounding towns, there are hardly any cases and very few deaths compared to Minneapolis, St. Paul, St. Cloud, and large communities like that.

My oldest sister Alice's husband was just in a semi/ pickup crash, and his passenger was killed. He is in critical condition, and she is the only one that can see him for just a short period every few days. They are being very careful. So hospitals are being very strict about visitors so as to not spread this COVID-19 virus.

We do not know at this point if schools will reopen in September or not. We will keep up with this pandemic as I'm writing my story of my life. Praying for all that are struggling.

Our area schools are opening person to person to start. We have already canceled the fifth-grade orientation as our county is seeing more cases all at once. So far forty-six cases, zero deaths, but cases are spiking. It is getting real now as we have not seen the repercussions of this terrible disease.

As of now, there is no cure or vaccine, but they are working hard to find one. We are seeing positive tests in a daycare and among close friends, but so far we haven't had to quarantine…yet! My husband, Rick, is not real healthy. He has had two back surgeries this year and is healing from that. He has A-fib, heart trouble, and also kidney stones and arthritis, so we stay pretty close to home. We did venture out this week to Carlos State Park in August with some of his relatives. We each stay six feet apart as much as we can, no hugs, and wear masks to use facilities. It is so beautiful here by the lake and a real good place to think about what to write next. There are only fourteen that could make it because of COVID. It scared a lot off as large groups are not recommended. His brother Wayne; cousins David, Angie, and Josh; daughter Shona; son and partner, Vernon and Amber; his sister Dorla; and Karl. Shona brought the three grandkids— Adrian, Olivia, and Emma. We had a blast learning to kayak for the first time for them. This is our yearly reunion on Rick's side. We go to a state park each year. It's so much fun and a good time to reconnect. We had a great time and always cherish our time together. This park is only an hour from us, so it was convenient for us.

Schools have now decided to go to distant learning. COVID has spiked in our area. They are being so cautious, and I feel it's very much common sense. The kids will survive. It's just going to be very different and not convenient for a lot of parents and caregivers. School will be taught online until further notice. I will keep COVID updated as I write more story.

SURVIVING LIFE AND
C◉VID-19

CHAPTER 1

Mom and Dad
The Early Years

My mother, Mary Baustian, was asked for her hand in marriage to my dad, Glen Curfman. They were close neighbors. It was on her eighteenth birthday, and they were at the movies. That was in August of 1947. On June 26, 1948, Glen and Mary were married in Fosston, Minnesota, at 10:30 a.m. at the Catholic church. It was a small wedding, and they had pictures taken in Bagley, Minnesota, at the studio. From there, they went to her parents' farm in Bagley and had dinner and reception. Then they went to a motel in Bemidji by the lake for their honeymoon. My mom had (five) brothers and sisters. My dad had eleven brothers and sisters. Families were large back then, and they lived very simple lives.

CHAPTER 2

Murder on a Small Farm

My mom's parents were neighbors to my dad's parents. That's how Mom and Dad met. So when Mom left home and married my dad, Grandma and Grandpa sold their farm. Mom was youngest and last to leave. They moved toward Bagley and sold their farm to Carl and Enger Baglien. The next year, Carl went missing, and so the Cornfield Coquette story begins. My other grandpa, Alfred Curfman, helped solve the crime. He lived a quarter mile away from where the murder took place.

CASE OF THE

Cornfield
Coquette

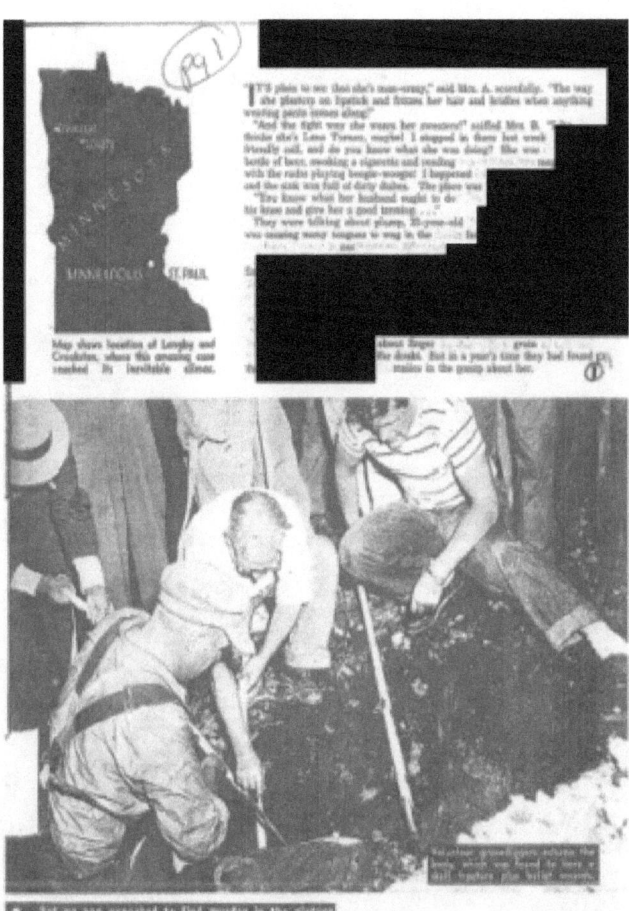

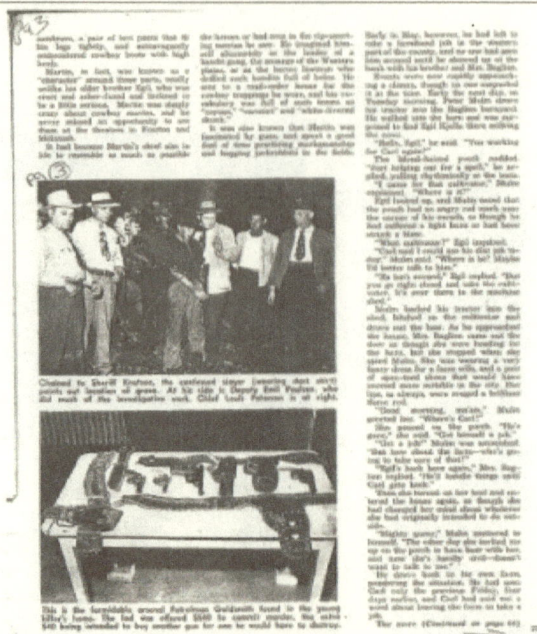

Coquette, *which means* a seductive woman who uses her sex appeal to exploit men.

This is a true crime story that affected my grandparents on both sides. I can remember them talking and being taken back by it even after years later. We were not told about it as kids for specific reasons. You will learn why as I recollect what happened back in summer of 1949.

My grandma and grandpa, Baustian, lived on a farm by Lengby, Minnesota. They raised all six kids there. Grandma and Grandpa Curfman lived a mile from them on another farm. That's how Mom and Dad met as neighbors. My mom got engaged to my dad on her eighteenth birthday at the movies. They were married June 26, 1948, and relocated to their first home in Solway, Minnesota. It wasn't too far from their families either. Glen got a job there as a custodian, and Mary helped in the kitchen at the school. They were happily starting their family here.

Since Mary was the last to get married and leave the farm, Grandma and Grandpa realized it was time to sell and downsize. They sold it to a couple with one child in the spring of 1948. Grandma and Grandpa moved to Bagley, Minnesota, at that time to another smaller farmhouse. Forty-two- year-old Carl Baglien had moved with his wife, Enger, age thirty-three years old, and thirteen-year-old son Kenneth. They had formerly operated a farm only a dozen miles to the West, and reports filtered in from that sector that Mrs. Baglien was a "queer one"!

The neighbor, being hospitable and hardworking, a solid and thrifty lot, had taken the rumor about Enger with a grain of salt. They gave her the benefit of the doubt. But in a year's time, they realized that there was a lot more truth than malice on the gossip about her. They still felt a woman should not necessarily be condemned for having a smoke, a beer, or listening to jazz music. But doing all that at the same time might not be a good way to act, and no good could come of it. The talk continues as time goes on.

One incident, my Grandpa Curfman heard, was one of the other neighbors was asked by Carl if he could take him to town to see where this missus was. The neighbor agreed. They checked out Lengby, the small town close by, but his car wasn't there. They drove to Fosston to locate her and found the car parked at one of the taverns. He was understandably angry but tried to conceal it as the neighbor drove him home. Why wouldn't a hardworking farmer be upset when he knew full well she should be home cleaning and having supper on the table not to mention leaving her young son home? The neighbors, including my grandpa and grandma, were pretty sympathetic to Carl. The neighbor woman tried to reach out to Enger, but she was quite antisocial in their eyes. Grandma said that was pretty unusual. They all looked out and helped one another in need.

On June 24, 1949, another neighbor reported that he went to Carl's farm to borrow a cultivator. When he drove in the yard, he noticed the missus on the front porch, sipping beer and moving to some music. "Hi," she called, "beer?"

The neighbor declined with a thanks. He asked where Carl was. She answered, "Over in the barn I guess. Why don't you come up on the porch and rest awhile?"

He explained he was in a hurry and drove to the barn. "That woman," he told others, "had the shortest shorts, which showed skin on her legs and thighs and a knitted polo shirt that accented every curve of her chunky body, and she asked me to have a beer with her." It was a Friday, and Carl was busy fixing and working the farm with his own two hands. He asked Carl, "I was wondering if I could use your cultivator next week sometime? If that's all right with you."

"Tuesday's fine," Carl cheerfully told him. "I'll have it ready first thing in the morning."

They had shared equipment occasionally. A month earlier, he had borrowed him the manure spreader. Carl did have a hired hand, Egil, who helped them.

He drove out of the yard and caught the missus out of the corner of his eye. He couldn't help feeling it was quite peculiar. Carl was a fine farmer, and it was hard to understand that his wife didn't pitch in with the farmwork. It wouldn't do a woman any harm to help with milking and spring planting. A neighborhood consensus.

Bank Business

Monday, June 27, Enger was seen walking into the McIntosh Bank seventeen miles northwest of Lengley. She was accompanied by two young males. One was Egil, the hand Carl had hired to help him on the farm. The other was Egil's brother, Martin. Egil was twenty-one, and Martin was nineteen years old. Handing over the bank account book and withdrawal slip, the teller knew her as they had banked there several years. He counted out the money and asked her how Carl was.

"Oh, Carl's fine," she replied. "I won't be seeing him for a while. He's finished with planting and took a job aways away." A few customers in the bank were quite amused by Martin's attire. He wore a sombrero, a pair of Levi's pants that fit his legs tightly, and high-heeled, extravagant, embroidered cowboy boots. They chuckled as Martin was known as quite the character around those parts. The word was he loved cowboy movies, and his chief aim in life was to resemble those heroes or bad men in what he saw. The more he looked and acted like them, the better. He got his cowboy trappings he wore from a mail-order house. He used words like *cayuse*, *varmint*, and *white-livered skunk*. He was also known in the community as having a love of guns. He bagged rabbits and practiced his marksmanship in the past. No one had seen Martin for a few weeks as he had taken a job as a farmhand in another part of the county. Funny he showed up at the bank with his brother and Enger. By the way, Egil was more erect and sober faced and inclined to be much more serious.

The neighbor that needed to borrow the cultivator went back to Carl's farm on Tuesday to get it. He drove into the barnyard and walked up to the barn. He found Egil milking the cows. He said hello and asked, "You working for Carl again?"

Egil nodded, "Just helping for a spell," pulling at the cow teats.

He went on to tell him he had come for the cultivator and asked where it was.

Egil looked up, and the neighbor noticed a red mark by the corner of his mouth. It looked like a light burn or maybe a strike or blow to the mouth. Egil asked, "What cultivator?" and he told him he had been there Friday, and Carl said he'd have it ready for him. The neighbor asked where Carl was, and Egil just said, "He isn't around." He then told him where the cultivator was in the machine shed and to go ahead and take it.

The neighbor hooked it up, and as he was leaving the farm, Enger was on the porch dressed in a fancy dress and open-toed shoes along with flame- red lipstick. He paused long enough to say good morning and ask where Carl was. She said, "He's gone. Got himself a job." He then asked who would take care of the farm. She replied, "Egil's back here again. He'll handle things until Carl gets back."

She then turned and went in the house. The neighbor thought this was quite a change from last time. Now she's civil, no beer, and no invite to the porch. He drove back to his own farm, wondering why Carl hadn't mentioned anything during their conversation last Friday about taking a job. It was quite peculiar but then chalked it up to maybe easy-going Carl had finally gotten a belly full of the woman. Maybe he was clearing out in order to pursue his own sanity. He put it all out of his mind for the time being.

Friday, July 1, Enger went to the bank in McIntosh. She was alone this time. She asked the teller if he'd cashed a check for her. She told him, "Carl's got this new job, but even with Egil with us again, we've got more than we can handle. We have decided to sell some of our cattle." The check was from a large St. Paul commission house. It was payment for twelve heads of cattle. Since it was a very sizeable amount, the teller decided to show it to the cashier.

The cashier realized Carl and Enger had a mortgage with the bank of Fosston, and part of this check would go toward paying that. A phone call to the bank in Fosston confirmed his belief. He then had to tell Enger regretfully and explain to her the mortgage matter would have to be straightened out.

She was quite angry and exhaled a cloud of cigarette smoke. Even with taking care of the mortgage, she demanded her part right now.

They told her she would have to go to that bank and clear

the matter with them, and she finally stomped out in visible resentment.

The neighbors were now very puzzled in the township with Carl's sudden departure, Egil doing the work, and now half his herd being slaughtered. Like my grandpa said, he knew from Carl he was building his herd to market milk.

One farmer boldly drove into Carl's farm. He found the place empty. The fields were not tilled or cultivated. The weeds were tall. He figured if Egil was looking after the place, he was doing a very poor job of it.

It was a puzzle, all right, but nobody wanted to be nosey or inquire the reasons for it. If a man and woman couldn't get along or were letting their farm go back, well, it was too bad but their own affair.

That was about it until on July 10, another neighbor, who had adjoining land, went to bring his cows from the pasture; there were six too many. He recognized that they were Carl's. He drove them across the field to his neighbor's place. On the way, he found four more and brought all ten back to Carl's farm. When he entered the barn, a pair of horses pricked up their ears. Their interest clearly showed they needed to be fed. The mangers were empty, and the stalls were so filthy dirty. They couldn't have been cleaned for days.

The neighbor was appalled at such neglect. The cows needed to be milked, so he went to the house and knocked on the door. He kept knocking with no avail. There was no car around, and it became evident no one was there. So he went home and sent his hired hand to take care of the animals. He then telephoned the chairman of the township board and told him what he had found that no one was there to tend to anything. The chairman made several calls to surrounding neighbors and found out they all wanted to know what was going on with Carl and Enger. Many people were confused and concerned. He felt with the feedback, it was a matter worth looking into.

The Investigation Begins

Finally, he called the police chief of Fosston, Minnesota. He agreed it was out of his jurisdiction. He sent all the information to Crookston, Minnesota, the county seat, forty-five miles west.

They got on the job the next day and sent a deputy to investigate and collect information. He stopped in Fosston first, where he discussed the case with the chief of police. The chief felt maybe it's just one of those family squabbles but also replied it wouldn't take long to find out.

They sent a deputy and patrolman first to the couple's farm. It was locked up tightly with only the sound of the windmill creaking forlornly in the wind. The place had a complete lonely aspect about it.

The two then made the typical trip around the neighborhood and talked to several farmers who knew them. They found almost every one of them were deeply puzzled and more than a little suspicious. The whole business looked quite fishy to them, and all concurred that Carl was not the kind of man who would run off and leave his farm hanging.

The Interrogation

The investigators learned of the couple's marital problems and that the missus was no farm wife; she just wasn't cut out for it. They then heard about the unexpected slaughter of half the herd, so they drove to the bank to verify this.

"That's right," the cashier told them. "She was here on July 1 with a check made out to her. We could not honor it, and they had a mortgage to pay on for the cattle." The teller also told them she had been there days before that and drew out $150 from their account. He mentioned that the two brothers were with her that time. "They all left together," he went on to report.

What started out as minor and routine to the officers began to loom in their mind as a first-class mystery. They had questions of why a woman would handle a cattle deal. That's a man's business. Why would Carl clear out without a hint to anyone? They both found it quite peculiar.

The two officers continued inquiring in the vicinity of the couple's farm. They turned up nothing new until they interviewed Alfred Curfman. He is my dad's father and lived only half mile away on his farm.

Talking with him, Grandpa said, "You know, I don't like this business of Carl being missing. It makes me wonder about those shots I heard a while back."

They asked him, "You heard shots? When was that?"

Grandpa told them it was about two weeks ago. He got up in the middle of the night because there was a thunderstorm, and he was checking the windows. Some were open, and it's then he heard the shots. They were coming from the direction of their farm. He thought it queer to hear shots going on that hour of the night. The officers concluded that two weeks earlier would put the time of the shots around June 27. Several neighbors agreed no one had seen Carl for the last time since June 26 that Sunday.

The officers continued their inquiries. They knew that the couple had relatives in Winger, fifteen miles from Lengby. They also had relatives in Grand Fork, North Dakota, sixty-five miles to the northwest. They also learned of the neighbor getting the cultivator from Carl. They interviewed him again and told him, "Even if it seems unimportant, you need to tell us everything you know."

He told them he didn't think Carl would just up and leave like that. He also said he had something important but kinda personal. He then told them about the red mark on Egil's mouth. He said it looked like a bruise or burn. The officer asked what he thought it was from. He said, "Lipstick, I'm sure of it." So some woman with bright lipstick was kissing him.

The officer said, "Who do you think the woman was?" they asked him.

"I can't say for sure, but his missus lays it on with a trowel." They asked him if he knew of an affair, and he said, "All I can say is that the missus seemed like the kind of woman who liked to shine up to men."

The new details left the police considering that Carl could have met his demise. It would explain why Egil showed up at the farm the moment Carl disappeared. There was also the possibility of an external triangle, and murder was a disturbing possibility. The investigators made their report, and the sheriff listened intently. Their conclusion that day was to settle it one way or another.

The next day, they went to the Baglien farm to see if there were any signs of violence or perhaps a grave. They were also going to do their best to locate Enger and the hired hands. While at the farm, the sheriff and deputies found no sign of blood or any sign of the ground being disturbed. They looked in the barn, examining every hand tool that could have served as a weapon. Everything was in its proper place, which led them to think they might be seeking clues where murder did not exist.

They moved on to examine the possibility of a romance between Enger and Egil. They questioned their relatives in Winger and Grand Forks. They had not showed up there, and they didn't seem to know much. They did voice their suspicions as they knew Carl just wouldn't leave like that.

Some neighbors revisited and told them of sighting of Enger and Egil at the bars in the different small towns. One had seen them parked at Sand Hill Lake Road. It was the sheriff's opinion that though the evidence was circumstantial, it would be wise to bring them in for questioning.

The next morning, July 14, the sheriff checked once more with the Grand Forks police. They reported back that they had located Enger and Egil. They had been staying with their relatives but had left there with her young son with them. They found out Martin (Engel's brother) was working in another farm not too far away. The next day they went out there, and to their surprise, they spied a young man and a chunky woman chatting with another young man in a sombrero. A small boy was hovering in the background. "There they are," the sheriff muttered. The four turned to stare at the officers. The officers got out of their car and walked toward them. The sheriff identified himself and told them they were looking for Mrs. Baglien and Egil K. "Are you them?" he asked.

The woman glanced at him cooly and said, "That's right." She asked what they wanted.

Egil chimed in and asked, "What's this about?"

Then the sheriff looked toward the other young man and asked if he was Martin. He said, "Yes, I am." Martin told them his brother was there to borrow his car, but he had told them no as he needed it himself.

The officers put the missus, Egil, and the young son into the police car. She said nothing, but her jaw was hard. Egil grumbled that they had no right to take them like this. It was pure silence the rest of the way.

The sheriff knew very well only these people could give the answers to whether a murder had been committed or not. He was personally convinced the answer was yes and that they needed Martin's car to make a getaway.

They took Mrs. Baglien to a separate room to wait. They then began questioning Egil. He at once admitted he had stayed with Enger in Grand Forks. They then had taken a bus across the river to East Grand Forks, Minnesota. They then proceeded to hitch a ride to the farm they were picked up at. They asked him how they got to Grand Forks in the first place. He stated that they drove Enger's car. They asked him where her car was now, and he responded that they had sold it. "That was Carl's car, so how could you sell it?" They asked. Egil realized he was trapped and admitted he signed the title. That's forgery, they told him. Then he said to them that a few days before the Fourth of July, Carl left the farm and asked him to look after the family. He said Carl didn't say where he was going or anything. He hadn't seen him since!

The police were not buying his implausible story. They pressed on about a possible affair with Enger. He finally admitted that they had been lovers in secret for months. His defenses began to crumble as they asked him where Carl was. He broke down and said Carl was dead but that he didn't kill him. He told them Martin had an argument with him and killed him in the road in front of the farm.

They were not sure of this story and thought it to be a stall on Egil's part. As this point, the sheriff sent two officers out to pick Martin up. They felt he wouldn't want to be accused of murder. They needed his side of the story.

The state's attorney was present when Martin was brought in for questioning. He clumped into the courthouse in his high-heeled cowboy boots, looking like anything but the heroes he admired in the Western movies he watched. He was scared, and being pea green with little urging, he told one of the most bloodcurdling tales in Minnesota crimes history.

He started by telling them he got drunk and didn't know what he was doing. They told him to continue, so he did. He told how his brother Egil had fallen madly in love with the missus. Enger had asked Carl point-blank for a divorce, but he angrily refused. Egil had made the same request, to no greater success.

On June 24, Enger begged Martin to come to the farm. The next morning, he did just that. She took him aside away from where Carl was working on his tractor. She told him there was only one way to get rid of him, and that would be to kill him. She asked Martin to do the job for $540. He asked her why the extra $40. She said he'd have to buy a new gun after he got rid of the murder weapon.

Martin and Egil both stayed overnight that Sunday night, and Enger kept urging them and waved the offer under their noses.

Martin told the officer that he was a handyman and that he always carried a .22 caliber pistol with him. It was in his car, but he had no intention of using it.

That Sunday night, Enger suggested they all go to Ebro and have some drinks. They spent several hours there drinking and talking. They came up with a plan to get Carl in an argument, beat him up, and then run off with the missus.

They all left the tavern around midnight in the midst of a thunderstorm. Martin admitted he was drunk. When they got to the farm, he carried out the murder.

Martin then showed authorities where they had buried Carl's body in the cornfield.

The authorities knew Martin was the one who was crazy about guns but found it hard to believe that Egil had no part in the slaying. When the county coroner examined Carl's body, he came up with the information to substantiate the belief Martin had not acted alone.

There were two bullet holes, but in addition, his skull had been fractured by a blow inflicted by a heavy weapon. They had the evidence that if Martin fired the gun, he couldn't have been swinging a club at the same time. They needed to talk to Egil. While talking with Egil, he was sweating profusely but finally admitted his part. He told them he had grabbed the car crank and struck Carl on the head during the struggle. "We then buried him," he told them.

Armed with this information, they brought Enger Baglien in and confronted the plump, defiant woman with the detailed statements made by the two boys. She quickly realized that any further denial was hopeless.

Enger gave her statement, confessing her illicit love affair with Egil. Sobbing, she said that she asked Carl for a divorce, and he refused. She admitted she loved Egil and had offered Martin $540 to get rid of her husband. She told them she had no part in the actual slaying but heard two shots as she ran into the house after slamming the door. They realized those were the shots my grandpa Alfred Curfman had heard that night during the storm. I am so proud of Grandpa for being a big help in solving this terrible murder. They might have gotten away with it without that detail.

The next day, more evidence was collected at Martin's home. There they found two .28 caliber pistols, a .38 caliber revolver, and a German Lugar. 38 as well as two gun holsters, all belonging to Martin.

In his cell, Martin was visited by his father, who asked him, "Son, what have you done?"

He told his dad he got drunk and didn't know what he was doing. His father just shook his head sadly as he left. He knew that the woman was to blame, not the boys. However, they were all accountable for their actions.

In September 1949, all three defendants—Enger, Egil, and Martin—went to trial. They, all three, entered a guilty plea. Because of technicalities, Egil was able to plead guilty to second-degree murder. The other two pled guilty to first-degree murder. In the end, it made no difference as in Minnesota at that time, there was no capital punishment. In a speedy trial, all three were sentenced to life in prison. It was the harshest punishment possible. In the courtroom, a woman spectator remarked, "If it hadn't been for that woman, those boys wouldn't have to spend their lives in prison." But as someone said, *if* is the biggest little word in the whole vocabulary.

When my other grandparents, John and Theresa Baustian, heard about all the facts and murder on the farm they had sold the Bagliens, they felt bad and wished they had never met them. I remember them talking about it as we grew up, but I never really put together how it must have made them feel. I learned more after becoming an adult and reading the articles and stories later in life about it.

We were not told about this murder until we were adults. My mom and dad thought it best because this is the same place and house where we warmed up waiting for the bus each and every day. They felt it might have creeped us out to go there if we knew. We only knew this place as a haven to warm up. I'm glad Mom and Dad had good instincts back then. Mr. Clausi also never ever said a word and seemed to love it there and always welcomed us each year.

My resources for this incredible murder were my parents, grandparents, and *True Detective* Magazine at https://www.newspapers.com, found on Google. Another source was at https://www.findafindagraveCarl Baglien1906–1949.

I googled first of all, "Murder in Lengby, Minnesota, 1949." That did list that Enger Baglien lived from 1916 to 1985. Here I found an article in the *Minneapolis Star Tribune* dated July 15, 1949, edition about the case also. I do have pictures from *True Detective* magazine.

The headline in the *True Detective* magazine was called, "Case of the Cornfield Coquette." I didn't know what *coquette* meant, so I looked it up. It explained how tongues were waggling about the wayward wife. The definition is a seductive woman who uses sex appeal to exploit men. Many felt that is exactly what she did.

CHAPTER 3

Mom and Dad Continues

My mom always said, "It's a great time to be alive." Continuing with Mom and Dad's union…

Mom and Dad lived in Solway, Minnesota, for their first year or so. Dad was a custodian there, and Mom was starting their family. Alice was born, but they soon realized it was too small and had mold in the basement space they rented. So they bought with a trade of a pickup as the story goes. They got Grandpa Curfman's farm, and that's where all of us were raised. Grandma and Grandpa moved to Fosston.

They had many challenges. First off, my dad had lost one of his eyes as a child. Somehow a screen door with a heavy spring had hooked his eye. He ended up with a glass eye and got diabetes at a young age also. By age twenty-nine, he was blind and was losing a leg. We grew up with this but really didn't think much of it. He still did construction with his dad, and he never seemed to complain. He did go to the twin cities to learn how to read braille an use equipment that helped him do his job. My mom was very healthy. Thank God for that. It balanced it all out.

They were such kind and loving parents. In the next ten years, they had eight of us children.

We grew up on our 160-acre farm by Lengby, Minnesota. There was a lake way out back, but we were forbidden to go near it. It was on the farthest corner of our property and very deep. We know we lost cows to it for sure. We had ponds and hills, strawberries and raspberries that grew wild.

We milked cows, maybe twenty or so. We had pigs and chickens and, of course, pets. Our kittens and dogs had plenty of attention. We milked the cows by hand and made our own butter. Mom and Dad sold some milk and cream too.

Our life on the farm was self-sustainable. We always had meat and grew lots of vegetables. I loved when we put up haystacks. Not sure if that caused me my allergies, but it's a strong possibility. Poison ivy was not fun.

We had such fun times too. We got to go swimming at Lengley Lake most summer days when chores were done. Little did we know that was Mom's way of cleaning us up. We had no running water yet in the house. Just a well outside. We were pretty poor, but as a child, we never knew it. We also got to go catch sunfish and walleye in the lake, fishing with wooden poles and hooks on a string. Boy, were we good at it. Many fish fries for us. Sometimes extra for the grandmas and grandpas. In the winter, we had the Strawberry Hill for sledding. We made a toboggan out of a car hood. Doesn't sound like the safest venture. At the time, we thoroughly enjoyed it. One time we did crash into the swamp. I might have loosened a few teeth, but they were okay.

To continue with where I fit in our family, Tim was born eleven months after Alice. He had a food deficiency, so he was given certain foods to help with that. Ted was born a year later in February 1951. Theresa followed in May 1952. Guess who's next? Me. I was born September 8, 1953. So here I am.

When I was three months old, I had my first brush with death, so as the newspapers reported, and the story goes this was what happened.

CHAPTER 4

A Night of Terror Reported by Mary Motl (My Mother)

There! She finally had all the children settled and the baby asleep. Sharol Ann was three months old, and she had really been fussy all afternoon. Gosh, it was already four thirty and getting dark out. She would have to light the lamp and get busy making supper. Oh, golly, she had forgotten to get water in. Out here in the country, they had no electricity or running water, but one got used to it. The temperature sure seemed to be dropping. Mary looked at the outdoor thermostat, and it was down to eighteen degrees below zero. It sure was a good thing Glen had brought in plenty of firewood for the night. She wished he was home. He had left about three o'clock to go to the home of the neighbor, John Nelson, who was their fire insurance agent. They had been waiting for him to come and renew their fire insurance, but word had come by a visiting friend that John had been sick with the flu. So Glen figured he'd better go and get the policy renewed as they sure didn't want to be without fire insurance. When he left, he said he'd be back in time for chores and to milk the cows and for Mary to stay in the house as he worried about her falling or getting hurt outside.

She got the gas lantern and decided it needed to be filled. Quickly dashing out to the entry, she brought in the gasoline and carefully filled the tank and then pumped it up with the built-in air pump. There it was, ready to be lit. The mantle looked kind of wiggly, but it was getting darker, and Sharol was starting to fuss again, so she quickly lit the lantern, and everything seemed much better with the nice bright light pushing away the darkness. She hung the lantern up on the

sturdy hook Glenn had provided in the ceiling by the kitchen window.

She told the kids that she had to go out to the well house and get a pail of water, and they should watch Sharol and talk to her if she wakened. Alice a "big" girl of five years old, was always happy to be allowed to take care of her baby sister. Tim, four years old, and Ted, three, were pretty good if not left alone too long. Also, Theresa, two years old, was content to help Alice rock the little cradle for Sharol.

Mary had the children set on the steps of the open stairway that curved up to the upstairs bedrooms from the kitchen. They loved to sit there and play and watch her go about her daily chores.

Mary hurriedly donned her warm chore jacket, scarf, boots, and mittens and again cautioned the kids to just stay right there and she would be right back. She put wood in the stove and lit her outside lantern to guide her way to the well house. Tim wanted to get his coat and cap and come along, but she said no, it was getting too cold, but maybe Daddy would let him go along to the barn when he got back.

She took a last look at Sharol and went out the door with her water pail and lantern. She had to cross the front porch and then down the steps. The well house was only about one hundred yards away.

All at once, she heard a terrible boom and found herself running back toward the house. Flames were visible at the kitchen window, and Tim was standing in the front porch, yelling, "Mommy, Mommy!"

Rushing back into the kitchen, she saw Sharol's blanket burning, and she quickly beat out the flames with her mittened hands.

The gas lantern was lying on the stairway back of the children and was flickering flames. She grabbed the lantern and threw it back out the front door.

The only other things burning were the kitchen curtains

and a few paper bags on the cupboard. The only light she had was the old outside barn lantern, but she finally got the children quieted. She then realized that it was extremely cold in the house.

Looking around, she saw that every window in the house had blown out and were gone. It finally dawned on her what had happened. The gas lantern had exploded!

The wiggly mantel must have come off, shooting a direct flame on the gas tank of the lantern. She quickly asked the children, but they were so frightened they had no idea of what had happened.

Mary knew she was in really deep trouble, five small children, ten below zero, a house with no windows, and at home alone with no telephone to seek help.

First of all, she knew she had to keep the kids warm, so she took them all to the downstairs bedroom; windows gone there too! She got their snowsuits out, and Alice, Tim, and Ted struggled into theirs, and she got Theresa bundled into hers.

The kids kept crying because it was so cold and getting colder. She still wasn't sure what to do to keep them from freezing. She thought of taking them to the barn but didn't know if she could manage to keep them warm there either. She made them all get into her bed and piled quilts and blankets around them. Then she went and filled the stoves with wood and tried to hang blankets over the windows, but her fingers were so stiff and cold she couldn't make them stay up.

Tim wouldn't stay with the others on the bed but kept trying to help her and finally kept tugging at her and said, "Mommy, let's take the sled!" Why hadn't she thought of that? She wasn't sure she could harness the horses, but she had helped many times and knew how the harness was put on. But it was three miles to the nearest neighbor! Well, she had to try.

She could feel a little warmth from the stoves but knew they could not stay there very long, so she told Alice to keep the other three in the bed, and Mommy was going to get the horses and sled.

She found another lamp and got that lit so they wouldn't be in the dark. Then Mary and Tim hurried out to the barn to hitch up the horses to the box sleigh.

Her troubles still weren't over though. Babe, the bay mare, was easy to get the bridle and harness on. Tim held the lantern while Mary finished buckling up the straps (he knew which ones went together too!). Then old Dan decided that he wasn't going to have a bridle put on him. She pushed and pulled and tried everything to get his head down, but he kept getting meaner. And meaner. All at once, Tim shoved the lantern over to her and said, "I can get it."

Up the side of the stall he went and climbed right up on Dan's head. He had the bridle on in no time. She knew they had to hurry because the kids were alone in the house. She led Dan out, and Tim brought Babe out. The horses didn't really like getting hitched up when it was so dark and cold. It was very difficult to get them to stand still, but her "big boy" sure knew how to help.

They finally had them hitched up, and she drove right up by the front steps and ran in to see if the kids were okay. Sharol was still sleeping, and

Theresa had fallen asleep, but Ted and Alice were crying because it had taken about twenty minutes for her and Tim to get the horses and sled. She also noticed that the big woodstove was really getting overheated.

With all the windows gone, the wind blowing in had made the wood burn fast and hard. A stove burning that hard could start a chimney fire. She grabbed the baby and wrapped her extra carefully and had Alice and Tim bring her bottle and diapers. She finally got them all down in the sled box and covered up with quilts and blankets. She glanced at the clock as she went out the door, and it was only six o'clock.

It seemed like hours since this nightmare had begun and less than one hour had gone by since she had went out the door to get the water. Tim would not get down in the sled by the others but stood by her side as they started down the road. She couldn't believe the kids could be so quiet; they must be just so darned scared.

As they were going along, she wondered what Glenn would do if he got home and found a dark house with all the windows out and no family there. It took them about twenty minutes to get to their neighbors' house. She drove the horses and sled right across Basil and Thelma's front yard to the front door. She started yelling and calling to them. Basil came out wondering what all the fuss was. It took a few minutes to explain what had happened, and while doing so, they got the kids into the house. By this time, Mary was crying so hard she could barely speak. Basil was going to go out and tie up the horses, but she absolutely insisted on leaving after the kids were quieted down. She felt she had to go back because Glenn would probably be back by now and would be terrified not knowing what had happened.

She finally convinced Tim that he couldn't go with her. It was now twenty-five degrees below zero.

Basil made sure she was warm enough and gave her an extra parka to put on.

The horses were hard to drive as they wanted to get home to their warm barn. As she turned the last curve to go up the driveway, she saw the headlight of a car coming behind her. Glenn drove into the yard behind her and jumped out to find out why she was out with the horses and sled.

She excitedly told him all the terrifying events of the last few hours. As he held her close and his quiet strength filled her troubled mind, she realized whatever the next day would bring, they would face it together and always be thankful for their family was safe and sound.

Wow, I'm so thankful I had a big brother Tim to help save me and a strong mother who did what she had to do. Of course, I don't remember any of this happening, but who would want to? Lucky, lucky, lucky.

Mrs. Carlman and Baby

SURVIVING LIFE AND
C😷VID-19

CHAPTER 5

My Younger Years

So now you know at three months old it's only going to get better. I don't know if being in a fire made me more careful or not. I have always been nervous around fire over the years. I am so glad I was spared as my life has been so good.

Being born as a middle child was a great blessing. It worked well to my advantage. I could act like a big girl if I wanted to or a baby if necessary. Mom told me I was carried around a lot by the older brothers and sisters until I was two years old.

I don't remember Paul, the next one in line, being born, but I do remember Evelyn and Audrey as the little girls. We were so connected with one another throughout our younger years. We had to depend on one another for a very self-sufficient lifestyle.

I guess we were poor but never knew that until later years when we had a lot more money and possessions. That was later in life. I realize now how wonderful electricity and plumbing really was when I turned thirteen years old. We now had one bathroom for the ten of us. The boys chose to use the outhouse probably because there was five girls. Boy did we love that bathroom. I will also never forget how great toilet paper was compared to the old hard Ward's catalog. It might have been Sears Roebuck catalog. It's funny how you don't know things are rough as long as you are loved and taking care of one another. I still wonder how Mom and Dad fed us all even with our self-sustaining farm and getting commodities, which included flour, sugar, rice, oatmeal, cheese, powdered milk, and beans. Our family knew just how to stretch it to feed us all, and believe me, we ate good.

I remember Mom canning chicken and other meats and putting away vegetables to get through the long winters. We had fresh cream that we separated from the milk in the cream separator. We could drink it or put it on fresh strawberries, raspberries, or blueberries that we picked in the summer.

I was only four years old when my dad went totally blind, but I barely remember that. I thought he was always blind. This changed a lot of things for Mom and all of us. Dad had to go to Minneapolis to a blind school to learn some things over and how to read braille. He was sick a lot of the time due to his diabetes, which also took one of his legs. Gangrene had set in, and it had to be amputated. So now he has a wooden leg to walk in and get around the house. I got to play in it when he had it off his stump. I would stick my little foot right in and clomp around. I think Dad let us do this so he knew where we were at. I don't know how he did it, but he knew which one of us was in it.

I remember the long rides in the old station wagon getting to all the appointments at that time. It just seemed normal.

As years passed by, I finally realized later on that not all dads had these issues. We had wonderful neighbors and relatives and friends to help our family through this time.

Our grandparents, Alfred and Sophie Curfman, were my dad's mom and dad. They loved to play cards and lived in Fosston, Minnesota. Teresa and John Baustian were my mother's parents, and they lived in Bagley, Minnesota We lived right between them ten miles from either direction in Lengby, Minnesota. We were very close to our grandparents and spent a lot of holidays and birthdays with them. With ten of us and more, there was always some celebration. They were very much a part of our lives. We all learned many things from them and treasure them to this day.

I absolutely loved school. It was so fun to walk to the bus and have friends on the bus and in class. We walked a little over a mile, and yes, there were hills. The school gave all eight of us kids free lunches all of our school days because the bus couldn't come up our driveway. There was definitely nowhere to turn around for a big bus. We loved that time together especially in the spring and fall. In the winter, we had a neighbor that lived about a half a block from the bus stop. His name was Mr. Classe. He lived in an old shack of a house with a wonderful warm wood stove. We we're always welcome anytime to warm up there in the winter months. I'm sure some of us would have frozen to death without his generosity. To this very day, I still remember how cozy and warm it was to warm our hands over that red-hot stove. His house smelled so bad, but we didn't care as it was a life-saving time. I don't know how old he was, but I think he was very old but oh, so very kind. He had no wife or children and was a man of very few words.

One of us kids would watch for the bus, and when spotted, we would all head out to the bus stop. On occasion in inclement weather storms, wind, and rain, it didn't always come. We would then get to walk the mile home again. We had no phones to call to know one way or the other. Sometimes the bus was just running late, but we had already headed home, so no school for us that day. We we're always excused as it was out of our control. *No bus, no school!*

This farm and house that Mr. Classe let us warm up at was the same place that that murder took place years ago. We we're never told about that until we moved off our farm and didn't need that lifeline anymore. I am so glad we didn't know at the time as I think that would have been creepy. I am sure Mr. Classe knew, but being an old man of few words, he never said a thing.

Summer seemed to fly by each year. We got to go swimming at Lengby Lake, where we all became pretty good swimmers. We never had swimming lessons back then and just jumped in and learned. It is definitely one of my favorite memories. When we were done swimming, Mom and Dad would give us pennies to go to the concession stand. Each piece of candy or Tootsie Roll or sucker was a penny. What a great treat.

As each year passed, we would get more and more responsibility doing chores and errands. It went according to our ability and age, of course. I finally got to sit on a little wooden stool and milk cows. That was actually my favorite chore. We all just pitched in and got things done. Our capabilities were endless. We put up hay, butcher chickens, pickled eggs, chopped and carried wood, shovel manure, cut trees down, fix fences, and list goes on and on. Us kids had little fear of anything.

CHAPTER 6

My Second Brush with Death

My second brush with death was when I was ten years old. We were swimming at Lengby Lake, and I jumped off the high board twenty feet up off the big tower as it was called. All at once I got caught in a whirlpool, and it started sucking me down. Every time I would come up, I tried to say help, but not much came out. My brother Tim was right by me and thought I was playing around until five or six times of up and down, then he realized I was in trouble. He reached out and grabbed me by the hair and pulled me to the shallow water. I survived again. Thank you, Tim. I did spit and sputter for a while, but I was fine. I don't know if Mom and Dad ever knew because we didn't want them to take this fun time away. Things like that we kept to ourselves. We also did not overreact to everyday things that could happen with ten in a family.

My little sister Evelyn was diagnosed with type 1 diabetes at age five, and I do remember her having to go to the clinic to get that under control. I rarely ever went to the doctor, and that was the story for all of us. With my dad being diabetic and now Evelyn, we just all took it in stride. It was normal to all of us. As little as she was, she handled it like a big girl.

I do remember one hospital stay for myself. I was about eleven years old, and I got a very severe allergic reaction to poison ivy. I had it all over my body and even internally, but eventually after a few weeks it went away. To this day I am still very allergic to oak, ivy, and sumac.

My brother Ted was injured somehow by falling on a mower sickle blade. He cut his arm wide open in that accident. He had to go to the clinic for stitches but turned out fine. I just remember seeing a lot of blood and fat in his arm. We definitely had guardian angels all around us.

CHAPTER 7

Farm Life

We were a Catholic churchgoing family and went almost every Sunday. I loved church just like school. It was always uplifting with the singing and routine. I even wanted to be a nun when I was about twelve but changed my mind when I started liking boys.

Our family did a lot together. We all loved music, and Mom and Dad would load us all up in the station wagon and go to the Lengby Community Center dances. I could do waltz, polka, and schottische at a very young age. Mom and Dad were not drinkers at all, but some of our neighbors and people we knew would head to the end of the block to the bar. I didn't know that people got drunk and stupid until I was much, much older. That was probably a good thing. At the end of a long night of dancing, they would serve sloppy joes and chips to everyone.

Most of our friends had large families also. One neighborhood family was the Erkys. We spent a lot of time there and would go get water in milk cans from their natural well that they had there. It was very fresh water, but I'm not sure why we went and got it. I just remember having fun at the well and never asked very many questions.

Then there were the Bakkens. We went to their farm a lot to play, toboggan, and sled. It was like a potluck all day and overnight sometimes. It was great to grow up with great family friends, and sometimes we got to stay there because our dad would be off to blind school. He learned many things there, including learning his construction trade over again. It was unbelievable what he could do even without his eyes. He could shingle roofs and help build or tear down old buildings. Mom was always supportive and picked up the slack whenever possible.

I do not remember my parents ever fighting. They had a good relationship and respected each other totally. They were both good role models.

Oh, and then there's the relatives. We had aunts and uncles that would share with us and send boxes of clothes from their kids to us It was like Christmas in September. I never felt deprived as we had such a good support system. I don't remember going to stores to shop. Mom sewed most of our clothes along with Grandma helping with cute dresses. I loved our hand-me-downs from my older sisters as they outgrew things.

We had three bedrooms upstairs in our house. One bedroom was for the three boys and one for all five girls with only one large bed. It was cozy as we all slept together to keep warm. I recall that the windows in our bedroom were so covered in ice and snow that we couldn't see out of them. I could also feel the cold winter wind coming through the cracks. The other room was for all the extra clothes and storage. I don't think that room was insulated at all as it was pretty cold. If we were running short on something, we could go dig through the storeroom boxes and see what we could find. We could never stay in there very long as you could see your breath. We learned to go dig through there in the warmer weather. I remember Mom occasionally going through it for material to make quilts out of whatever she could find.

When we were home, we always ate meals together. There were too many of us to eat in between with the exception of cookies or bread in the afternoon. I still love homemade bread with lots of butter. I don't ever remember going hungry as we were a family of plenty.

Now as I'm getting older, I was allowed to stay in town for things after school. I like running so I would run around the track after school and go to Aunt Ellen's and spend time with them. My cousins Larry and Delvin were great entertainment and always so welcoming.

I also babysat for my cousin Melford and Gloria for their two little boys, Kevin and Kyle. I loved staying in town and felt so lucky. I will never forget their hospitality.

So you see, we had a great family and grew up appreciating the little things in life. Time together was precious.

Oh, I can't forget our playground. We had acres to explore and roam endlessly. Our front yard was full of fun times together. We played games like Ante-I-over. This is where you would have half the kids on one side of the house or garage and the rest on the other. We would throw a ball over the building, and if someone caught it, they could run to the other side and try to tag someone on that side. If tagged, you are now on the other side. If not, you run to the other side, and you are safe. If the ball wasn't caught, you would wait to hear the words "And ante-I-over" and play until everyone was on one side. Then we would start all over again. It was kind of a guessing game as you didn't know if they would be coming over to tag you or not. It was so fun! We also played kick the tin can in the dark. In this game, a can was placed on a rock or a piece of wood in the middle of the yard. One person will guard it while the rest scattered and hid. If you had a chance, you would run out to the can and kick it. If the guard caught you, you would help him guard the rest. If you kicked the tin can, the game would start over. We also played a lot of baseball with the neighborhood kids and relatives. With such large families, there was always plenty of people to play. Life couldn't be any better than that. I definitely loved growing up on a farm.

This is one of the only colored pictures of all of us before our dad died, 1964 or 1965.

COVID-19 Update, October of 2020

It is now the end of October 2020. My best friend got COVID. She was sick for about a week and quarantined for two weeks. She is good now. Her husband had it too. They mostly had sore throats, headache, and fever. A few of our neighbors have also gotten the virus and some at Hope Chapel, where I attend church. With only twenty to thirty people, being a country church, we skip a pew and only put a few people in each one. It is nice to be able to go to church again.

Another neighbor is in St. Cloud Hospital and having a lot of trouble with COVID since he has underlying conditions. We pray all our friends and neighbors survive this ugly virus. There is no vaccine or cure as of yet. Many more are getting tested. Todd County next to us has 605 cases testing positive with three deaths. Otter Tail County has 625 positive cases with seven deaths. The sad part of this whole thing is you can be walking around with it and not even know you have it. Some people have no symptoms, which makes it even harder to detect. Most people that get the virus will run a fever, have body aches, and lose their ability to smell or taste. Many report having respiratory distress, and pneumonia. It seems to affect the lungs the most. It doesn't seem to affect children as much at the present time. We pray all are safe and recover from this big bully. More cases are being reported as of November 2020. Things are changing in a matter of one day or a few weeks.

This is also an election year. Donald Trump and Joe Biden are neck and neck. A lot can change if Trump doesn't win. This is a historical race, and we just got word that Joe Biden is our new president. There are rumors that the election was tampered with in the counting of the votes. I guess they will work that out in the future. It was a big disappointment to many.

CHAPTER 8

Dark Times

I was now thirteen years old. My dad was sick a lot, but we were so used to it that it seemed normal. Mom had to take him to Saint Paul to get his wooden leg adjusted and to make sure there was no pressure spots. With his brittle diabetes, it had taken a toll on him. This particular year, I remember him being much, much worse off and on. We all still went to church, and this was the year I got confirmed. I really was getting close to God and felt his presence often, I even wanted to be a nun during my confirmation classes. It felt so good, and I would get warm and fuzzy feelings as I learned to pray. Prayer came easy for me as I was taught there's no right or wrong way to pray. I just would speak from my heart. I also thank God every day for what I have.

I had got the idea of being a nun because my mom's sister was one. Her birth name was Evelyn, but her sister name was Sister Karen. She was a humanitarian and helped so many people, especially young women. She also served our country and took care of many hopeless, helpless, and needy people. She was a role model to many. I was confirmed and still considered following in her footsteps. There was a lot to consider, and I wasn't sure I could give up not having a family. I guess time will tell!

I was in ninth grade now and hadn't even thought about boys. This was high school, and a lot of my friends already seemed to like them. Coming from a farm girl's life, I guess I was pretty naive. We still went to dances on the weekends, and this particular year we made Christmas candy with some good friends in Lengby. They were the Vasilics. We knew them quite well. We learned to make hard candy. She would pour a batch of wintergreen hot candy mixture on a marble

slab. We waited until it cooled, and then we would all start cutting with scissors. We would make many different flavors, including licorice, chocolate, vanilla, peppermint, and many, many more. I like the almond the best and the memory of making it altogether. They had a son named David, and he would tease and try to tickle me. I blew him off as being a stupid boy. Little did I know he was flirting with me. It took me a while to figure that out. My friends pointed it out to me, and I took it from there the next time.

My dad was hospitalized quite a few times that next spring and summer, September of 1967. I had visited dad at the hospital in Fosston along with the rest of the family, but this time it felt different. He was very sleepy and tried to figure out who was talking to him. He would get mixed up, which was pretty unusual. Normally in his blind state, he could pick us out by our voice or the way we walked up to him. I knew something wasn't right. Mom never talked to us about sick people or death. She probably was in denial as our dad was only thirty-nine years old. She was a very strong woman, which made us all strong also. That night I went to bed, and for the first time in my life, I knew what worry was. I had never felt this way before, and next thing I knew I was in deep prayer. I just wanted everything to be okay. I was in the middle of my thoughts when all at once a heavenly angel appeared above our bed. The room lit up, and the angel said, "Don't worry, everything will be okay."

Teen Years Continued

It was very uplifting. You would think I would have been afraid, but I wasn't. I had a feeling of peace come over me, and I accepted God in my heart and life that night. My sisters said that they saw nothing and told me I must have just been dreaming as we got ready for school that next morning. It was now September 8, my fourteenth birthday. I hadn't remembered till I got to school as my friends were singing to me on the bus and at lunch. Wow, I was fourteen years old.

All at once, there was a message for me to come right to the office over the loudspeaker. When I got there, my brothers and sisters were there also. We were told we had to get to the hospital as Dad needed to see all of us right now. So off we went, not knowing it would not be what we expected or the last time we would see him alive. We didn't know what was happening until we got to his room. It was very quiet, and the nurse was checking his blood pressure and vitals. Mom was standing holding his hand, and tears were pouring down her face. Then the nurse left, and Mom gathered us all around and told us to say our goodbyes to our daddy as he was not going to live much longer. So we each took a turn to touch him and cry and say our goodbyes. It was a bittersweet moment. As we all finished, he kind of came around and said, "The angels are coming." He then looked up and took his last breath. There again it felt like a dream to me, but it was so calming and peaceful at the same time.

Our dad was gone at the very young age of thirty-nine years old. But boy, did I believe in God's gentle touch in our hearts from that day on. From there it's kind of a blur. I knew the next step was the funeral, and there were lots of people and so much love and caring among us all. Mom was strong as usual and did comfort us the best she could. She just continued on running the farm with eight mouths to feed, and life just went on.

Three days after our dad's funeral, another tragedy happened. Uncle Howard, dad's brother, was killed in a car accident. Grandma and Grandpa Curfman now have lost three siblings in a very short time. A younger brother, Harry had died of diabetes earlier. They had also lost an infant daughter years before. Here we all gathered again with the cousins and Aunt Ellen and the rest of the family at another funeral. It made me realize how precious each day really is and that anyone can die at any age. It definitely was a rude awakening.

Life did go on, but oh, what a change. None of us had very many coping skills if any at all. I remember my older brothers being quite angry and quite disruptive in many ways. Back in those days, there was no counseling for anyone let alone children. Boy did we all grow up fast.

We had a lot of friends and family that got us through that first year without Dad. My sisters and I were always close, but this brought us even closer. School was always a good place for me, and I always wanted to teach kids from a very young age. I actually wanted to be a physical ed teacher as Mrs. Carlin was a real role model during this time. Her family ran the funeral home, which I didn't realize then, but she took me under her wing and was such an encouraging lady. I liked all my teachers at Fosston High School, but she stood out and helped us all. I was in tenth grade and fifteen years old. We have sewing class and typing this year. I loved to sew and cut up material to make for myself and others. I didn't care much for typing. What a great life lesson I would use a lot throughout my life. We also had a great cooking class and learned how to prepare meals quite well.

I still get to stay with Aunt Ellen, Cousin Larry, and Cousin Delvin when I want to mostly because I'm older and in track after school now. I loved being in sports!

CHAPTER 9

The Move

My mom was moving on already. She had a boyfriend named Bill, but she said they're just dancing friends. He was a little rough around the edges, I thought, compared to our dad. Then she met Everett, and she fell hard. Without any warning, she sold the farm and everything on it, and we moved to Plummer, Minnesota. They got married, so now we had a stepdad. *Uffda*. We only lived there for a few months above the laundromat.

I got along with him okay in the beginning, but so many things changed quite quickly. Mom and Everett got jobs in Thief River Falls at Arctic Enterprises making snowmobiles.

I can only remember Teresa, Paul, me, Evelyn, and Audrey being there. I really don't know where the older three brothers and sisters were—Alice, Tim, and Ted. At this point was where I lost track of a lot of my siblings and didn't even realize it till years later. They would catch me up as I have asked each of them to write their story from that point on to add to my autobiography. I can't wait to see where and how they got through this time in our life.

Now we move on to Thief River Falls, and Mom and Everett got a place on State Avenue on the south edge of town. It was a cozy house with a big yard and lots of room. I met good neighbors right away. Marie lived next door and more friends down the block. Wow, it was so fun to have a great friend right next door and hang out with and ride bike. We spent many hours together. She was a year younger but just as mature. We spent many days and nights together, and her parents were so good to me too.

Meanwhile, my mom is now married to a man who treats her quite poorly. He was like a raging lunatic most of the time. I didn't like how mean he was to Mom, and they fought all the time. He was very physical with her also. I wasn't used to the fighting and bickering, and I've never had to deal with that. One night he pushed her into me, and I got angry and threatened to leave. Mom said, "Just go before someone else gets hurt." I did just that and went to Marie's house. Her mom said I could stay there for a while. I loved it there, but I also knew I had to not overstay my welcome. It was now August, and school would be starting soon.

CHAPTER 10

Third Brush with Death

I decided to go visit a relative, and that's when another incident happened. While spending the night there, the male party decided to pay me a visit in the middle of the night. I had my own bedroom, which was on the opposite side from theirs. I felt very uncomfortable around him but had no idea what he was capable of. The next thing I knew, he was covering my face with a pillow, and I couldn't breathe. My fight-or-flight response kicked in, and I managed to scream in the middle of the struggled. I remember his breath being horrid, and his body was all sweaty. I do think he was drunk or on drugs. He ripped my nightgown off me, and I was so scared I thought I was going to die. This would be my third brush with death. His wife had finally heard the ruckus and came to save me. She just screamed at him, and he ran out of the room yelling he was just goofing off. I even knew better than that, and what he was doing was sexual assault. She felt so bad, and since he didn't get too far, she just dismissed it and promised he'd never do that again. We sat up till early morning as I couldn't believe that for a minute. I knew in that moment I didn't plan to ever be around him in my lifetime. There would always be distance between us, and I kept it that way until he passed away. Even to this very day, the least he should have done was an apology. Although I would have never trusted him again.

Back then I knew nothing about calling the police or even telling someone else. Secrets like that were just hushed up. His wife drove me to Thief River Falls the next morning, and I never went back to their house again. Little did I know how much an incident like that can affect you down the road. Even in relationships that were good, it was hard for me to trust a guy. I always felt they could get aggressive, so I had my guard up most of the time. I also am very claustrophobic whenever I'm in a situation, where I'm in an enclosed space like caves, MRIs, or even masks. If I feel at all like I can't get out of something, I start to panic, but over the years, I've learned to not put myself in those situations. I decided right then living with relatives or even thinking about asking was not an option for me. I also could not tell anyone as I thought they'd send me home. I knew my support system was gone with not living at home and brothers and sisters dispersed all over the place. The people I had always counted on were not around anymore. I sure missed what I had since Dad died. I then learned real fast that my friends were my go-to people, but also learned I couldn't trust all of them. Life lessons seemed to come easy for me. Thank God!

CHAPTER 11

Gaining Independence

I now moved on and got my first official job and apartment. My apartment consisted of a small kitchenette with a stove and fridge. On the other end of the room was a couch and bed. I also had a small table and two chairs. It was sooo cozy. It cost me only $35 a month, and everything was included. Marie's mom helped me as I only had $20 to my name. Their family also gave me items for my place, like blankets, sheets, and dishes. Most things came with the apartment, which helped me a lot. The $15 I borrowed was with the condition I had to get a job. The next day I went to look for work.

I had never had to do that but thought, "How hard could that be?" My plan was to just ask. I applied at one grocery store, but right away they said I had to be sixteen years old. I was two weeks away, and they said they would let me know when I turned sixteen. I realized my best bet was to just walk in a place and ask instead of an application. So I stopped at two different restaurants and at the Rex Café right downtown. I met Vi Henning. She was a real tiny woman with long black hair and actually looked like a witch, dressed in all black. My friends had mentioned that to me and that no one liked her. She sat down with me, offered me a Coke, and asked if I had ever waitressed. I told her a little at my mom's café, and I had served people at church functions. I also said I was willing to learn. She asked how old I was, and I said sixteen. I didn't usually lie, but I was pretty desperate to get a job to support myself. She turned out to be a mother hen who taught her little chicks, and we were very good friends along with teaching me the ropes. I waited tables, cleared, worked the malt counter, washed dishes, and learned how to make change. I did all that for a whopping ninety cents an hour. With all the tips and my paycheck, I had no problem paying my own way through two years of high school. I loved it and lived quite well.

I went to Lincoln High School and also was picked to be on the dance line team. We were called the Prowlins. It was so much fun and helped me make a lot of really good friends. They were so welcoming and were wonderful classmates. Somehow it's hard to believe I could be all that I could be with paying rent, living alone, working, and finishing high school. I was loving life but at the same time missing my family. Mom never did try to stop us and knew we were strong enough to make it. In her own way, she was protecting us from Everett's outbursts. *My* little sisters said he was good to them, and I think he was because it was what he could handle. I had such a good upbringing that I never thought it odd to just move forward. It was just the way it was.

I did go out a lot as I had no curfew. That was nice but also made me be accountable for any repercussions I would encounter. There was no one to wake me up for work or school, so I learned real fast what my limits were. I also didn't like drinking or drugs, so that helped. We all loved to dance, and many weekends were spent in some woods somewhere having what we called keggers. We would blast the music so loud that sometimes, not very often, the neighbor would turn us all in. The cops would come, and many of us would flee to the woods. Some would get hauled away for providing the booze and for the noise we made. Basically they would just break it up. I remember a few times we just continued a few hours later with the music down low. Oh, what great memories we made back then. My dilemma back then was not driving so depended on friends for that. I will admit there were some questionable drivers but somehow I survived.

I found a second job my senior year mainly because I needed more money for food, clothes, and just the essentials. I also bought a bike so I could get around town faster to work and school, although I preferred walking. It's a habit that has been lifelong. The store I worked at was mostly weekends and was called Tiny Tiger. It was so much fun as I got to order products and face the shelves when they came in. It was located right beside the Rex Café. Both my bosses worked with my hectic schedule as they knew school was a priority for me. I loved that little store. It was like a small Ben Franklin store with just about anything you could imagine in it.

I had met a few guys, but no one I really liked. Most of them have been immature or drank too much for my taste. Then at a birthday party for a good friend, I met Jeff. He was so sweet, and we just connected right away. I loved his family, and they loved me. We dated my senior year, and then he went in the service. We kept in touch by writing letters and an occasional phone call to his parents. We had no cell phones back then, so I would try to be at his house when he called. He seemed to like the army, but we both missed each other a lot. He made it home for Christmas and asked me to marry him. He gave me a beautiful ring, and I was in heaven. He was cute, a gentle soul, and for sure my first love! What a great year for me.

Now I was nearing graduation, and Jeff got to come home. On the phone, he said he had some news to tell me. I was just so excited that he would be here with me for a while. He did like it in Germany and had made some friends. He sat me down at his parents' house and told me things I didn't want to hear. He really felt that he was asking way too much for me to wait four years and not date others. Wow, I didn't see that coming. I was crushed, but we both agreed it was probably the best at this time. His parents were sad, but I kept in touch with them for years. We promised to keep in touch, but that didn't happen either. I missed him a lot, but life goes on.

CHAPTER 12

Graduation

I graduated from Lincoln High School in 1971. Our class was around 270 students, so I didn't know everyone but had made many good friends in those two years. I did call my mom and Everett so they could come to the ceremony. They made it, which I was thankful for, and they took me out to dinner. It was nice since I hadn't seen Mom for a long time. I had missed her during these years but also understood her situation. I guess what I missed most was having someone to direct me on how to get into college or getting my driver's license. Those were two milestones I had no help with and didn't realize it until years later. My priority was in survival mode. I had little money to pursue my dreams and now was a pretty street-smart kid.

I started dating again, but no one compared to Jeff. I had fun anyway, and one day instead of riding my bike to work a hot rod car pulled up to me and asked me if I wanted a ride. I jumped in, and that's when I met Les. I had hitched rides quite often, but this guy took a shine to me and me to him. He turned out to be quite free-spirited. He was also a risk-taker, which kept things interesting. We dated several months. He took a lot of chances and was pulled over for speeding a few times. I started to feel unsafe, and I got tired of his recklessness, so I broke up with him. I know he was tired of me not enjoying his ways. It was exciting at first, but after a while, it scared me! Now I have experienced a sweet, kind soul and a rebel. I did date a few others but knew right away they were not my type.

By now I have lived in quite a few places due to others not paying their share, and moving to bigger and better apartments was always exciting and a new adventure. I even lived in a five-bedroom house, and my sister Theresa lived there too. We would see each other once in a while, but she was engaged and had gotten pregnant. That made it hard to spend time together. It was still nice to have her close at the time. I would say I must have moved fifteen times in those four years. Each time was new friends and new experiences, and I wouldn't change any of it for the world.

CHAPTER 13
Brothers' and Sisters' Lost Years
Evy and Audrey

Evelyn Faye Curfman was born August 14, 1956, in Fosston, Minnesota, to Glenn and Mary (Baustian) Curfman. She was raised on a farm by Lengby, Minnesota, with her three brothers and four sisters. She attended school in Fosston. After the passing of her father, Glenn, her mother, Mary, married Everett Motl, and she lived in Newfolden, Minnesota, for a brief time. Evie returned to Fosston and graduated high school in 1974. She met the love of her life, Maurus Karboviak, as he would come in for coffee at the Little Café, which her mother and stepfather owned and where she worked, next door to the Fosston Light Plant, where he worked. After graduation, she moved to Thief River Falls, Minnesota, where she worked as a waitress at Woolworth's lunch counter. Evie returned to Fosston in 1975 and married Maurus on June 7, 1975, at St. Mary's Catholic Church. She then returned to waitressing and cooking at the Little Café.

In 1976, they moved to Finley, North Dakota, when Maurus accepted a job as a lineman with Sheyenne Valley Electric Cooperative. In the summer of 1976, Evelyn worked for Northern Pipeline Co., gluing pipe together for Dakota rural water users in Griggs and Steele County areas. In 1977, their son Richard was born, and Evelyn became a stay-at-home mom. In 1981, their daughter, Jacquelyn, was born, and she remained a stay-at-home mother until the children were in school. During her time at home, she occasionally took up babysitting other children and was known for decorating many wedding, anniversary, retirement, and birthday cakes. She then took a job as a teacher's aide with Finley-Sharon School and affectionately became known as Mrs. K., a title she truly cherished while working with children. Although she only had two children herself, she considered each of the school children one of her own.

Evie worked as an aide for twenty-five years, retiring in 2015 due to failing health. She also volunteered at St. Olaf's Catholic Church teaching confirmation classes. Other volunteer activities included being a first responder for Finley Ambulance. Upon Maurus's retirement from Nodak Electric Co-op in 2016, they moved to Sauk Rapids, Minnesota, to be closer to their two grandchildren. She truly enjoyed attending the many concerts, plays, and hockey games that Emma and Alex participated in. Never one to sit still, she began volunteering at Good Shepherd Lutheran Home, praying the rosary with the residents in the memory care unit until COVID-19 ceased that activity. Always a talented, craft-loving person, she began using colored pencils, coloring pictures to share with all the residents at Good Shepherd. She had just recently completed this project. Evie never wanted to run any of Maurus's saws, but she helped with hand sanding and varnishing hundreds of prayer crosses she and Maurus made over the years. This was one of her most cherished hobbies.

She is survived by her husband of forty-five years, Maurus of Sauk Rapids; son, Rick, and daughter, Jackie (Filip) Johnson; grandchildren, Emma and Alex Johnson, all of Sauk Rapids; sisters, Alice Winder of Detroit Lakes, Theresa (Marvin) Stark of Green River, Wyoming, Sharol (Rick) Mason of Verndale; brothers, Tim (Donna) Curfman of Alexandria, and Paul (Deb Pfiefer-Curfman) Curfman of Fosston; sister-in-law, Jan Curfman of Prescott, Arizona; and numerous cousins, nieces, and nephews. She was preceded in death by her parents; daughter-in-law, Jenny (Rettig) Karboviak; brother, Theodore "Ted" Curfman; sister, Audrey (Rick) Simmons; brother-in-law, Vernon "Beans" Wander; and nephew, Dustin Simmons.

In Loving Memory of Audrey Gayle Simmons

Audrey Gayle Curfman was born on November 26, 1959, in Fosston, Minnesota, to parents Glenn and Mary (Baustian) Curfman Motl. She graduated from Fisher High School in Fisher, Minnesota, in 1978. While in high school, Audrey was part of the speech team and earned numerous trips to the state speech tournament.

Audrey attended Northland Community College in East Grand Forks to be a clinical technician. She worked in Crookston at the Midwest Vision Center for several years. She had various jobs over the years working at REM with disabled adults, which she really enjoyed. She most recently earned a degree from Rasmussen College as a medical transcriptionist in 2008.

Audrey married Rick Simmons on August 6, 1983, in Fisher. Audrey had three sons—David, Darren, and Dustin—whom she dedicated her life to raising. She also had a stepdaughter, Jodi Simpkins.

She spent many summers at the lake taking care of Dusty's special needs. She loved being a mother and spending time with family at the lake fishing and riding pontoons. She also loved to have any children with special needs to come to the lake to enjoy the outdoors. She spent recent years with her grandchildren Henry, Owen, and Jason, also at the lake or family gatherings. Audrey had a special gift of wanting to help others be happy. She was an avid collector of cookie jars, which she enjoyed very much.

Audrey Simmons passed away on September 18, 2012, at her home on Lake Sarah near Erskine, Minnesota at the age of fifty-two years.

She is survived by her husband, Rick of Erskine, Minnesota; sons, David (Jennifer) Simmons of West Fargo, North Dakota, and Darren (Sarah) Simmons of Fosston, Minnesota; stepdaughter, Jodi Simpkins; three grandchildren, Henry and Owen Simmons of West Fargo and Jason Winter of Fosston; seven siblings, Alice (Beans) Wander, Tim (Donna) Curfman, Ted (Jan) Curfman, Theresa (Marvin) Stark, Sharol (Rick) Mason, Paul (Deb) Curfman, and Evelyn (Maurus) Karboviak; three brothers-in-law, Rich (Raenelle) Simmons, Buck (Pam) Simmons, and Mark (Bonnie) Simmons; and one sister-in-law, Rose Simmons. She is also survived by many nieces, nephews, great-nieces, and great-nephews, and great-great- nieces and nephews.

She was preceded in death by her son Dusty in 2008; her mother, Mary Mod, in 2011; father, Glenn Curfman, in 1967; stepfather, Everett Motl, in 1996; grandparents, Alfred and Sophie Curfman and John and Theresa Baustian; nephew, JR Simmons; and several aunts, uncles, and cousins.

May her soul and the souls of all the faithful departed through the mercy of God rest in peace. Amen.

Evelyn's and Audrey's Lost Years

On the farm was only twelve years for me. I always remember everyone referring to Audrey and me as the little girl even though I was only eight years younger than Alice. Mom never let me out of her sight unless one of the older girls would watch me. Alice told me this in 2020. There was nothing known about diabetes back then, so we never knew when I'd pass out. I told Alice I never asked for this disease, and I apologized for being so difficult to handle. I have always looked at it as a special blessing from God, and that's what has formed my life to this point. I was diagnosed at the age of six years.

Audrey and I were childhood soulmates. We always played together and always got to go to town with Mom and Dad. Mom would drop us off at Grandma Sophie's and then come get us when their errands were done. I loved it at Grandma and Grandpa's house, but I was a little afraid of Grandpa Alfred as he seemed to have a dark side. I'm sure that's just a childhood perception. Grandma did normal things with us when we were there. She would wash her hair in the kitchen sink, and I remember it being all the way down to her waist as she combed it. She would then put it up in a bun. They had a Siamese cat named Linda. She was very finicky and would only let me pet her, not Audrey! Maybe Audrey pulled her tail or something. We got to play with her old trunks upstairs. I remember old coats hanging up with real fur collars on them. She had two bedrooms up there. The west one was always for Uncle Sam and his wife when they came to visit. The east room also had a full-size bed just in case someone else came to stay. She had handmade quilts on the beds. I remember the smell of Grandma's bathroom, always a musty air freshener. She kept a really, really large pine cone on the corner shelf by the tub. It was a gift from Sam and Ruth.

I remember getting to go through the dining room buffet drawers. She kept linens in one drawer, and the bottom drawer was full of old newspaper articles. In there was the story of the murder that took place on the farm next to where we grew up and where our mother lived as a child. The wife had an affair with the hired hand, and they killed him and buried him in the woods. Uffdah!

I also remember in the dining room Grandpa sat in an old armchair and always spit his tobacco in an old coffee can. Yuck! He loved playing cards, but Grandma always refused to play. One time we showed up, and she was finishing Grandpa's hand of solitaire. As we walked in, she pulled the tablecloth over the cards. Dad told us to never say anything about it but insisted she played this game often.

In her living room, she had an old, out-of-tune piano. She never complained when we pounded on it. The only time we couldn't play it was when her soap opera was on, *Days of Our Lives*. That was quiet time. She kept family pictures on top of the piano.

Sometimes she let us go through her jewelry box in the downstairs bedroom. I remember lots of brooches and pretty sparkles. We even got to wear some.

After Grandpa died of leg cancer, I remember Grandma moving into a board and care home uptown in Fosston. Then she got an apartment, which was the same one our mother lived in till she passed away. Grandma had moved on to a boarding home care in the old clinic in Fosston. Kendall and Nelson was her caretaker. She also lived for a short time in a house at the mini park by the hospital. When she was there, she had two birds named Jackie and Jamie, after her two youngest great-grandgirls at that time.

I don't recall a lot about Grandma and Grandpa Baustian. Grandma Teresa was not comfortable watching me, but they did come to our farm a couple times a month, usually on Sundays for special occasions. Grandma and Grandpa Curfman would come on opposite Sundays. Grandpa Baustian, John, loved to wander around the farm and try to fix things the boys would mess up. I would wander with him, and he'd always show me tricks to fix things, such as a bottle of Coke to dissolve rust off almost anything. Grandpa loved cars also. It always seemed like he had a different one quite frequently! Grandma Teresa loved to cook, and she often, in the summer, would cook lunch for all of us. They would go to mass with us, and then we would go to their house for the whole afternoon. They lived on a little farm with the lake on it. Grandpa always had a neatly stacked wood pile for the wood stove. He let us play with that as if it were Lincoln Logs. The only rule was to stack it back up when we were done.

I remember their house in Bagley the most, which was right across from the lake and on the other side of the street a Jack and Jill store on the corner. The fairgrounds was only a stone's throw away. That house was a tiny house living before it became a thing. Grandma always left games in her buffet. I loved Rack-O the best. They always had a nice big garden, and Alice and Sharol would go stay with her at different times and help out. I think Grandma was sickly also.

I remember the Christmas after our dad died. Aunt Phyllis and Uncle Ed, Mom's brother, came to our house to visit. They brought lots of little gifts for us. She said every time she went grocery shopping, she'd throw a few things in the cart. We got pencils, pens, crayons, and even socks. They lived in Omaha, Nebraska, which I'm sure had large stores. Mom fixed the largest turkey Aunt Phyllis had ever seen. She didn't cook much and kept raving about the wonderful smell the turkey gave off. After that big meal, Mom would leave the carcass out on the counter, and we would all pick on it all afternoon. Aunt Phyllis was the biggest picker of all! What a funny memory.

Aunt Betty and family would come to the farm too. That was Mother's sister. Her boys Bill and Bob were quite young and were enthralled with the electric fence. They stuck their tongues on it, which had to hurt. I am sure Tim and Ted had something to do with that, haha.

Back to Audrey and me. It always seemed like it was just us. Everyone left home shortly after Dad passed away and Mom married Everett. We moved to Thief River Falls for a year, and then we moved to Newfolden. It was a tiny off-the-grid shack. I remember my brother Paul getting in serious trouble with the law. He was sent to Lino Lakes to get reformed. It worked as he's the best brother, husband, father, and grandpa you could ever meet. Mom and Everett did buy a large trailer home and drilled a well on the farm, so we now had water. Before that, we would go get a cream can full of water from the neighbors. We lived there about three years.

In our formative teen years, Audrey loved to party, even back then. I remember Mom and Everett leaving us alone out there a lot. They would run into Thief River Falls for bingo and pick up supplies. Sometimes Mom would drop us off at the Laundromat to do the many loads of laundry, while they were at the VFW playing bingo. Audrey would love to just run away. I think it was her game. I was fourteen years old, and she was eleven.

Our school with split. Audrey went to Viking, and I went to Newfolden. We did ride the same bus though. Mom and Everett had to be at work at Arctic Enterprises by 6:00 a.m. ten miles away. Mom would wake me up at five to make their lunches and make sure I had my meds gathered to take to school. I couldn't go back to sleep because she was afraid I might not wake up. I would stay awake and listen to records. Then I would get Audrey up about 6:30 as she was not an early riser. We would then catch a bus at seven or seven ten at the end of the driveway.

We had four moose that lived right across the road. We would often see them and always were afraid of them. They never did come check us out though.

In 1973, we left Newfolden and moved to Bagley for the summer. They couldn't find a place for the trailer house until August in Fosston. Mom and Everett purchased the Little Café in Fosston.

Alice, Tim, Ted, and Teresa all lived in Fosston. Sharol and Paul lived in Thief River Falls. I was now starting my senior year, and Audrey was in ninth grade. Audrey still liked to party. Mom left me in charge of her a lot. By then we had moved to the trailer court by the old A and W at the end of town. I worked lots of hours at the Little Café, usually with Teresa.

Theresa had been married to Duane, but now she then was divorced. Her kids, John and Brenda, were really little. Later, she met Larry Oak and got married. He was killed in a train accident on the railroad tracks in Fosston. Theresa later moved to Wyoming, where she still resides with her third husband, Marv.

Back to me. In 1973, I met Maurus Karboviak just before I started my senior year. He worked as a lineman for the city of Fosston, and the light plant was only two doors down from the Little Café. They would come in every day in the afternoon for coffee. I knew he was the one. But just to be sure, after graduation, I moved to Thief River Falls and lived with Sharol and Ralph for about three months. We just took a little break from each other, but it didn't take long to know we really were meant to be together. In September, I moved back to Fosston and lived with a classmate. She was not easy to live with, and she stole things from me. I then moved in with another classmate, where Ted and Deb lived. He had a little bungalow on his property, and it worked out very well.

I married Maury in June of 1975, and we bought an old house not far from Ted's place. We lived there one year, and then we moved to Finley, North Dakota. Maury had got a lineman's job for a rural system. We had two children, and after forty years there, we moved to Sauk Rapids, Minnesota. Since retiring, we wanted to be closer to Jackie, our daughter, and her family. We would now see our granddaughter and grandson every day. We have the best son-in-law, Philip, who rounds out their family.

Rick, our son, was still in Mayville when we moved to Sauk Rapids two days after his wedding with Jenny. It was a dream. Sadly three days after the wedding, she suddenly died in 2016. It was a very hard time for all. We offered to move back to Mayville as we hadn't even unpacked anything yet. Rick said no and had friends and family there to comfort him. After four years, he decided to move to Sauk Rapids too. Now we are all together, and we love it here.

Evie and Mom

I was always Mom's shadow. She always seemed to be in the kitchen. Eight kids, no wonder. I learned everything I could, and Mom was a good teacher. I remember doing a lot of cooking even at age six! I loved it! I hated the barn and outdoor chores.

Mom also taught me how to sew when I was eleven years old. I loved it. I learned on Grandma Teresa's treadle machine. We learned to can together too even though she was frightened of it. A canner had blown up on her in her first years of marriage. I still recall Mom baking five loaves of bread each day. We always had bread after school before chores. I still recall that aroma.

After school, my job was to fill the kitchen wood box. I could carry four to six pieces, and it took four trips. I remember one time at Christmas time, the boys filled the stove too full, and the chimney started on fire. We had to open all the doors and windows to cool it down inside. Grandma and Grandpa Baustian were there at the time, so they helped.

I wanted to mention that I recall in July of each year it was always haying time. Audrey and I were too little to help with that, but Mom would have us carry a mason jar full of water out to all the rest of the kids. I am sure it was only to make us little girls feel like we were helping. I remember it being so very hot out there.

The old farmhouse we lived in had a few leaks in the roof. We had to set pans in our bedrooms to catch the drips. The wallpaper was falling off the walls in our room too, but it was our room, and we loved it.

Mom and I both loved crafts. I remember at Newfolden, we got into fabric painting classes. We made lots of pillow cases, and we even did one large tablecloth together. That was a great time together.

I even crochet an afghan, but it was not for me! I hated it

but kept it, and my granddaughter Emma loves it. Go figure.

Mom and I even got into dying material and reupholstering furniture. We reupholstered a living room couch, and I loved doing that stuff. It was a natural thing for us to do. We were going to dye ten yards of material, but luckily we found ten yards of tie-dyed at a cheap fabric shop in Thief River Falls. That couch is a great memory for me.

I also got to babysit for John and Sandy Lubitz, our neighbors in Newfolden. I only did that in the summer months. I had to watch their boy, who is two years old, and cook for John's carpentry crew. Sandy liked our tie-dyed couch so much she had us put mock velvet on her couch cushions. It turned out beautiful.

Mom taught me how to drive when we lived in the shack. Everett never knew she let me take the car to the neighbors to get milk from them. There I would get milk and gallon jugs from their milk room. It was only three miles away, and one day he caught me driving change. He was not very happy with me. He didn't seem to relate to children very well.

Evie and Dad

I don't remember a lot about my dad as he passed away when I was just eleven years old. I do recall he helped Grandpa Alfred with a lot of tearing down of old buildings in Fosston. Our red grainery was built with one of them. I don't remember him not being blind. He did lots of things that blind people usually don't try, like sawing wood and helping stack hay. He loved going to auction sales and loved cars. I remember getting to go to Spring Lake almost every night to swim after the chores were finished in the summertime. Dad would sit on the park bench and talk to everyone. Without running water, it was their way to clean us all up. A cheap bath for all eight of us. I learned to swim at that lake when Tim threw me off the big tower dock. I then learned to dog-paddle out to the tower. I don't remember our dad ever being in the water. Mom never went in either.

Dad loved when people came out to the farm. It reminds me of Paul and how much he loves to have people out to his farm. One day Uncle Ronnie came screaming up the driveway in an open ragtop car and a beer in his hand. Dad came unglued with him and read him the Riot Act, which I hardly ever saw him do.

Dad loved music, especially at the dance hall in Lengby. He recorded all the big bands on his big tape reels. He also played the harmonica, and sometimes the bands would let him join in with them. He had a mini type accordion, which was called a concertina.

I remember him going to blind school to learn his trade and braille in the summers. That's where he met Jim and Carmen Frazier and family. They became lifelong friends. I wish Dad would have been around many more years.

Evie and Paul

Audrey and I were always the closest when we were little. All my brothers—Tim, Ted, and Paul—seemed to always be outside doing something on the farm. We all played a lot together, but that's about all I remember.

In later years, I took care of Jason and Jamie when Josh was taking treatments for his cancer. Paul was living in Fisher, Minnesota, and Julie had left him for good. I remember Jamie was only one year old, and they stayed six weeks. Another time they stayed for a whole month. It was summertime, so we spent a lot of time in the public baby pool in Finley. It had the best pool ever!

Evie and Ted

I remember when Ted was in a bad accident with Deb and the kids. He ended up in Grand Forks hospital for about six weeks or more. I would drive there really often to keep him company. One day a nurse asked if I was his wife as they needed a signature for something. I knew things weren't good between them, but that was a real wake-up moment for me. They divorced shortly after that. Ted loved life, and it wasn't long before he met Barb. They were engaged, but she died of cancer before a wedding could be planned.

Ted loved being married and soon met Becky and married her. They were married for quite a few years. He actually adopted her daughter, Renee, and even after they parted, he never gave up his relationship as Dad to Renee.

Ted met Jan shortly after that, and they were married for twelve years when he suddenly passed away in 2019.

He loved his mules and horses and did tons of things with them for other people's joy. Jan always pitched in and helped. They bought a Cinderella carriage and did lots for people with that. He also went on lots of wagon train rides where Mom was the camp cook. Ted also loved cooking and having visitors and hosting the Curfman Christmas party at his farm.

Evie and Tim

Tim and Donna have lived in many different places. That made it harder to keep up with their life. In our younger years, we did lots of tenting together with them. We all loved tenting and roughing it. Tim has always been in construction, and Maury would help him with some of his carpentry projects. They have stories to tell.

Evie and Sharol

We have always had a special relationship. When our kids were young, we would always come for Easter as it was the only weekend Maury would have off. Sharol would cook a turkey and all the trimmings. It was quite the spread and so good.

I remember one time Sharol gave her dog a haircut in the yard, and the wind picked up, and there was doggy hair everywhere.

We also did some camping. One year we went to Medora and Roosevelt National Park for one whole week. Jackie was one year old, and Ryan was two years old. I remember the campsite was quite rustic, so there were no showers. So we put the little ones in a cooler to take their baths. It worked quite well.

Sharol and I also went down the same career path. We both worked at school, loving and teaching the little children. That gave us a great connection over the years.

I know you have these memories too, so that's all I'll say!

Evie and Alice

Then there's Alice. She left right after her graduation to work at McIntosh Nursing Home as an aide. I was only ten years old, so I don't recall much about her. I know her married life wasn't good.

When time allowed from Maury's demanding job, we would run to Fosston to see Mom and always tried to see Alice too. We would often bring her boxes of meat as we always butchered beef each year. Sometimes we brought necessity items also. She never had enough for those little kids, and Lynn was a worthless cause. She did finally divorce him after many years.

Later on in life, she married Beans. Oh, his real name was

Vernon. After twenty-five years of a nonexistent life, again she called me in the middle of a blizzard New Year's Eve of 2019. She had finally walked away and would take a break to figure things out. She stayed with us in Sauk Rapids, where she was safe for the time being. After a few weeks, she found an apartment in Detroit Lakes, Minnesota, and took it. I am so happy you love it there.

Evie and Theresa

Theresa and all my sisters were very close living on the farm. As we all moved forward after Dad died, I lost track of her. She moved away and lived in Thief River Falls. She got married there and had two kids. She got a divorce and moved away for many years with her third husband, Marv. He was older than her, and he passed away in 2021.

Another memory just came back to me. Mom worked as a waitress for Thelma Manning at the Third Street Café. I was at her side at that job also. Thelma needed a dishwasher for two hours over the lunch hour and asked Mom if I could do that. Mom said yes. It paid $0.50 an hour. Wow, a dollar a day. That was a big allowance for 1970! I remember saving every dollar, and at the end of the summer I bought a china set at Bostwick's on their clearance counter. I used that scat until we left Finley in 2016. I remember it cost me $40. I got my used out of it.

I was about fourteen years old, washing dishes. I remember meeting Esther, a lady that ran the Woolworth's lunch counter. She had to ride in with her husband as he worked at Arctic Cat the early shift, and she didn't go to work until ten. She would sit and wait for her shift to start, and I sat a lot with her until I would go wash dishes. She was from Grygla.

When I moved in with Ralph and Sharol, I needed a job, so I went to Woolworth's and asked Esther if she'd hire me.

She instantly remembered me, and she gave me the assistant lunch counter manager job. I also became best friends with her niece Brenda at Grygla when I went to Newfolden School. Our schools were in a co-op together for three years. Funny how our paths crossed again. Brenda ended up marrying Paul's and my best friend Jerry Albaugh from Newfolden. Small world!

I just thought of this memory about the café Mom and Everett bought in Fisher, Minnesota. Audrey was a senior and pregnant with baby David. Ray had walked out on her just before their wedding. Mom thought a move would be a good thing for Audrey. It turned out after a few years she met Rick Simmons, and the rest is history. I was living in Finley seventy miles away, and Mom would often call me to come help her with cooking for the snowmobile club. They always wanted steak at their clubhouse. They paid her a lot and were good big tippers. Shortly after that Mom and Everett got divorced, and she moved back to Fosston.

I need to mention one other job that I did. While living in Finley, I worked for a carpenter that built new houses. He was a really big, heavy man, and it was hard for him to do the varnishing and staining. He hired me to do that, and it paid really well. I also put new wallpaper in the local bank in every room. I also did some wallpapering in the local funeral home. I loved all my jobs I've had all my life but especially my para job at the school for twenty-five years. The hardest job I ever had was working part of a summer when we moved to Finley as a pipe gluer on a water pipeline.

Over the years, I really got into the scrapbooking craze. After completing one hundred albums for friends and family, I had enough and no longer do it. In retirement, my newest love is adult coloring. It is so calming and relaxing and fun.

My favorite color is blue, yet I just love yellow roses. My favorite flower is lily of the valley.

Lastly I just wanted to mention our summer trips when

we were young to Itasca State Park. Those were fun day trips. I remember the buffalo and Tim totally convincing me that the Indian chief that sat at the tourist area by the headwaters was really a chief. We always got to stop at Merseth's store and pick up bologna, fresh white bread, and a huge bag of puff corn. Mom would make Kool-Aid in a big gallon pickle jar and bring it to drink. Lastly we would catch mass at the chapel outside the entrance of the park. It's still open, and Maury and I enjoy going there when we go to the Long Lake family reunions even to this very day.

What a great life. We had in such a large family.

*****

Response to Evie's Story

I learned so much about you and Audrey that I didn't know before. Your family is going to love this, just like me. It seems we were all older than what we really were when we left the farm. I know now that we all had just grown up so very fast.

I am so glad you felt you were a special blessing having diabetes at such a young age and that it was not an affliction. Throughout your life you dealt with the disease with grace even in your very last days on this earth.

We all miss your encouraging words you gave many times to all of us. I have been so thankful that you moved to Minnesota your last five years. It was hard when you lived in Finley, North Dakota, to keep up with your family life and what you were doing. I can tell by your memories and account of those missing years we had as kids that you were the best sister to Audrey that you could be. We know since she was the baby of the family, she needed all that and more from you. We all thank you for that.

I didn't know you got to go to Grandma and Grandpa's as often as you did and learn so many experiences from them. We were all so very lucky to know our grandparents like we did. I love that Mom took the time to teach you and Audrey and show you so many, many things.

I did not know you and Audrey lived in places like that after I left home. I always thought you had it better off than me without realizing you had no running water and no bathroom. You obviously had to take responsibility in each and every situation.

I, too, loved that little café Mom had in Fosston. All of us kids in one way or another enjoyed that.

The memory of when you met Maurus was definitely a good one for all of us. He was the love of your life right from the very beginning, and we all knew it. You together have raised two beautiful kids and now get to enjoy your two special grandchildren.

I know the hardest and saddest time for your family was when Rick lost Jenny three days after they were married. It still seems unreal to all of us, but life goes on for everyone even in a bad situation. Rick has handled it well and is moving on with his life. We are all so proud of his strength.

I remember when you were in Thief River Falls with us. You are so easy to have around, and that was a special time for me. I was so glad and happy to read about the life lessons you learned from our mom and dad.

It was so refreshing to read your connection to each of our brothers and sisters over the years. I am sure they will all appreciate that.

You have always been a great little sister. I am still upset that you went to heaven during the 2020 pandemic. It doesn't seem like you're gone since we couldn't see you, grieve, or have a funeral at all during this time. It certainly was out of all our control, and we all wish you were still here. Sometimes you are in my dreams, and that helps me a lot. You will live in our hearts forever.

I am so very thankful you got to be a part of my book and got your script to me in just a few months before you passed away. I miss you, Audrey, and Ted every day. Until we meet again.

Love,
Your big sister

*****

Paul's Story

Where to begin?

I guess what I can remember from the earliest age. I am the third from the bottom of eight children. Alice, Tim, Ted, Theresa, Sharol, me, Evelyn, and Audrey, right? That's the oldest to the youngest. As I reflect from then to now, it seems just like yesterday. We lived on a farm about three miles out of Lengby, Minnesota. It had a population of about one hundred people at that time. Today it is still about the same population. As I remember we didn't have a lot of money. We always had food and the basics and everything we needed. I remember Grandpa Alfred Curfman coming out to shoot the pig so we could butcher to have meat in the fall into the winter. We would then butcher and put it in the freezer to keep. Grandpa would drink a cup of the warm blood as he cut the jugular of the pig. I thought that was pretty gross. I was only six or seven at the time. I guess it was an old German custom. We had many adventures on the farm. We owned a variety of animals: cats, dogs, horses, cows, sheep, pigs, chickens, ducks, geese, rabbits, and hamsters. That gave us a good supply of milk, eggs, butter, and other things we needed without having to go buy things at the grocery store. Mom always cooked good meals. My job was to help with chores and haul wood into the basement for our large wood furnace. That would keep our house warm for the winter. The large wood furnace was taken out of an old school in Newfolden, Minnesota, about eighty miles away. It worked very well in our old farmhouse. It seemed like endless days of carrying wood in the basement to supply the monster stove.

In those days, both grandparents would come out and help on a regular basis. Grandma and Grandpa Curfman would come out a little more often than Grandma and Grandpa Baustian. We had a Minneapolis Moline tractor, which had what is called a saw rig mounted on the front with a very large blade that would feed an eight-foot log of wood. Grandpa was in charge, and one of us kids on the other side of the blade helped to cut the wood about fifteen to twenty in length. It seems a little dangerous now! Then it seemed like it was just what had to be done. Grandpa Curfman was missing a few fingers from both hands, and I always kind of wondered what happened. I never dared ask him.

Grandma and Grandpa lived ten miles away in Fosston Minnesota. It didn't seem to bother them to drive to the farm to help us. We had lots of other chores to do also. Tim and Ted were more in charge of the cows, which we had about twenty to twenty-five most of the time. I was a helper but most of the time was milking the cows by hand. Sometimes the girls would help too. We milked at 6:00 a.m. or so and again at 5:00 p.m. The milk had to be kept cold, so we went separate the cream from the milk in the cream separator. We would put the cream in a separate can. It was worth a little bit more than the milk and would be taken to Fosston to be made into butter at the creamery.

Each and every day we would get up at five and do chores, have breakfast, and then head to school. I went to school in Fosston Inskip kindergarten right into first grade. Yes, we did walk uphill and down a mile to the bus stop for real. We all seemed to get to the bus on time, so Mom must have been a good manager. Speaking of our mother, she helped some outside when she had to but mostly did the cooking, cleaning, washing clothes, sewing mittens for winter, and anything else that was demanded of her. I still remember that our mittens were made from old clothes, mostly wool. We never had cold hands. As for Dad, I always remember him being blind. He told me once I was kind of his eyes, so I would lead him by dad holding on to my arm. He also had a foldable white cane to use to feel in front of him for danger. This wasn't easy as he also had a wooden leg. The story I was told is that a horse stepped on his foot, and because of being a diabetic, it got infected with gangrene. They removed his leg below the knee. He then was fitted with an artificial leg, a term used back then. Now they call them prosthetics. I remember Mom and Dad taking lots of trips to the Twin Cities for all his medical issues I got to go with a lot of the time.

We always had older cars to drive. Dad had a love of cars, and that's probably where I got my love of cars even to this day. One of the earliest cars I remember was a 1956 Ford that was green. It had a wooden shelf built over the back seat that we could put a pad on. It would take most of the day to get to Minneapolis, and I would get to sleep on that pad. One trip I remember is when we stopped at a restaurant, which also had a gas station combo back then. That was common. It was a real treat to get the biggest pancake I had ever seen. We very rarely got to go to eat at a restaurant. It was just something we couldn't afford. So whether Dad was going to get his leg checked or going to school to learn, we had precious time together.

Sometimes he would have to stay there, and we'd go back to get him in a couple weeks. Dad made many good friends at school, and on occasion they would come to the farm to visit. Our favorite family were Jim and Carmen Frazier along with their kids. They were from Inver Grove Heights, a suburb of Saint Paul. His friends were also blind, and they all agreed as carpenters that their hands were their eyes. Carmen and Mom became very good friends for life. Jim had a garage converted into a shop for woodworking. Dad and I would go into the totally dark shop, lock the door, and you could hear power saws and other wood tools at work.

They would be in there for many hours, not letting anyone in so they could continue to turn out tables and other furniture. Jim also had a contract to make wooden stakes to use in road construction. They had to be made with just certain specs. When they would come to our farm at least once a year or more, we always looked forward to that. Linda Brian Susan and Gwen were always so excited to see a farm being from a big city. So we played hard and ate well. We would always round up the horses and go riding. We had anywhere from six to twelve horses and Shetland ponies.

I remember on one of their trips to our house they were in need of a better car. So dad helped them find a 1956 Ford Ranchero Wagon. It was a nice red-and-white car I think. It had a V8 engine with what they called Hollywood exhaust pipes. They rumbled real nice. Carmen was kind of a wild one, and I recall she loved those pipes on that 1956 Wagon.

For many years we had people from the school for the blind come and visit at our farm. One other person that visited was Mel Hataloma. I think he was from the Duluth area. I don't remember too many things about him. On one occasion, he was at our house, and he went out to use the outhouse. Someone finally went out to check on him to make sure he was okay. When they found him still in the outhouse, he was trying to recover a kitten that had fallen down into the poop. Well, needless to say the blind guy was covered in poop, but the kitten was okay. Everyone had a good laugh, and Mel got cleaned up. There was one other person I remember coming out to the house. He was a full-blooded Cherokee Indian. He whooped and hollered a lot. That's what I remember about him.

We had many friends and neighbors that also visited us, and we visited them.

One family we were close to where the Bakkens. Harvey and Betty had five kids, and we did a lot of sledding at their farm south of Lengby. Harvey was also a carpenter, so Dad had a lot in common with him. They had Great Hills for sledding and tobogganing on. We would go out at twenty below zero, never get cold, and even stay out after dark. We then go back to the house and enjoy eating whatever they had cooked up. On one occasion, we were going home quite late, and they forgot me at the Bakkens. I gotta stay overnight and went home the following day. Holidays were mostly spent at home. We would have big meals with Grandma and Grandpa's from both sides, many brothers and sisters, friends, and neighbors.

Moving on to the last year of our Dad's life in 1967. That summer was spent building a fence along the driveway for the cattle. It seemed like a big project Dad, even without his eyesight, would oversee it. We dug the holes with a hand-post hole digger. The fence project took us into late August of that year, and school started in September. I was twelve years old at the time. I remember getting called from school to go to the Fosston Hospital, where Dad was not doing very well. He had been hospitalized I think a few days before the problems with the diabetes got worse. He was only thirty-nine years old. Us kids all went to the hospital to say our goodbyes. He died on September 8, 1967, which was also Sharol's birthday. But on the other hand, it reminds us all of what a good and caring Dad we had for a short time.

After Dad passed, we stayed on the farm for the fall and the winter. During that time, Mom had met Everett Motl. She married him, and we moved to Thief River Falls Minnesota. He had been working for a mink farm near Crosslake, Minnesota. They both got a job at Arctic Enterprises in Thief River Falls, so that's why we moved. I never really did have much confidence in him; he seemed like a goofball. I tried to make the best of it. Mom seemed to be happy about having a man in her life. We did have an auction at the farm and sold everything except the cars and the furniture and, of course, all our essentials. Mom had bought a new car in Fosston, a

Ford Fairlane 500. It was red. I never was much for Ford's, but I like that one. We moved to Plummer, Minnesota, and lived in an apartment above the Laundromat on Main Street. I worked on my tree house right up until we left the farm, one reason I didn't want to move. Mom and Everett did find a house in Thief River to buy. The house was on State Street by the Hartz warehouse. As time went on, Everett became more and more of a problem. He was very controlling with all of us. I usually just ignored him as much as possible. I think we lived there for about two years. We got to know the neighbors. They were the Doughertys. Their kids were close to our ages, so I hung around with them and got to know Thief River Falls. We would ride our bikes around and explore the city.

Everett didn't like us to hang around with them. One time one of us fell from the tall ladder going up to the tree house. It was close to the neighbor's window, and somehow it broke. He was a crabby old man and didn't like children. One day when I was at school, Everett and Henry, the old neighbor guy, tore the tree house down, and I lost my tree house. Not long after that, Mom and Everett bought a farm by Viking, Minnesota, close to Newfolden. It was about fifteen miles from Thief River Falls. They sold the house quickly and got forty acres at that location. It was very small. It had no running water or sewer, but Mom made the best of it while still working at Arctic Cat in Thief River Falls. In 1972, I think they were able to purchase a fourteen-by-seventy mobile home. It had two bathrooms, three bedrooms, running water, and everything we needed. Mom was so happy to have a nice house. I was going to school in Newfolden and had a car and driver's license. I didn't spend a lot of time at home but went to school in ninth, tenth, and eleventh grade in Newfolden. I had a job in Thief River Falls at a gas station that was open twenty-four hours, so I went to work at night and school during the day. I had a nice 1956

Chevy Belair two-door hardtop. I even got to work on it at shop class in Newfolden School.

Well, that summer brought some problems, being raised on my own so much. Some of us boys from school got in trouble drinking beer. One of our friends decided to break into a bar in Newfolden and take a case of beer. Needless to say, we all got in trouble, being we were in the truck he had taken from where we worked. Jerry Alba and a few others walked about eight miles in the dark to Jerry's house. We did not want to be involved with that. In the meantime, Galen, the one who took the beer, ran in the ditch with the truck. He told authorities that we were all involved in the break-in. The cops had found him in the truck. He was passed out. Well, that led to a court date. They decided to send me away to get help. Back then, it didn't take much to be sent away. Off I went to Lino Lakes by Onamia. That is where they evaluate you for a few weeks and then decide where you go from there. After a short time observing me and the reasons I was sent there in the first place, they sent me to a camp called Thistledew. It was located near Cook, Minnesota, by Eveleth. That was a six-month program, but I really liked it there. It was more like going to camp in the summer. We were required to get up at five to start our day. Each week we could choose to work outside or take kitchen duty for a week at a time or longer if you wanted to. That's where I learned a lot about cooking. My boss's name was Geno. He taught me a lot. Many of the other kids didn't like him, but we were best of friends. He was kind of crabby if you didn't pull your weight. He had one of the nicest kitchens I've ever seen.

We had so much to do there. We actually got to go fishing, learn DNR stuff, kept up with our schooling, and many other fun activities.

When winter was over, we were required to go on what was called a challenge before we could be sent home. April 1, we started our training getting up at 5:00 a.m. and doing a five-mile run. May 1, we left on her 350-mile canoe trip with about twenty kids, two adult counselors, and seven canoes driving to the Boundary Waters, setting sail, so we thought! The first day was walking our canoes thirteen miles up the Pigeon River against the current to toughen us up. There was a lot of whining from the city kids. Because I had kitchen experience, I was the cook on the trip. You could not take any canned goods, only things that were disposable without damage to the environment. They did allow dried meat, pancake mix, fruit, and vegetables. We drink the water right from whatever lake we were on. We would be up by 5:00 a.m., pack up, eat, and back in the canoes by six thirty. We would travel twenty to thirty miles a day by canoe in the Boundary Waters. The trip was to take a month. We could also fish and eat all the fish we caught. The fishing was great!

Midway on the trip, we are required to stay by ourselves on an island on Lake la Croix. It had one hundred or more small islands, and the reason we were there was to help us reflect on why we were there and think about things. We were given a tarp, a small amount of food, sleeping bag, knife, fish hook, and line. That was about it. I spent three days by myself on my very own Island. I didn't catch any fish, but it was a good experience, and it went fine. The trip ended May 30 after 350 miles on the water. We were all ready to be sent home, and all in all, it was a good six months.

After returning back home, I stayed only a very short time. Everett by that time had become very eccentric and out of control. He was spending money they didn't have, and Mom was not used to that. She was always so good with money.

I continued to work in Thief River at many different summer jobs. One job that I liked was at the alfalfa pellet plant. My friend Mike Kal Sagan was the manager. He told us it was very hard work unloading hay bales twelve hours a day with very few breaks. He threw a perk in by letting us have all the free pop we wanted. Four of us said yes and were paid $10 an hour. That was unheard of in the 1970s. Normal wages at that time were $2 to $4 an hour depending on your skill. I did quite well that summer but worked very hard. The next summer, I was able to get a job with the city of Thief River Falls with the sanitation department (garbage truck) I was seventeen years old at the time and wasn't turning eighteen until March. They asked how old I was, and I said eighteen, and they never checked. I would fill in for other workers when they took vacations and for other reasons. That next fall, I was able to get a job at Streiger Incorporated. They built large tractors just out of Red Lake Falls, Minnesota. One of my friends, Russ Holton, worked there, so we took turns driving from Thief River Falls. I had rented a small house in Thief River Falls at that time. The working conditions were not good at the factory. It was very cold outside, and the factory was made in a very old barn. It was so cold we could hardly work. I work through the winter and left in the spring.

I then worked at a gas station called Fast Gas. It was a twenty-four-hour station as was most in the 1970s. I owned a 1953 Chevy two-door, which was in very good shape but had a very weak engine. The engine finally went out. I traded it off in Red Lake Falls for a 1966 Impala 55. It was the nicest car I had ever had. I worked at fast gas for a while cut the end of that summer, and I think it was 1974. I still had that Super Sport 66. At that time gas was only $0.26 a gallon, so driving around a lot was a given. Theibert Buik Still has the 1953 Chevy last I checked in 2019. I always wanted that car back, but as I understand, it was taken apart to restore and never ever finished. As far as I know, it's still sitting in storage at the Theibert Farm.

I spent a lot of time in Thief River Falls at the club, it was a pool hall. There I met a couple friends, and we would go to concerts. I met a band called Jacania. They were from

Thief River Falls, and I became friends with them. They were brothers, Marlow and Terry Dunham, and very talented musicians. They were into rock and roll, and I think some drugs too. Drug stuff was going on all over in the 1970s. Seems a lot of people I knew were into drugs, but I never really wanted to go down that road. I tried it a few times but didn't like it. Later that summer, I ran into Marlow and Terry, and I asked them how the band was doing. To my surprise, they said they had given up the life of drugs and rock and roll and realized there was more to life than having a band and doing drugs. They said Jesus had made a difference in that change. We talked a long time that day. They lived in an older mansion-like house on Labree Avenue in Thief River Falls and had started a new Christian band.

They invited me to come over and listen and watch their practice sessions. Well, I thought about it, and a few days later, out of curiosity, I went over to the house. They sounded very good.

Marlo showed me some more guitar chords. I already knew some chords, and over the next few weeks, I went over there quite often. I always really liked them, and this brought us closer together. They had a furniture shop in the big house. They would refinish old furniture for people. They needed some help, so I was glad to lend a hand. Eventually I moved into the house, which was called the Miracle House. There were eight or nine bedrooms, a common kitchen, and they had a pastor living there. His name was Oliver Urdahl (Ollie). There were about fifteen to twenty people living there. I moved in and worked in the woodshop. Ollie had a farm at McIntosh, where his parents lived, and I would go out and help with farmwork too. That summer of 1976 was very busy with all the stuff I was involved in. It was kind of nice to be a part of that community.

In the spring of 1977, I found out there was a job opening at the Ke Wells Bottling Company. It is now owned by Pepsi

Cola. I was hired the very next day I applied. They put me to work as a route salesman. It was a lot of lifting and miles on the road, but I had no problem with that. The job went really well. Eventually myself and another friend I met at Miracle House, Rick Lindsey, moved into an apartment in Thief River Falls. Rick was a very talented musician and a songwriter. He also worked at a paint and glass shop. We lived there for a few months and then moved into a house a friend from Hutchinson had just bought on Dewey Avenue. Another friend, Paul Lasha, worked at the tire store in Thief River Falls. He said he had a date with a girl from Fosston. I asked him what her name was. He said Julie Fisher. They came over to the house. We played games and had a few beers. They really never hit it off. So I started dating Julie. She was in school at that time for cosmetology. I was still at Pepsi route sales. Julie and I dated that year. We went to concerts, car racing in Brainerd, and fishing. Looking back, I think she was just in it for the fun. In July of 1978, we were married at the Catholic church in Thief River Falls. Growing up as a Catholic at St Mary's in Fosston, I knew the routine. The Catholics seemed to think they could work their way to heaven. I never did understand the robes and garb and rituals growing up. Just thinking about what my good friend Marlowe told me, that's as simple and as hard as believing John 3:16. This is my view on the subject. Everyone is entitled to their own opinion.

Julie and I lived in a rented house in Thief River Falls. In 1979, Jason came along. Julie didn't work and stayed at home taking care of the baby. My Pepsi job was not financially enough, so we struggled. To top it off, there were changes in the management. It was purchased by the Pepsi company, and technology was changing. The economy was changing, so everything was getting very expensive. Groceries, gas, and just everything was skyrocketing. I got laid off from Pepsi and had to draw unemployment for a while. It was half the amount of money I was used to making. The next spring, I was able to get a job at Northern Insulation Incorporated. It was right outside of Thief River Falls, and my friend's dad owned it. Due to everything going up in price, the government had programs for people to insulate their homes. So we had plenty of work to do. It was very long days, many overnights, and long distances. Some of the locations were in Baudette, Eveleth, and even into North Dakota.

In March, Josh came along. Everything seemed fine, but when he was two years old, he developed a tumor on his spine and on his butt. By then we had moved to Fisher, Minnesota, to work at my mother's café there. I also work for Ross Farms part-time. It turned out Josh had to have surgery at Children's Hospital in Minneapolis. They removed a two-pound tumor from him. It had attached to his spine and tailbone. It was cancerous, and there was a chance of paralysis. He was hospitalized for about a month or more. He was started on chemotherapy with a catheter put in his chest to receive the dose directly in his heart. This would require twenty-four-hour care. Things at this point were not going good with Julie and myself. With all the stress, she just walked out without any warning. I didn't even know where she was. Jamie, our daughter at this time, was just a small baby. I was home alone with three kids trying to take care of them with special needs for Josh. He needed daily shots and dressing changes. Needless to say, I had no time to work, no money coming in, and had to go on county assistance. Josh was doing okay but had to make trips to Minneapolis for more care and checkups. I had a 1964 Cadillac that we made the trip with many times. I actually still have that car, but it's just sitting in the pasture. I'm not in too good of a shape to move on to what happened next.

Needless to say, a divorce and custody battle begins. Court was in Mahnomen, Minnesota, with many court dates. The decision was made that Julie would get the kids.

I remember the judge saying women should take care of the kids; men should work. Well, there I was, with a house payment, no job, and many bills to pay. I had to let the house go back to the bank, and I moved to Fosston with Mom. Mom was working for a combined insurance company at that time and was on the road a lot. This was not what I wanted to be doing, but here I was in Fosston. It was now 1981.

I was able to get a job helping my brother Tim in the construction business. With very little money and a lot of bills, it was very tough. Eventually, I was able to get a job at a new car lot that has just opened up, something I've always wanted to do. It's now 1983. The car lot was in the old creamery in Fosston. The owners were also building apartments in the back, and I was able to help with that. I now have a little more income.

Mom was still working at Combined Insurance and was still on the road a lot. She decided an apartment would be easier for her. We started looking for something. We made a deal on a trailer house in Fosston. It was more room when I had the kids. Things were looking up. Julie had the kids in Thief River Falls, so I was able to get them on weekends. In the summer, a coworker from the car lot, Rick, moved into the trailer with me.

In the fall of 1984, the apartments were done and move-in ready. Rick and I saw a car pull up, and they were starting to unload their trailer end. So being helpful, we went over and gave them a hand. To make a long story short, it was Deb and her parents. She had just taken a job at Fosston School as a special ed teacher. We help unload her stuff, and my friend Rick said he kind of liked her. Being new in town, he invited her over to my house to have a few beers. It turned out Deb and I actually hit it off with a lot of things in common. She was from Southern Minnesota and a farm girl. I really liked her right away. She was very smart and easy to talk to at that time. I had been seeing a girl from Bemidji, but she was just more of a friend than a girlfriend. That just kind of stopped. Deb and I started dating. She would stop at the car lot every day to just visit me and tell me about her day. I heard from my friend Doug Hoilman that she was a very nice girl, and he said he thought she really liked me. It really hadn't dawned on me just because she was so easy to visit with and talk to. She actually cook me supper on one of our early dates. It was very good. Deb became a very special person in my life. She made me happy even with all the stuff that was going on in my life. She was very accepting of Jason, Josh, and Jamie when those weekends came around. She was more concerned about doing the things with the kids instead of her own things. I always loved that about her. She kind of had a boyfriend but broke it off with him. I respected that. He came to see her for a weekend, and that's when she told him. I was so happy. Shortly after that, it was Thanksgiving time, and Deb was going to Blooming Prairie for the holidays. She had a 1977 Ford Galaxie, and I was kind of worried about her, being she was going by herself. We talked on the phone every day she was there.

That Friday a huge snowstorm hit all of Minnesota. I was so worried about Deb making it back to Fosston. We had no cell phone back then. Deb made it back by Wednesday the next week. By then Deb and I had become inseparable.

As months went on, Rick moved to a small trailer next to mine. Deb and I talked about her moving in with me, and we decided to do that. Shortly after that, we went out to Moran's restaurant for supper. We had a nice supper and a bottle of wine. We talked a lot and Deb actually asked me to get married. I enjoyed her so much and loved being with her, so of course, I said I wanted to get married. We set a date of August 17, 1986. Shortly after that, we were able to buy a new mobile home and some land south of Fosston. We bought the mobile home in July and were married at our new house in August. It was a beautiful outdoor wedding.

I continue to work at Apple Auto, learning the sales end of the business. Money was a little tight, but we made it work. She was always putting others before herself. I've always loved her for that and respected her. As time went on, the kids would come on weekends, and Deb's family would come visit also.

Apple Auto was eventually moved to Bemidji, Minnesota. That was in 1987, and I drove back and forth. I moved into a salesman and manager position at the car lot. Deb's job is going well at the school.

In 1988 our twins, Angie and Leigha, came along. Deb was so proud to be a mother and through the pregnancy as usual was so strong. My sister Alice came to our house to take care of the twins while Deb and I worked. It was so nice of her to help, and we are so eternally grateful for her doing that. The girls were two months early and very small. They weighed only three pounds each and had to be on heart monitors for six months. Deb and I both were working as hard as we could to keep the bills paid. Deb never complained and was the best mother I've ever seen. Jason, Josh, and Jamie were so proud of their new sisters.

I continued to work at Apple Auto until I was offered a job at Donlinger's. I would be a salesman for new and used cars. I made the move on August 23, 1992, my mother's birthday. It was a good move and a lot more money than I had ever been making. I set many records in new and used car sales.

In 1994, we decided to build a new house on our property and had plans drawn up. Just as we were ready to start, we found out there was a farm on the east side of Fosston that was for sale. So we went to look at it. It was a lot more than what we thought we could afford, but after looking at the numbers, we made an offer. We waited, and they came back with an offer we couldn't do. We went back and forth whether to build or buy. In the middle of negotiating, they called on the farmhouse and said our offer would work. They had one condition though. They wanted to stay there until January 1 of 1995 and would pay us rent for that extra month. So we agreed. We moved in on a very stormy day, but we got it done. It was so nice to have a big house.

By this time, the twins were five, and we had added Kelsey to our family, and she was three. We settled into our new home, and we're glad to have all the room. I continued at Donlinger's until the economy went bad in 2009. I got laid off after almost twenty years. I stayed home and collected unemployment and got caught up on a lot of work around the farm.

The following summer, I started a car lot in the old Haugstad building with the Carlson boys. They operated a repair shop at that location, something I had always wanted to do. In 2013, the car sales were slower due to the bigger dealerships taking the bulk of the sales. I was offered a cooking job from six thirty to one thirty at the grade school. That schedule would free me up to do the car lot and work at the school, Also it was nice to be where Deb worked.

In August of 2018, I was working in the yard trimming trees. I have done this many times. I was up in the tree thirty feet on a ladder when the branch snapped back and took me and the ladder thirty feet down. Deb was helping me, so she blocked my fall somewhat. The ambulance was called, and they took me to Fosston Hospital. I was in the emergency room and found out I had broken my femur and fractured my pelvis. Both wrists were fractured, and I had cuts and bruises. I was flown to Fargo, North Dakota, by helicopter. There they rushed me into surgery and put a rod and some other stuff to fix my leg. I spent the next ten days in the trauma center. I was then sent back to Fosston in a swing bed for about a week. Finally I was able to go home but had to have a wheelchair there. Deb stayed home from work and helped me adjust and take care of me. I started to get better slowly. In November of 2018, we went to visit Kelsey and Trent in Bismarck, North Dakota. We arrived Friday, and on Saturday, we shopped and did a few other things and then went back to Kelsey's. After supper, my ankle was swelling even with ice it wouldn't go down. Yeah. So off to the emergency room we went. The doctor checked me over and did an ultrasound. They found a blood clot in my leg. I spent a week in the hospital in Bismarck. Finally I got back home and slowly recovered.

The summer of 2019, I was getting along okay. In 2020, I will finally retire. Deb is planning on retiring in 2021 Our future plan is to travel some and see more of the kids and grandkids. Our kids are all successful and doing very well. That's all anyone can ask for. Thank you for letting me share my story for all of our family to see.

Love,
Paul

*****

My Response to Paul's Story

Thank you, Paul, for filling in those years when we kind of lost track of each other. A lot of your memories on the farm came back to me, like the wood scene, the animals, chores, and grandparents. We can both agree we had a great farm life. Our parents taught us well and set the tone for us to be good parents someday and very hard workers. We also had a great support group, including friends, neighbors, church family, and grandparents. I love the analogy of our dad: "His hands were his eyes."

I loved reading about the places you worked and why. Boy, we all had to buck up and survive. I never knew all the trials you and Evelyn and Audrey endured but so glad to know now.

I do remember the rumors when I'd be at a party or hanging out with roommates about you. The story was you were on drugs and got sent away. I never believed that for a minute. I'm so glad you wrote about how Gaylen got you and your friends in trouble. Sometimes you're just in the wrong place at the wrong time. The way it turned out though was so inspiring. You had to tough it out and grew into the person you are today. I have always believed in the tough love rule. If we enable friends and family, it only hinders their growth.

I do recall you staying in at the Miracle House and playing in that band. I also know you were happy there. I didn't have to worry about you then. I moved on and was married in 1972.

I remember when Josh had the tumor and how scared we all were for him and your family. Even with your marriage in trouble, I didn't worry because I knew how strong you were by then. God is so good in times of troubles, and we are so blessed to have Josh, Jamie, and Jason in our lives. I love that you moved on and met Deb. She's a gem and such an asset to our family. It was fun to read how you met and thanks for sharing that. I hope your kids will enjoy reading this part of my book.

I will never forget when Angie and Leigha were born. What a blessing they have been for all of us. Then Kelsey came along to finish off your super family.

Our family has always been so thankful for your strong family ties. I want to thank you for being the glue that held us altogether as our family grew. You always open your home for reunions and campouts even to this day. I know you think nothing of it, but we do. Not to mention the way you cook for all of us. None of the rest of us did that. We are also thankful we could be as close or closer than most families just because of your and Deb's hospitality. Mom, like the rest of us, was always so proud of you for doing that.

Your kids are going to love your story.

Now since we're retired, get your bucket list ready. Rick and I hope to travel with you and Deb on Route 66 and many other places.

Love,
Your big sister

*****

Theresa's Memories

My name is Theresa Stark. I am Sharol's older sister, fourth from the top. I am one and a half years older than her. That made us very close as we grew up. We had a big farm we were raised on with lots of great memories to share.

Our dad was blind but still worked in the construction business along with his dad, Grandpa Curfman. They would tear old buildings down and also build new buildings for others. One section I remember them salvaging became a bedroom for Grandma Curfman as they couldn't do stairs anymore. Daddy had to go back to Blaine School in the Twin Cities to learn his trade all over again. He also learned braille. He learned to dance again and walk as he had one leg amputated. We got to go to dances as a family at the Lengby Community Hall. Our neighbors and friends would all gather there on Saturday night, and we would have a great time. We would stay at Aunt Ellen and Uncle Howard's house in Fosston when our mom would take him back and forth to blind school. He made good friends there stop. One family, in particular Jim and Carmen Frazier, had four kids and would come stay on the farm with us. Jim was blind also, but he and Dad would build cupboards or benches or anything to keep busy while they were there right. Mel and Mack were two other good friends he met at school. They were also blind. When they would visit us, they spent a lot of time helping with the needs of the farm. They would join in trips to haul cans of water from the neighbors' spring well. They all loved to keep busy. We had no running water, just an outhouse as a bathroom. We also did not have TV. So we usually listened to the radio. Another hobby my dad had with carving diamond willow sticks. He made beautiful things out of them.

We went to church on Sundays and got to go to a two-week vacation Bible school each summer. That made for a strong religious foundation. Our dad was confirmed at the same time as some of us kids. I thought that was pretty cool, and so did he. He would read with Mom from the Bible to all of us. She was definitely his eyes many times.

In the fall and winter, we all worked together cutting logs all over our property. We had to get the popple. On the one side of the lake, we would cut popple trees. We could never go near the lake as it was deep and dangerous. We would take the horses around through Willie Weimer's land and pull out the logs, then return home to unload. Dad would unhook the logs, and back we'd go for more. We would load as many logs as we could lift onto the wagon, but there were some we couldn't lift. Willie, the kind, old hillbilly that he was, seemed to always show up to help us. He would also bring us apples for free. One time a load landed in the creek, and there he was helping us reload. My job was to mark the logs with a stick to be cut the right length. We got a whopping $8 a cord or so. We got more if we peel them.

I will never forget the beauty of the woods in the fall, especially out back of our house. Of course, we got enough wood to heat our house for the winter. We would then throw the snowy firewood in a hole through the dining room floor into the basement. We would then go pile it up later. It was nice to do that because it was by the big wood furnace where it was very warm. The money from the wood was for Christmas and to make it through the winter for all the essentials. Sometimes we got ice cream for helping.

In the summer, we all helped put up hay. We had a hay rack, and I got to do the dump rake. Then we would put the hay into haystacks. They were like a teepee shape, so the contour of them shed the water off. When we would go load the haystacks with pitchforks, we would see a lot of mice that made their homes there. That's why I hate mice! In the fall, we would also pick potatoes and put seven to eight hundred pounds of them in the basement. That would get us through the winter. We would go behind the harvester and pick as many as we could get. They were free. In the spring, we would go to the dark damp corner of the basement and get rid of all the smelly rotten potatoes that were left. None of us liked that job. Evelyn and Audrey never had to help with that because they were the little girls.

On the farm we had cattle, pigs, horses, dogs, and cats, which kept us quite busy with chores. We would round up the cows and could usually find them because Betsy had a bell around her neck. One time on the way home with the cows, I looked up, and there was a baby bear. I don't think we ever made it home as fast as that day. We had stopped to pick berries, but that day we came home with none. We had a special hill called Strawberry Hill. That was our best picking spot our entire life on the farm. We milked the cows by hand, but with so many of us, it went really fast! Ted and Sharol would squirt milk in their mouths right from the cow! Eewww. They would also squirt it to feed the cats. The cats loved that! A truck would pick up the milk cans and take them to town, and we'd get a milk check. Sometimes Mom and Dad would haul the cans to the creamery. They would bring home head cheese and blue cheese and take some to Grandma and Grandpa. They all loved it on crackers. Linda was one of our best milkers but also quite a menace. She ate a bag of feed once and had to go to a back Stantion and poop for several days. What a mess! Another time we couldn't find her, and she had got out into the woods for three days and had her calf. We always put cows in the barn to calve. She definitely had a mind of her own. She also ate too much, and the vet had to come stick a needle or trocar of some sort in her stomach and deflate her. She was okay again! But in the end, she wandered off to the lake and drowned. We also had a cow named Alice, haha.

To keep our food supply plentiful, we had a big garden and canned a lot of food. We also had a big chopping block to butcher chickens. I hate it when we chopped their heads off because it was really gross. They would flap around and spew blood all over. One Thanksgiving Mom decided to butcher the big red rooster. He was way too tough to eat. So the dogs and cats and pigs were very happy! I recall different dogs that we had but especially Lady. She got hit by the hay mower, and it cut one of her legs off. The vet had to treat it with a huge bandage and said when she chewed it off, it would be healed. We fed her molasses and milk to help heal it also. When Lady chewed it off, she was healed!

It wasn't all work. We had great friends and neighbors. Mom taught us to sew some things, and we also learned sewing in school. She sewed some shiny shirts even for the boys. We would get school clothes at Mrs. Haugen's store. We also got clothes from Aunt Clara. She had a daughter older than us. She would send a big box for all of us to share. Alice, of course, got first pick as she was the oldest, and it would fit her first. I was always jealous of that! We got hand-me-downs from others too.

Uncle Ed and Aunt Phyllis would come a lot of summers and visit us. They stayed in a cabin by Grandma and Grandpa Baustian in Bagley. Uncle Ed would hit golf balls into our fields and give us $0.25 a ball to go find them. It was a fun way to make money. Ed was my mother's brother. Her sister Karen who was a nun, visited us sometimes too. Uncle Leo and Aunt Rita and their son Timmy loved to come to Uncle Glenn's farm as he called it. One time when they were there with us, we got to go to the end of Bagley. We all ordered a small cone, and Timmy said, "I'll have the shrimp." We all laughed so hard because we had never heard of that.

Our grandparents on both sides were a big part of our young lives. One or both would come on most Sundays and be with us. They would bring birthday cakes for us and always a dish to share. Grandma Baustian made Ted a cake for his birthday. It was a coconut cake And before any of us could have a piece, he had eaten all the coconut off it. She was quite mad. I don't think he ever got another cake. Grandma Curfman would many times bring Jell-O dishes in a beautiful green bowl with bananas on top. She also made good hot dishes with macaroni, tomatoes, and meatballs, which stretched a long way to feed us all. When we stayed in town with Grandma and Grandpa, I remember his spit can. It really stunk! They lived in Fosston, and at times we would help them clean the house or do yard work. When their son Uncle Sam would be coming from California, we would clean the upstairs to. It was so old and dusty. It was so dingy we thought there was a boogeyman or a ghost up there. Sometimes we would find dead mice droppings, which made it very creepy. We never slept there but would clean up enough for them. We never slept upstairs, but Uncle Sam did. One year I got to go to the Iron Range with Grandma and Grandpa Baustian, and we planted a money tree. When I was ten or twelve, I remember Sharol and I getting to help Mom wallpaper. We got to write all over on the old stuff before putting the new stuff on. We also got to help paint an ugly, pukey green color in the living room. I guess it freshened up the walls.

Mama gave us perms before school started sometimes, and I remember our hair being very frizzy. We're not sure why she did that. Alice and Mom also showed us how to make Valentine's out of sample wallpaper books. They were pretty and fun to do. Back then you didn't go to buy things like that at a store. Some fun school times were when we got to go to the Shrine Circus in fifth grade. We got to eat at the Bratland Café when they picked us up after our trip. In third grade, I started crying because my rubber boots got wet inside. Even though I had plastic bags in them to keep them dry, I got wet. It made me mad. We had to walk to the school bus stop, and it was a mile away. The only lifesaving grace was we had a neighbor, Mr. Clause, that lived by the stop, and we could warm up there. He always had the wood stove fired up. We definitely would not have survived without his kindness. Sometimes we had friends or neighbors come home with us on the bus. They would get picked up later.

We had a really nice bus driver named Daisy. He would haul the oranges and apple boxes home on the bus for us that we got for Christmas. He also let us load Christmas trees one at a time to take to our classrooms if needed. Audrey, our younger sister, was a lot of fun. She believed the bunny that ran around the yard was the Easter Bunny. One day the bunny disappeared, and Mom and Dad told her he had to go to other houses for Easter. She also carried around her *Bozo*, which was a stuffed clown. She loved it. We would catch lightning bugs, and they really loved to watch them in the jars.

Sometimes we would help Dad carry things while they were building. I recall when they built our garage on the house we got to carry rocks by removing them first and using some in the cement. I dropped one on my foot, and it hurt for a very long time. I also went up on the roof when they were putting the shingles on, and I got so scared I've never gotten over the fear of heights.

I remember different cars that we had. We even got to work on some and painted a yellow one. The wind came up, and it ended up looking like sandpaper. One day when we got home from school, we heard that President Kennedy had been killed. Mom and Dad were sad, and we all prayed for their family.

With so many kids and animals, there were many days that things didn't go well. I broke my elbow one summer but still got to go to the lake. Of course, Ted had to splash me and got my cast wet, so we had to go to the doctor and get a new one. Sharol and I had the measles at the same time. We had to have our windows covered as we're supposed to stay out of any light. Ted and I were a little accident-prone. Ted was fixing or changing the sickle on the mower and slipped and cut his forearm wide open. It was so deep it didn't even bleed. Just fat and bone were showing. He had to go immediately to the doctor and get it sewed up.

I also jumped out of our tree house, and I ran a nail through the top of my foot. It was sore, but I was okay. My sisters and I were playing with washers and putting them on our fingers for rings. Well, they got stuck, and we had to go somewhere to get them cut off. Mom was not real happy with us.

We also got to go to the movie theater one time and saw *The Flying Nun*. They finally got a small TV when we were teenagers. Boy was that neat. The first show we watched was called *The Day the Earth Stood Still*. It was about a power outage in New York City. Dad would make us sit way across the room because people back then thought you could go blind from the TV light. We also watched *The Lawrence Welk Show* many times. So many things to recall, which has led me down a path of wonderful childhood memories. Thank you, sis, for letting me share.

Now to fill in the years we lost with each other forever when dad died on September 8, 1967. Mom worked hard to keep up with all of us all alone.

The next year, she met Everett Motl and married him. We sold the farm and moved to Thief River Falls. There they would work at Arctic Enterprises. I graduated from Thief River Falls in 1970. Sharol and I had an apartment together briefly, and I worked at the Rex Café. I had medical issues and then got a place of my own. I got pregnant, and it was a traumatic pregnancy. John was born in 1971. I had to stay in the hospital, so he was placed in foster care until I was well enough to take care of him. I got another apartment in the same house as Sharol. There one of my friends, Myron, lived in an upstairs apartment. Another guy named Duane Strandlian lived in one of the other apartments They were both welders at Arctic Enterprises. In November of 1971, I married Duane, and we moved a lot. When he would get laid off, we would move to Bagley. Then back to Thief River Falls for work, we moved back and forth as layoffs happened. Brenda was born July 13, 1972.

My life with Dwayne did not work out, so we divorced. I landed in Fosston and worked for my mom at the Little Café. Donna babysit for me. I met and married Larry Oak in 1975. I had a floral shop consignment store any ceramic shop. Larry and I divorced in 1991. I moved to Green River Wyoming and married Marvin's Stark on November 23, 1994. I ran a consignment shop until I had new health issues. I still taught landscaping painting at the senior center and also in Rock Springs. It was so popular sometimes up to twenty people and even youngsters as young as five years old and oldsters as old as ninety-four. I had a hard time keeping up with them. My friend Viola still has her card table setup and has painted for twenty years. Some of the students have taken a lot of classes. They even go to Las Vegas to get in-depth classes such as portrait paintings. They say they never forget their humble beginnings though. Most of them paint on their own now and make Christmas cards, gifts, and pictures for their families and homes. I am not teaching anymore, but it was fun to recall such a fond memory.

My family consists of Marv, my husband in retirement; my son Jon Oak and his family and children; Jessica, married to Chris Willis; and my four great-grandchildren—Kaden,

Savannah, Cameron, and Riley. Sarah is married to Sherman Rogowski. They have two children, Steven and Sarin. Bobby Ann, Jonathan, and Samantha round out the rest of my grandchildren. My daughter Brenda Foster is married to Bill Foster. She has two children, Gabrielle Hope Schmidt, born in July of 1998, and Christian, born March 30, 2001. Bill has three children—Brittany, Lauren, and Sydney Foster—and one great-grandchild. Brenda and Bill both work at Cass Lake Public Schools. Jon is on his own now and living in Wadena, Minnesota. Thanks for asking me to share, Sharol.

*****

My Response

Thank you so much, Theresa, for filling in a lot of the blanks for me to share in my book. You are so good at details of our life. I don't recall a lot of it, but some of it came back to me. I do remember Ted's accident and the incident of the washers as rings. I know now that wasn't really smart. I also now know where your life took you and made you who you are today. I'm so glad we keep in touch every week by phone because you still reside in Wyoming with Marv. I do watch over Brenda and Jon a lot because you live so far away.

Since I've been writing my book for the last three years, a few things have changed as I finish. I'm so sad that Marv died this last year. But at the same time happy 'cause it brought you back to Minnesota to us. We get to enjoy doing things together with you and Alice in retirement. Since you and Alice now live in Detroit Lakes, Minnesota, only forty-five miles away, we have already done so much together. I hope we get to do a lot more and share our retirement years together. We are truly blessed to have each other again.

Love,
Your little sister, Sharol

*****

Tim's Story

(This contains memories of Ted as well because Ted had passed away before writing his story for my book.)

I was born on January 18, 1950, at the Fosston Hospital. Mom and Dad lived in a rental house on Schamburger Farm six miles east of Fosston. Mom said it was twenty below zero when I was born. Alice was eleven months old then.

My very first memory is being hauled to the hospital when I was two and a half years old because (Black Eye) the dog bit me in the face. I had pulled his hair. He was a white sheepdog with black hair around one eye.

Ted was born just after I turned one year old. We grew up close. The grade school was built in 1956, so Ted and I started school the same year. He went to kindergarten, and I went to first grade. By this time we had three more sisters; Teresa, Sharol, and Evie. Also another brother Paul. Audrey was born three years later in 1959. I remember sitting on Dad's lap and steering the car as we drove Mom to the hospital to have her. That was ten miles away. Dad was blind, so he ran the gas and gears, and I steered the car. That makes eight of us kids in just ten years.

Dad had lost one eye in a screen door accident when he was six years old. He had a glass eye to replace his real eye. He had changed his first and middle names around as kids in school called him marble eye. His birth name was Marvel Glenn, so he changed it to Glen Marvel. He was severely diabetic and lost his other eye and his right leg when he was twenty-nine years old. He was blind when Audrey was born.

We milked cows by hand, cleaned the barn, and fed the cows and pigs and chickens. We worked hard from the time we were five and six years old. We did chores before and after school. I learned to drive tractor when I was seven, and Ted drove the Ford tractor through a shed when he was seven. We used the horses in winter to do the hay hauling and barn cleaning.

When I was twelve, I started working with Grandpa Alfred Curfman. We dug graves for Carlin Funeral Home and did various fix-it jobs around Fosston. I was paid $5 a day, and that was a lot to me at the time. Grandpa was a fair and honest man. I learned a lot from him. Alfred is our dad's father. Us three boys cut pulpwood in the summer to sell at Bagley and firewood for the wood stove at home. We were just thirteen, twelve, and eight years old at the time. Mom would drive the truck to Bagley, and we would get $20 for the logs. We went to the Mrs. Olson's thrift store in her garage and got our school clothes for the year.

When I was sixteen, I worked in the summer for Uncle Howard along with my cousins Melford and Ordell. We did remodeling of houses and other buildings. I also worked with them the summer of 1967.

For fun at home, we would go sledding and tobogganing on Strawberry Hill. We went ice skating on the stock pond, where we usually had a campfire to keep warm.

One or two of us would get to go along with Mom and Dad to Bagley depending on how good we were. We knew if we had been real good, we might get a nickel ice cream cone at the A&W on the way home. We took family trips to Bemidji and Itasca State Park almost every summer. Ted and I had horses, and in the summer, Dad's brother Harry would come out and ride horse with his new wife Ruth. This was in 1965 and 1966. Harry died in 1966 at the age of twenty-seven from diabetes.

On Saturday September 4, 1967, I met Donna Locken at the dance in. Lengby. She was there with her sister Ardis and her husband, Clayton, from Erskine. Donna lived three miles west of Winger. Ardis said I could take Donna home, so I did. On Wednesday September 8, our dad died from complications of diabetes. Donna never got to meet him. Dad's brother Howard died in a car crash the day after our dad's funeral. Donna and I dated until December of 1968 when we got married. I was going to tech school in Thief River and working at Arctic Cat. We moved to Winger in the spring of 1969, where I was assistant manager at Willcox Lumber Company. We rented a farmstead for $25 a month. Mike was born in July of 1969.

In 1970, we moved to Lake Park as I transferred to Willcox Lumber there as assistant manager. Melanie was born in November of 1970. In 1971, we moved to Audubon, where I worked for J&S Cabinets, building custom cabinets and cabinets for Dynamic Homes of Detroit Lakes. We bought a 1971 Liberty mobile home for $3,600 brand-new.

Grandpa Curfman died in 1973. He was seventy-nine years old. He was a great mentor to me.

Missy was born July 13th 1976. What a joy!

In 1974, we moved back to Fosston. There I started my own construction business, remodeling and building houses. I had my business for twenty years until 1994 when we moved to Alexandria, Minnesota. There I attended Alec Tech for three years. I got a degree in professional sales and sales and marketing. In February of 1997, we moved to Duluth, where I took a job with Lighthouse for the Blind. I was a customer service and public relations representative. They downsized in 2000, so we moved back to Alexandria. Here I worked at the A&W, Dollar Days, and Dollar District. I was hired by Walmart in 2006 as a building maintenance and worked there until 2015 when I retired. Donna and I have bought and sold three different properties in Alexandria and are currently finishing our new house east of Alec. We enjoy buying and selling anything and everything! Fun hobby!

In retirement, we are enjoying our five grandkids and two great- grandkids.

I just had my seventy-second birthday on January 18,

2022. My sister Alice will turn seventy-three in February 2022. Donna and I will celebrate our fifty-fourth anniversary this year and would like to go to Branson and Nashville again. We have lots of fun on bus trip tours even though we are retired we keep very busy.

Your brother,
Tim.

*****

Response to Tim's Story

I am so glad you could fill me in on some of those lost years. When we were young, so many different things happened to each of us. I hope my autobiography helps you to see how my life was back in those years we lost together. We all move forward, and that's really what matters.

It was very neat to read your early memories of the dog and our mom and dad. I love the part where you drove the car with Dad to take Mom to the hospital to have our sister Audrey. You are way too mature for your age. I do know that living on the farm and learning how to work together as a large family taught us all how to survive. I did not know how old Dad was when he lost his eye that was replaced with a glass eye. I can see why he changed his first and middle name. I'm sure his life at school was better at that point. It was nice to hear that you got to work with Grandpa Curfman a lot as a young man. What a great way to earn money digging graves together. It was good to hear that the pay wasn't great, but it was fair.

I do remember helping with the wood hauling and going to Bagley to get school clothes each year. We didn't have department stores back then, like we do now, that's for sure!

I'm glad we both remember the days of sledding, tobogganing, and ice- skating. We definitely knew how to make our own fun. I think that's why we all love camping, fishing, and the lake life as that's what we' got to do for free. Lengby Lake will forever be in our hearts and never forgotten.

It was too bad Donna never got to meet our dad. I didn't know you met her right then just a few days before dad died. Our poor Grandma and Grandpa losing so many of their children before they passed on. I'm so glad you learn lessons from our dad and Grandpa and pursued building your life literally. You are so good at construction remodeling and all the things you learned and know. I know it hasn't been easy with you being legally blind, but you just keep on keepin' on. It truly is your love to build things.

You have worn a lot of hats and still continue to do so. I'm glad you and Donna are enjoying retirement and making time for fun in your life. It was so fun when we all had our seasonals at Lake Victoria by Alexandria. Such good memories together along with the bus trips.

Rick and I love your new house you are finishing as I write my story. I say, "Remember to stop and smell the roses," which I know we all know how to do that! You're a great big brother.

Love,
Your little sister

*****

Ted's Story

Theodore "Ted" Curfman, of Thief River Falls, Minnesota, passed away peacefully on Friday, May 24, 2019, at his home at the age of sixty-eight.

Theodore "Ted" Curfman was born February 17, 1951, in Fosston, Minnesota, the son of Glenn and Mary (Baustian). He grew up on a farm by Fosston. Ted graduated from

Fosston High School. Following graduation, Ted moved to Minneapolis and got a job the very next day.

In December of 1969, Ted was united in marriage to Deborah Harthun in Fosston, Minnesota, and together they had three children.

In 1992, Ted married Rebecca Pagnac in Fosston, Minnesota. They raised their daughter Renee together. During this time, Ted also started bringing his mules to different events, giving rides to people of all ages.

On April 1, 2007, Ted was married to Jan in Prescott, Arizona. With God in their relationship, they had a spiritually enriched twelve years together, serving the Lord and community.

Ted had many different occupations. He wanted to be a farmer, but his dad passed when he was sixteen, so he did construction, scrapping iron, working with the beet harvest, was a rural mail carrier, did some farming, was an auctioneer, and served in the National Guard. Along with his wife, Jan, Ted was co-owner and cooperator of Curfman's Critters. Together they worked side by side for twelve years. Ted was very passionate about his mules and cared for all of them. Ted was also known for his horses and the pony rides at fairs. Twenty years ago, he bought his white mules, George and Gracie, in Missouri. He had a JD covered wagon, a sleigh, stagecoach, large red, white, and blue trolley wagon. Ted even built a smaller trolley. In 2016 alone, Ted and Jan had thirty-six events, bringing Curfman's critters to town parades, weddings, birthdays, and more.

Ted enjoyed his volunteer work. He helped with the TRF Area Food Shelf, where he helped with fundraising and volunteering and delivered and handed out food at distributions. Ted was a large help in the search for the current building. He also played Santa at the Holiday Train, provided equipment for the fair parade, and traveled to Haiti, where he built chicken farms with the church. His other favorite volunteer work included helping with church activities, the Big Brother Little Brother Program, St. Hilaire Lions Club, the Sons of Norway, and being a sober companion for several people in AA.

Ted's relationship with his Lord Jesus Christ was very important to him. A man transformed, in 2006, he walked into the Evangelical Free Church in Thief River Falls and asked the pastor to pray to have his anger gone. Ted was truly transformed, and from then on he was on fire for Christ. He was baptized on July 2, 2006, at 12:21 p.m. in Sand Hill Lake, near Fosston, Minnesota.

Ted is survived by his loving wife, Jan Curfman; children—Daniel (Kristi) Curfman, Matthew (Althea) Curfman, Christine (Riley) Fish, and Renee (David) Houske; stepchildren—Roxane Gilbertson, Dan (Karen) Pagnac, Amy Hyslip, Nathan Erickson, and BethAnn Donarski; grandchildren—Alexandria, Laura, Sadie, Belle, Noah, Tia, Gabrial, Keanon, Kathrin, Shavonda, Jeremiah, Jack, Kallie, Logan, Brielle, McKynzie, EdWyn, and Evangeline; great-grandchildren—Jazzmynn, Tristan, Riley James or RJ, Harley, and Harmony; siblings—Alice (Vernon) Wander, Timothy (Donna) Curfman, Paul (Debbie) Curfman, Sharol (Rick) Mason, Theresa (Marvin) Stark, and Evelyn (Maures) Karboviak; and many nieces, nephews, relatives, and friends.

He was preceded in death by his parents, Marvel Glenn and Mary Curfman; grandparents, Sophie and Alfred Curfman and John and Theresa Baustian; sister, Audrey Simmons; nephew, Dustin Simmons; and grandson, Travis Curfman.

In Loving Memory of
Ted Curfman
February 17, 1951–May 24, 2019

Anyone who was down and out,
Ted was there to help them out.
The mules were his joy and pride;
And Jan was his wonderful bride.
Ted was the best friend one could find.
We had twelve great years together, and twelve more
I wouldn't mind.
We were married in 2007 on April Fool's Day
In Arizona and honeymoon and back to Minnesota to stay.
He's in heaven and has no more pain.
He's laughing and telling stories again and again.
Whenever I see a red pickup,
My tears seem to show up.
I miss you every day and night.
Wish you were here to hold me tight.

Love you forever,
Jan Curfman, his wife

*****

Response to Ted

Your life story is your obituary. I would have much rather had you write about your life, but this will have to do. We all know you loved to tell stories, and I wish you could have shared some in my book.

I know you worked hard all your life and were a very loving brother through the years. I wish we would have had some time together in retirement, like we would always talk about at reunions. We do have many good memories to share, and you will never be forgotten. Until we meet again.

Love,
Your sister

*****

Alice's Memories

I give my sister Sharol Mason permission to use the following writing in her book.

I was the first child of my parents, Glenn and Mary Curfman. I was born in Bemidji, Minnesota, on February 2, 1949. My mom said she named me Alice because she knew a nice lady named Alice.

My dad was the janitor in the Solway School. When I was born, Mom took me upstairs to show me off to the students there. My parents had to move out as the basement apartment was damp and unhealthy for a baby.

I grew up on a farm east of Lengby, Minnesota. In the next ten years, our family was joined by my three brothers and four sisters. Now there were eight kids and Mom and Dad.

The girls slept in a large room upstairs with two full-size beds. Two of us slept in one bed and three in the other bed. I can remember sleeping in the middle as it was nice and warm. All three brothers slept in the room next door.

Here are a few memories from the farm.

One day my dad said I could have a calf. It was a brown-and-white one. So I named her Coco. Every day I tried to go out to see her. One day I went to see her, but she had been sold. I thought she was my calf. I was only about ten or eleven years old and didn't realize she was not my calf forever.

As the oldest girl, I was almost always in the house. My mom was outside helping my dad. I was expected to clean, cook, wash clothes, bake, and take care of the siblings.

When I was eleven years old, my grandma and grandpa Baustian came out during the week. I was washing clothes in an old wringer washer. My grandma went ballistic and screamed at my dad that I was too young to be washing clothes for ten people. *My* dad kicked my grandma and grandpa off our place that day. I was so upset I accidentally ran my hand into the ringer! Later that week, my grandparents did come back.

One day I was in the house babysitting and working. I had to go to the outhouse. While I was outside, I ran down to the shed my mom and dad were building. I was only outside for about four or five minutes. When I came back, I found the refrigerator tipped over on the floor. My brother Ted had swung on the refrigerator door and tipped it! My mom and dad came running into the house.

My dad thought that someone was under the fridge, so he lifted it up. That is a horrible memory for me. I was screamed at and told that it was all my fault! I received a whooping for that. I'll never forget that.

A fond memory was to run to the milkhouse at separating time. That is when the milk is separated from the cream in a machine. Many times I would take a tall glass and fill it from the skimmed side of the separator. Oh, how I loved that milk!

In my teenage years, I was busier and busier with more and more responsibility!

When I was seventeen years old, I met Lynn Bursheim at a dance in Lengby, Minnesota. It was November 27, 1966, on my sister Audrey's birthday.

In 1967, I graduated from Fosston High School. On September 8, 1967, our dad passed away from diabetes. It was my sister Sharol's birthday that day.

I married Lynn on May 4, 1968. We had five children together—Bruce, Laura, Brian, Marcia, and Christopher. Most of our married life we lived by Winger, Minnesota. Then in the town of Fosston, Minnesota, in later years. We divorced in 1990.

In 1995, I met Vernon (Beans) Wander. We were married September 6, 1995, in Bagley, Minnesota. Our house was on the White Earth Lake, east of Waubun, Minnesota. On September 6, 2020, we will have been married twenty-five years.

*****

My Response to Alice's Story

Thank you, Alice, for sharing what you could. I didn't know how you had met Lynn. I also didn't know where you were born. I did not realize you graduated the spring before Dad died either. I wasn't aware of how much responsibility came with being the oldest girl. I respect the fact that you didn't want to share all the hardships of the past as you told me. I'm sure you have more memories than the rest of us. I'm sure since I'm the middle child, a lot has escaped me. *It* could be that my guardian angel protected me from a lot too.

You have five great children that I'm so proud to call my nieces and nephews. Now that we're all in our golden years, I'm also glad we have more and more time together. This last year has been a doozy with COVID-19 and all the struggles it brought to all of us. You have stayed strong, and I'm very proud to tell you that.

This is how it went on that dreadful day for you in July of 2020. I know you don't know all of the details, but I was in the right place at the right time. I was so glad I was the one who could come and tell you the news along with Brenda, our sweet niece.

To start with, I was at Brenda's house, helping with her hemp products. In the middle of production, literally pouring product into bottles, I got a phone call that would change your life forever!

The call was from a police officer from some county way up north. They asked if I knew a person named Vernon. I said, "Yes, that's our son." She continued to tell me that he had been in a terrible semitruck accident. They wanted to know where to take him for life support. I said what happened and where because none of it was making any sense to me. Our son Vernon would not or should not have been in that area. So I asked her, "How old is this person?"

The lady on the other end of the phone said, "I'd say about seventy-five years old or so."

My heart felt grateful as I said, "Well, that's not our son Vernon." I asked the nice lady to please check the driver's license. She took about five minutes before she told me it said Vernon Wander. Then I knew for sure it wasn't our Vernon, but your husband who we knew as Beans. He had gone up to his five-hundred-acre piece of land with his best friend and neighbor. After they finished mowing and were about to head home, a bad accident occurred as they pulled out onto the highway. Again, they had called my number (which was in his wallet for some reason?) to ask where he should be taken as he was going to need life support. The lady finally asked if I was his wife, and I told her no. Because she (the onsite EMT) was only able to be in contact with one person, which she said were their rules, we had to figure out where to send him. The EMT said she would give us a few minutes to call someone who could give the directive of where to send him. She said she would call me back shortly.

Meanwhile, Brenda knew she had Rhonda's phone number, who is a daughter-in-law to Beans. Brenda quickly called her and told the situation and that we needed Leon, Beans's son, to tell us what hospital to send him to. The options were Duluth, Grand Forks, and Fargo. Other places would take too long to get there, and he didn't have that kind of time. Rhonda quickly returned a call after speaking to Leon. They wanted him sent to Grand Forks, North Dakota. When the EMT called back, I told her the family requested to send him to Grand Forks. I also gave the EMT Leon's name and phone number that we had gotten from Rhonda so that the hospital would be aware of who to contact if anything further had to be decided. Leon, Rhonda, Brenda, and I all agreed that you needed to be told in person. Brenda and I decided to come tell you the news and then take you to Grand Forks to the hospital. We stayed in contact with Leon and Rhonda as we drove to get you. We called you to make sure that you were home and that we were coming for a visit.

When we got there, you seemed excited to see us but were also questioning why we came there on such short notice. It was then that we asked you to sit down because we had to tell you some bad news. With that, I explained what we knew to have happened so far and also that we were still in contact with Leon and Rhonda as they were on their way to the hospital already. We asked if you wanted to go to the hospital too. Your reaction was that we should leave right now! We helped you pack a bag, and you grabbed some cash and your purse, and off we went. Because of the pandemic going on, we were not sure of the restrictions the hospital would have until we got there. Once we got there, you were the only one of us who was able to go in to see him. Leon and Rhonda had beat us there and were already in the room with him.

Throughout the next days, he was unstable and needed several surgeries to survive. He remained in the hospital from the day of the accident until he passed away in November. Unfortunately, Beans never knew that his best friend was killed instantly in the crash.

I want you to know that I felt that Beans knew you were with him when you visited. I still to this day do not know why Beans had my phone number in his wallet. Maybe it's because God sends guardian angels to step in when they are needed. I hope we can always support each other in times of need.

I'm so glad you have found happiness living in Detroit Lakes but mostly for me! Because you only live fifty miles from me, and it is so much closer to visit.

All this happened in the middle of the pandemic. I know there is way more to the story, but the rest is only yours to tell.

Love,
Your little sister, Sharol

CHAPTER 14

A Stable Guy

The next spring. I met Ralph. He was four years older than me and had a good job at Arctic Enterprises. He was quiet and reserved and was friends with Jeff. They had the same circle of friends while being in the service. I had known him through the group, and he had just gotten out of the army. We both had come from big families and hit it off right away. We dated about five months and got married. We had a large Catholic wedding in Thief River Falls with five bridesmaids and groomsmen. He was not very outgoing, but at the time that was refreshing for me. He preferred to stay home a lot and worked nights. Most of my family made it to our special day. Now with the older siblings having already started their families, we were starting to reconnect. *We* also had bought our first house together so as to not keep paying rent. It was a beautiful three-bedroom with a fireplace, garage, and nice fenced-in backyard with a wonderful patio. We would grow into it in time.

Ralph was lead person in the fiberglass department and thought I would maybe want to work there. I applied and was hired to start the next week. I let go of my other jobs and worked under him from 1972 to 1980. It was a great job, which included putting decals on the snowmobile sides on an assembly line. I then learned to put the side vents in and eventually was moved to working as the hood inspector as they came off the line. There I would check each hoods for soft spots by using a rubber hammer. If I would find a defect, out the door they would go. If there were several in a row, the line would have to stop to fix the fiberglass mixture. Sometimes it was just a simple change to the sprayer to adjust thickness or the drying process. Either way everyone liked when we would get a few extra minutes to break. Of course, management did not and were pretty efficient at fixing or finding the problem. The best part of this job was not only the pay, but also the benefits were something we would never forget. They paid our family insurance each month completely, and it was super great insurance. We also would have a snowmobile each and every year to ride for personal use. Who wouldn't love that. They did it as an advertising strategy so as to show off their new and upcoming styles. We did pay $8 a year for liability insurance, which was a no-brainer. My favorite snowmobile was the Jaguar. It was small, fast, and easy to handle. Ralph liked the Panthers the best and would try new and different ones each year. Some other models were the Cougar, Cheetah, El-Tigre EXT, and the FireCat. We both had very good and lifelong friends from working at Arctic. We both loved working together and couldn't be happier. The only downfall was fiberglass was very itchy, so we would keep all our work clothes separate to wash. Believe me, you wouldn't want your towels or undies in the same load.

CHAPTER 15

Our Family Grows

It is now 1974, and we want to start a family. Joey, our first child, was born in August. *My* pregnancy was great, and he was only three weeks late. I didn't really like that but worked right up till he was born. I got eight weeks of leave and didn't have to go back that year as they had early layoffs. What a lucky, lucky time that was to be able to be home with our newborn. Joey was a fussy baby, but I thought that was normal and just embraced being a mom. I had always loved babies, but there is no better joy than your very own.

We were so blessed with two baby showers before Joey came along One was from the Arctic people, and we got so many generic things because back then you didn't know the gender until they were born. I loved that it was a surprise. My family also had one, and we got a crib and so many other useable items. We had also gone to a parenting class, and they had a drawing and gave away money and baby stuff. Well, the lucky person I am, we won the grand prize. It was just crazy and included a play pen, diapers, bags, toys, clothes that were either for a boy or girl, and a $200 gift certificate. We really didn't have to buy much for our boy.

I soon realized I needed my driver's license. I now had doctor appointments, and Ralph was at work, and I wasn't. I had no training but learned by going out on the country roads and then in town. Some of my close friends were a great help. I just hoped and prayed I would pass, and I did. It was one of the best things I ever did, but I just wish I could have done it sooner.

When Joey was about a year and a half, we got pregnant again. I never felt good with this baby, and we lost a little boy at five months along. He had died inside me at three months, and my body was trying to abort it as the nurse told me while losing him. I didn't like the term *abort* as I never planned it that way. She explained that there was natural abortions, and they are out of your control. That made me feel a little better, but I was very sad for a long time. Ralph, being a man of few words, was not much support as

I think he just didn't know how to feel or react to such an ordeal. I got through this very trying time.

In November of 1976, Amy came along, and I felt so good with her, so wasn't worried about another miscarriage. It all went well, and ten days late, here she was. She was a beautiful baby with a lot of dark curly hair and was healthy. That's all that mattered to me. She did sleep way more than Joey ever did, which concerned me, and I hoped nothing was wrong.

A few weeks later, I realized she was just calm and content. There were a few times I actually did wake her just to be sure.

We loved her so much, and Joey was the best big brother he could be. He never got tired of getting to hold her and help run for the bottle or diaper. We timed this perfectly again as I'm on maternity leave, and layoffs are in December, right before Christmas. I felt so blessed to be able to be home again with our newborn. God's plan was definitely working, and I treasured my time with her and Joey.

We soon found ourselves staying home more and more. Our friends were in the same boat, so we would all get together for card and board game night. It was usually on Saturdays or Sundays, and we could bring the kids to one another's houses. With being laid off for three or four months in the winter, it was a good pastime. We had several couples to host, so it wasn't much work, and we always brought a dish to share. We had such good friends. Sometimes we would watch sports teams play or go on poker runs. The poker runs were snowmobile runs down the Thief River and stopping at bars along the route and picking up one card at each place. We would each end up with a poker hand, and whoever had the best hand won the pot. Oh, you had to pay $1 for each card you collected. That's where the money came in. It was such fun times. The legion hosted this activity every week as long as there was snow and the river had the right thickness of ice. Of course, we rode our new snowmobiles and showed them off. Some of the riders did drink at each bar, so then they would be a passenger behind the designated driver. I didn't like drinking, so I was the DD most of the time. Also for me, it was more about the fresh air and freedom to ride that hooked me. With good jobs and good friends, I sum this time in our lives as the good old days. A time to remember.

Foster Care Days

We also, during these years, decided to do foster care. Yes, we were young but also knew there were kids out there who needed care and a home. Ralph had a troubled childhood and was from a family of fifteen children. Yes, his mom had ten with his dad and five more with their stepdad. He was even in an orphanage and then lived with his dad and stepmom. With so many kids, it was a tough time for them. His brother Orville was the most open about their life, and he and I had planned to write a book, but he was killed in a crash before it happened. Ralph would never talk about his life and carried it all inside. Even though it affected our life, it's their story to tell, not mine.

I myself chose to do foster care because at fifteen, I didn't have a home and had nowhere to go. I figured it out but had friends who weren't as lucky. They crashed many times wherever they could find a couch or floor. My places were always a place of refuge for anyone in need. The least I could do now was to open our home to those in need.

We got licensed, and we passed all requirements as everything in our house was up to date. We were thankful we had bought a big-enough house. We also had to go to many classes to learn how to take the best care of these children. We learned about fetal alcohol syndrome, ADHD, drug issues, and so many classes on behavioral management. This helped us to raise our own, foster, and respite kids. It also at times would help Ralph relate to and understand things that happened in his childhood. Believe me, his childhood trauma would trump mine any day of the week. Many times I would bring up counseling, but he wouldn't hear of it. He chose to bury the demons inside. He would come close to exploding in stressful times but never allowed himself to vent. I was thankful for that, and we worked hard to raise our kids to have it better than we did.

CHAPTER 16

Jobs in Jeopardy

Just when life was looking really good and we just had Ryan Ralph, our third child, things were about to change. Ryan was born April 24, 1980, and was such a bundle of joy. We are loving our family of five and living quite well. In May, we got word that Arctic Enterprises was in trouble. Many workers would either have to take a pay cut or get laid off. Well, a pay cut wasn't going to happen, so instead everyone went on strike. People got greedy and demanded more wage and pay. Ralph was in management and he knew the company couldn't do that, or they would go under. A strike didn't solve anything but went on for two or three months. We would get threats and even vandalism, but it was out of our control. I think people went a little crazy, and everything just got worse. In the end, Arctic closed the doors. Life can change in a blink of an eye, and now we had to figure out what we should do next.

We had no idea how long the shutdown would be, and the word on the street was probably never to be open again. When things looked gloomy, we knew we just had to pick ourselves up, dust ourselves off, and find a new job. It was again good timing for me as I was on maternity leave. I got lucky again and get to stay home with my newborn. I love God's plan. Of course, everyone was in the same boat, looking for work around town. We still applied to several places, adding ours to the stack of applications. During the process, we got wind that a lot of people were going to work in the oil fields out in Williston, North Dakota. We had never dreamed we would move let alone so far from family and friends. Ralph still applied and was hired almost right away with NL McCullough. He would be working on the oil rigs.

With a newborn and two other kids, I stayed behind and gave it some time to see if he could do this or not. What a change for all of us. When he got there, he really liked it and immediately started looking for housing. The pay was great, but housing was very expensive and hard to find because everyone was moving there. It took three months before he found us a two-bedroom apartment on the third floor of a complex. He took it and sent for us. Meanwhile, I already had our house rented to our good friends if and when I got the call to move. We moved there in August of 1980. The company had put Ralph up until he found housing for all of us. It was hard trying to care for three kids by yourself let alone packing up and moving all alone. I did have good friends help load the U-Haul and would have never gotten through it without them. I did downsize and left some furniture for the renters and packed as light as I could. It wasn't like I had never moved, but it had been a while.

CHAPTER 17

Williston, North Dakota, Here We Come

Well, the apartment was pretty small, and the kids adjusted so well. It wasn't too bad, but it was hard to go get groceries with three kids and get them all to the third floor through three flights of stairs and locked doors. I devised a plan and would take the kids up first and have the neighbor watch them until I got the groceries carried up. We all helped one another, which was a blessing. Everyone was from anywhere and everywhere, but what great people I met. A lot of them were the wives of the other oil field workers. We all babysat for one another and helped with rides and supported one another any way we could. Many days it was just plain exhausting especially when Ralph would be gone for weeks at a time out on the rigs. He couldn't help at all, and when the guys were home, they all wanted to drink and party. It was like they wanted to spend all their hard- earned money every chance they got. Us wives would go with it, but at the end of the day, someone had to take care of the kids, so most of us were the DD. I was not much of a drinker, so I could see that we got home okay. This lifestyle was not what I was used to, and I definitely did not like driving in a strange town and state but felt I had no choice. I know a few of the guys got DWIs, and that even back then cost them dearly. Ralph dodged that, but I really don't know how he did not get caught. I guess it was the guys' way of unwinding from being gone so much.

The kids adapted so well and had friends their own age right in our circle of NL McCullough friends. Joey was in school and had good friends there too. They all fit in right away. We would have picnics and go swimming and just play at one another's houses.

I joined a bowling league in the afternoons and met lots of good people there. I was offered a job at the bowling alley to babysit other people's kids while they were bowling. It was a great job as I could take my kids with me for the two or three hours I was working. My kids loved it, and it paid good. Plus each family would tip me so I could buy treats. That wasn't necessary, but it sure added up. I would provide a snack and play games and music. The little ones loved it, and I loved working with kids. I also got to bowl for free because I worked there. It was most definitely one of the best jobs I ever had, and they provided the room crib's mats. It also got me out of the apartment three or four days a week.

CHAPTER 18

Better Housing

We didn't really need me to work but soon realized we had plenty to get or at least look for a bigger place. That next summer, we found a trailer house and bought it brand-new. We hadn't sold our house back home but had great renters, and we were guaranteed the rent because they were on a HUD program. The rent came directly to us each month, and they weren't going anywhere soon. We found a lot on the edge of town for the trailer. The only downfall was there was no curb or gutter as of yet, and it was smack-dab in a field with pretty poor gravel roads. You had to see it to realize how desperate we all were to have a home. It would be at least a year before the curb and gutter would be put in. It was a trailer park of probably a hundred lots. We loved the location and made the best of it. Of course, it was the rainiest summer Williston had ever seen, which made for the muddiest mess you could ever imagine. We had to adapt to the situation. Everywhere you went, there was mud and people getting stuck and having to be pulled out. Most of us that summer came up with the best idea we could by letting the kids play in it in their swimsuits. I hope the kids remember how much fun that really was for them but not so much for the moms. In the evening, we would pick them up at the door and carry them directly to the tub. It was a system that worked but not ideal. For lunch, we had a little play picnic table right outside the door. If they chose to come in early, they had to stay in for the rest of the day. Who would have ever dreamed we would let our kids wallow like pigs in the mud. It was quite the memory though.

I am now meeting new friends in our new location and getting to know all the wives. We spent a lot of time

visiting and just getting together with the kids. One of our closest friends are Linda and Goody Godejohn. They had a daughter, Lynn, who was Joey's age; another daughter, Lori, who was Amy's age; and another daughter, Katy, who was, believe it or not, Ryan's age. We became friends so quickly with having so much in common. Another good friends were Shirley and Craig Edwards. I can't forget Linda Olsen and Mike. They all worked with Ralph on the oil rigs. All the fun we had together bowling with the gals, having barbecues and swim parties, and becoming lifelong friends. I also met Pauline Everson, and she and I hit it off right away. We we're on the same bowling team along with Linda and Linda. Us women looked out for one another and always looked forward to the guys coming home and getting to go out, of course, to the bars and drinking, but it was just what it was. It wasn't an ideal situation with them gone so much, but we made it work and made the best of it. I guess we all learned to go with the flow.

When Ryan was six months old, we noticed he ran into stuff and was banged up a lot. He also was not afraid of anything. I took him to the eye doctor and found out that he was very, very nearsighted. He got his first pair of glasses at eight months old. Everyone said he would not keep them on, but once he could see better, he would cry when I would take them off. He ended up having several pairs, increasing the strength as he grew. He always loved getting his new glasses. He loved the water and swam at eight months old. When I took him to a swimming class, all the other moms couldn't believe it. He was like a fish and didn't like to come up for air. Sometimes I would pull him up just in case. The other moms were dealing with spitting, sputtering, and crying. It was kind of a proud moment for me. Amy had a lot of ear infections and ended up with several tubes inserted in her ears. The doctor said she had chronic ear disease. He also told us it would probably cause permanent damage over the years. We doctored in Rochester, Minnesota, as they were the best. Joey was quite healthy and only had tubes in his ears one time.

I guess you could say we were settling in to Williston, North Dakota. We loved our new trailer house and all the room we had compared to the apartment. One thing I didn't like in North Dakota was the howling wind. It never stopped and was very annoying. We have been in Williston almost two years now, and it's a life, but I miss Minnesota and my family. We had visited Mom and Everett just before we left Minnesota. They were living in Fisher, Minnesota, before we left. Mom owned a restaurant there. They had a trailer house, and were doing okay. I had seen most of my brothers and sisters before we had left for Williston at different birthday parties for all our kids. We had also been to a few weddings before we moved.

CHAPTER 19

A Trip to Home in Minnesota

Now I was making plans for myself and the kids to go home to see Mom and Everett. I had a sub for the bowling alley job, so that wasn't a problem. I told the kids we would be going home to Minnesota to visit Grandma and Grandpa. Immediately Amy started crying and was so upset. She kept saying, "I'm not going." I couldn't figure out what in the world was wrong with her, but I knew by her reaction it was serious. She loved Grandma and always couldn't wait to go there. She cried for a few hours but finally told me why. We hadn't been there or home for two years, so she was only two and a half when we left. She said Grandpa woke her up from her nap in the trailer house and hurt her. I asked her how he hurt her, and she said, "Where I pee." I asked her again as I couldn't believe what she said. She said the same thing with more detail and that she didn't want to ever see him again. I knew by how scared she was that it had to have happened. I never doubted her for a minute because no child could think that up.

My next question was, what do we do now? My foster parent training kicked in, and as a mandated reporter, I knew what I had to do. There was a protocol to follow in any difficult situation. I just never dreamed it would or could happen to a two-year-old and remember so much two or more years later. It definitely was hard to understand or even comprehend when it was our own sweet little girl. I called Ralph at his work and told him, and he agreed this had to be reported. He would be gone for another two weeks, so he couldn't help navigate this situation.

We lived twelve hours away, and it happened in another county. My first call was to the Williston Police Department.

They were very helpful and gave me the number for Polk County in Minnesota. I then called the police department and told them what had happened there. They took all the information over the phone and assured me they would bring him in for questioning. They also said after that they would call me for the next step in the process.

I now had to call my mom and let her know what Amy had said and that the police would be calling them. She was just devastated and so sad but also told me he had gotten somewhat unstable. She was afraid of him by now as his mental illness had progressed. I told her to let the police handle it and not confront him. She did just that for her own safety.

Well, it turned out that we were home the next week, and they had questioned him before we got there. He admitted to all of it, but Amy wasn't the only victim. He had been abusing some of the neighborhood girls too. He gave them names, and those parents were notified. Many of them pressed charges, and he was charged with sexual assault with minors. My god, they were babies! How sick was that. They all ranged from two years old up to eight or nine years old. It turned out he was sent to a mental hospital for evaluation due to his mental issues over the years. I guess you could say he just wasn't all there. He did get some jail time and also some help with his illness. If I would have had a say, they should have thrown away the key.

My poor mom felt so bad and had no idea he was capable of doing something so evil. We did talk a lot while I was home, and I assured her it was not her fault. There were lots of tears on that vacation, and I strongly suggested she go to counseling. We talked on the phone a lot after I returned to Williston. She did reach out for a while, but when he got out and came home, she said it was never the same. She thought she could help him and was hoping he had got the help he needed. She ended up divorcing him after he turned on her and threatened to kill her while holding a knife on her. She knew then she wasn't safe. I think he was more than capable of killing someone in his fits of rage. We were all so glad Mom would be safe now. He was then put in a home that would help with his care. In the end, he didn't even recognize Mom or anyone he ever knew.

We did take Amy to play therapy, and she seemed to forget about it after a while. We also assured her she would never see him again. We were so proud that she was able to tell and help others in the process. It was so nice that none of the victims had to go to court or testify because Everett did confess and accept his consequences for his actions. That could have been so much worse if he would have denied. There are so many different kinds of predators, and all we can do is teach our kids about how they could be lured into danger and how to yell for help and tell if they can. There are bad people out there along with many good people. We need to get educated and at least try to keep our kiddos safe and stop abuse in its tracks.

CHAPTER 20

Housemates

We were in our third year in the oil fields. We had made good friends while living here. Ralph's brother Bill and Carolee called and asked if they could come live with us and look for work. So they moved in with us, and we had a lot of quality time with them. They were helpful with our kids as they only had one of their own (Jimmy). That was so nice for all of us. They started their job hunt right away, and Bill landed a job with the city. It was a smart job choice as we were hearing rumors that the oil fields were cutting back and not sure how long before a layoff would happen. They stayed with us several months so they would have rent or a downpayment for a home. We we're so happy to help them out and get started. Their timing was much better than when we moved here because with people already being laid off, there would be housing available for them. They found a place and moved out.

CHAPTER 21

The Boom Is Over, We Move On

The rumors were true, and Ralph got laid off, and here we were again looking for work. Our house in Thief River Falls had not sold and was still being rented, but the job situation was still very poor there. We knew Arctic Cat was still closed, so there were no promises there. We both agreed we wanted to move back to Minnesota somewhere, anywhere as the oil fields were just not for us. It was definitely a different lifestyle than we were used to. We loved the money, but money isn't everything when you never see each other.

Ralph got a job interview in Wadena, Minnesota, at a fiberglass mold- making company called Dow Light. He would be making burial vaults. He got the job there, and I guess we're moving to Central Minnesota. He went on a head and started work while looking for housing. It was a blessing that we had bought a trailer house as there was lots of places for trailers in Wadena. He and I found several choices to pick from, and we chose Pine View Acres. It was about a mile out of town with big backyards and maybe fifteen sites. The landlord was very accommodating and helped us a lot in this move. The best part of this move was being able to leave everything in the trailer house except for what I needed to get by until we would get there. Within about a month, our plan was put into motion. I packed the essentials for all of us. I paid all the bills and closed our accounts in Williston and headed to Wadena. Believe me, it was one long trip with three kids. The trailer house was leaving to get there the same day with the moving crew. We did have to stay in a motel for a few nights until everything was hooked up for the trailer house. It was a sad day leaving such great friends and hard for the kids to say goodbye to theirs. Some of our friends didn't fare as lucky as we did. Everything seemed to always fall into place. Even his work would be close to where we live.

I will continue my story now. We are back in the trailer park in Wadena, Minnesota. The landlord was a great guy, and his name was Maurice Schwartz. Our neighbors Dave and Linda Klinke had four kids, and three of them were the same ages and grades as our kids. They all rode the bus together and played a lot together. Michael was the same age as Joey. Amy was the same age as their Amy, and to keep them apart, we called their Amy as Amy K and ours just Amy. Then there was Kimmy, who was between Amy and Ryan. To round it off, there's Johnny, who was the same age as Ryan. How lucky can a person get? There were other kids in the trailer court and a lot of elderly people and single people too.

It's 1983 around Christmas time I decided to take a job selling Avon to make a little extra money and get to know my neighbors. They all seemed happy to have an Avon lady in the trailer court. Money was quite tight as we were used to the oil-field pay and had been without paychecks for a little while. I was able to get all our Christmas gifts for the kids through Avon that year.

Ralph's building up his business making the burial vaults. It cost more than he figured and also went in streaks depending on how many people died and how many vaults were needed each week.

Ryan was having trouble adjusting with all the changes that year. He was having trouble with his training, but once we settled in for a few more weeks, he was being a big boy again. They were all doing well in school and fitting in good. I was still looking for work with more hours in mind.

Ralph took a second job at Bell Hill Recovery Center. He made vaults during the day and worked nights at the recovery center. He took care of people in recovery of alcohol and drug abuse. That job took him away mostly every weekend. Not ideal for me or the kids.

I finally got a job at the Four Seasons restaurant doing waitress work. I worked during the day while Joey and Amy were in school, and I took Ryan to a daycare. Things were looking up, but I was still applying elsewhere for full-time hours. I made really good tips especially on weekends. I started a savings account to save money for a downpayment on a house sometime soon.

It's now 1984, and it's been a good year. We had even gotten to go see Mom a few times and other relatives when possible. The kids loved that and also seeing more and more cousins at weddings and special events. Life was good, and I was so thankful for my family.

I had met so many nice people where I work at the Four Seasons. One very nice lady, Norma Jean, was so good to help me and helped me fit in. We had become very good friends in a very short time. She was a little older than me, but you would never know it. She had taught me the ropes.

The owners of the Four Seasons were very nice to me too. They had older children than mine and gave me boxes of brand-new brand-name clothes when they outgrew them. It had helped a lot. It had never bothered me to take used stuff in time of need. I had done the same for others in need.

Boy am I missing our good friends and relatives out in Williston. I do not miss the rat race and the wind that came with North Dakota though. I heard through the grapevine that many of them have relocated and started over.

CHAPTER 22

Losing My Little Sister

I am stopping here with my story as we just got word, November 17, 2020, that my younger sister Evelyn just passed away. She was only sixty- four years old. She was the sweetest sister and person you could ever have known. She leaves a loving husband, Maurias; a daughter, Jackie, and Ricky, her son. Also a son-in-law Filip and two great, sweet grandchildren, Emma and Alex. Maurus and Evelyn had lived in Sauk Rapids the last five years. They were able make many memories with their children and grandchildren during this time. Thank goodness!

We're always close, but she had lived far enough away where if we saw them one time of year or special events, that was about it. I would also visit her when she was in the hospital in Fargo, which was more often than most people when they lived in Finley, North Dakota, for forty years. These last years have been wonderful as we were able to go see her whenever she was sick and anytime that Rick had appointments in St Cloud.

She had type 1 diabetes since she was six years old, which required four or more shots a day of insulin. She was so good with her own care and had a very supportive family. In her last years, she endured five or six heart attacks with stents required each time. We are not sure of her cause of death, but we all know it was due to her poor heart and diabetes. She also had stage 4 kidney disease. It just doesn't seem real as COVID is quite rampant, and no one can go see her as she lay there dying. The hospital wouldn't even let her own children in until the very end, only Maurus; one- visitor rule applied until her final day.

I was so thankful these past few years that we were both

retired and could spend so much time together. I would go to their house and visit her while my Rick was at appointments in St Cloud. We usually had at least a few hours to catch up and go shopping, and then we would all go out for dinner. We made so many lasting memories during this time. I had stopped in just a few months earlier with my pastor's wife from Hope Chapel from my church. We had gone to St Cloud to the Monsignor Gardens and just felt that day like I had to stop in. Little did I know it would be the last time I saw her alive. She was home but had just gotten out of the hospital and really didn't look very good. She was all covered up and had her feet elevated as they were swollen quite a bit. We all had to wear masks as not to make her any sicker or get COVID on top of her conditions. No hugs either.

Her funeral is today, but because of COVID-19 and state shutdowns, no one can go right now. It will be small with just Maurus, Jackie, Phillip, and Alex and Emma and the Catholic priest having mass for Evelyn. She was a devout Catholic and Christian person. Her faith carried her through her entire life. We'll be able to see it on live stream, but that just doesn't seem the same. I watched the live stream, but it just didn't seem real. I felt like it I was watching a movie, but since that's all we had, it did bring a small bit of closure. Maurus and his family are planning a celebration of life hopefully next summer. That will depend on where COVID is at that time.

It was such a sad time for all of us to not be able to comfort them and console them in time of need. Funeral homes are not the only places with strict rules and shutdown during this pandemic. Many restaurants, bars, gyms, and churches are at a standstill also. We can still get takeout, so that helps. It's like ordering your food and going through a drive-through. Businesses are closing left and right, and many people are collecting unemployment. People do not have enough money for food and other essentials. Churches are giving away free boxes of food to help them out. Food shelves are running out of product. Many people are going without health insurance and just your basic needs. It's a very trying time for all of us. The good news is they're working on a vaccine that may be ready in a few months or spring. Let's pray that they do find a vaccine! Enough about COVID-19!

CHAPTER 23

School Times

Ryan is in preschool now, and when he was tested for school, he didn't know his colors. We found out he is color-blind on top of being very, very nearsighted. His glasses are very thick, and his friends think they're sunglasses. He never takes them off except at bedtime, so I guess his friends will never know. One little boy even brought a pair of sunglasses and wore them for a while so he could be like Ryan. Ryan loved that.

Amy is in third grade and likes gymnastics. She had taken a dance class when we lived in Williston and loved that too. She is definitely leaning toward sports already.

Joey is in sixth grade and loves basketball. He is definitely an outdoor kid and spends most of his time outside with his friends. He loves Boy Scouts also.

I am still looking for a better job with more hours. I finally got a call from Wadena Deer Creek Elementary School. I got an interview, and it went really well, and I start in one week. I will be a paraprofessional in the TMH department, which stands for trainable mentally handicapped.

I was a little apprehensive at first but realized my training for daycare respite and foster care would really come into play. My first job was to take a little boy into the kindergarten room for one hour a day to try to help him fit in. They had just passed a law saying every child has to be in the least restrictive environment possible. So that means you need to take a handicapped child among his or her peers, or they will not learn as easily. I will call him little Johnny. He could barely feed himself, walk, or talk. He was quite severely handicapped. The philosophy means he would catch on from other children faster than being isolated. He was such a sweet child I fell in love with my job right away.

The rest of each day I would work in another building across the street from the school on his goals and objectives. We would string beads, roll a ball, swing on a special swing, and many other physical activities. There were three or four other students working on their objectives also with other paras and teachers. We also taught them how to feed themselves with assistance and use the bathroom. Some needed to be in diapers, and we learned how to take care of that. Even back then we had special equipment, including chairs, swings, and lifts. It made our job easier and was safer for them.

One of the little boys was blind, and I connected with him right away probably due to my dad being blind most of my younger years. We had such a great team and worked so well together. My coworkers were wonderful with filling me in and teaching and helping me learn what worked and what didn't for these sweet kids.

It was an ideal job considering the hours were the same as my kids' hours in their school day. I was off every time they were off school for holidays, conferences, and summers. What a dream job, and I loved it. I also could keep working and waitressing and saving money for a house. With both of us working two jobs, I guess you could call us workaholics at this time. I did have to drop my Avon route and just took orders over the phone. The kids just somehow fell into our chaotic schedule. They are so adaptable.

We bought a pop-up camper, and we're able to enjoy camping in the summers when Ralph had two weekends a month off. The kids loved it, and we all like the great outdoors.

We only had a large tent before this. It was nice to upgrade and not sleep on the ground anymore. It was always a fun time when we got the time to finally all be together. Summers we're the best. The kids love the outdoor pool that

Wadena provided, and we had several parks to pick from that had great playground equipment. It even had a baby pool. With raising three kids, two jobs each, and opposite hours, it wasn't ideal, but you do what you have to do to make it work.

Pine View Acres Memories from Others' Recollection

Dave and Linda's memories

In the last few weeks as I'm writing my book, I was visiting Linda and Dave and talking about what they remembered from Pine View Acres. They willingly shared a few memories I am including in my story. One of Linda's fondest memories was the golf carts, of course. It was a great way to get around, spend time together, and tear around the trailer court. She also mentioned all the bonfires we had at Paul and Judy's their next-door neighbor. We can't count how many hot dogs and marshmallows were roasted over there along with a few beers. She recalls Avon calling, which was more than a visit sometimes many hours. She reminded me that we are lifelong friends forever.

Dave remembered a lot of the neighborhood parties that went on back then. He said he loved his Crown or McMasters whiskey especially at the bonfires. He claimed the good brands of whiskey were so much better than the cheap stuff. I wouldn't know, but I took his word for it. Ralph was a beer drinker alongside, and I liked a glass of wine occasionally. Dave called my wine sissy drinks, and I agreed, but I always felt better the next day. Dave also recalls snowmobiling with all of us and all the fun and freedom that gave us. It wasn't always fun and games, they recall, but we all made it through those tough times over the years. To this day we all agree; if you're dealt lemons, make lemonade. What great times we all had.

My kids

Ryan, my youngest son, informed me about Maurice the landlord and how they spent a lot of time at his house. He had dogs, and he and Johnny loved to ride their bikes there on the way to the gravel pit and pet and give them some attention. I guess Maury looked forward to them taking the time to do that, and the dogs never tired of them. They would ride their bikes for hours on the trails to the gravel pit that they had created. I knew they did this but not that it would be one of their favorite memories. Ryan reminded me of the Go-kart they built altogether and would chase the golf cart with that all over the trailer court. One more memory was he had his first kiss at the trailer court with one of our neighbor girls. I know who she is to this day, but I do not have permission to put her name in here. They could only have been between three and a half years old to seven years old at the time, and Ryan says he barely remembers it. We had a good laugh while he was telling me this.

Joey, my oldest son, was eight years old when we were living there, and his best memory was the walk from the highway outside the court to home. He said he would play all the way home in whatever mud puddles or water or snowbanks he could find. I always wondered why it took him so long and way longer than the other kids. Joey said I would get after him because his clothes or snowpants were always wet or dirty. I really didn't care because I knew he was having the time of his life. He said the next best memory was making friends with the Jensens, Kleinkes, and Judds, and he is still having a lifelong friendship and connection to this very day with all of them.

Amy, my middle child, told me her favorite times at Pine View Acres were the golf cart rides and swimming at the gravel pit. They would journey on their bikes with her neighbor friends Amy, Kimmy, and anyone else who wanted to go and always made their own fun. It truly was a great adventure in the great outdoors. She remembers jumping from tree to tree and bush to bush to avoid the water and mud that was provided there. The area was quite swampy as she recalls. She also remembers she got a few kisses there just for giggles. She collected a lot of baseball and basketball cards and still has some to this day in her collection. One last memory was her dad made her a baby doll bassinet for her dolls. It was a baby casket out of fiberglass, and I wouldn't let her play with it if people were over. It kind of grossed me out, but she loved it. She told me I made her keep it in her closet unless I said she could play with it. I know she doesn't know why I didn't like it 'cause she was too young for me to let her know that I had lost a baby, and it just kind of bothered me. She will know now as she reads my book. Amy also has lifelong friends from those four and a half years spent at Pine View Acres. Believe me, your kids need friends like that forever. I can't stress it enough how important it is to help your kids be a good friend and to work at those relationships even at a very young age.

CHAPTER 24

New House Hunting

It's fall of 1986 and back to my school job. I went mainstreaming kids more and more. It was so rewarding to see their progress each year. I was still selling Avon in the neighborhood and at school and the restaurant. People just called me with their order, and I delivered. Worked great!

Dave and Linda had become good friends real fast, and the kids all got along so well. Life was good! We had saved up a downpayment, so we were really looking for a house now.

While working at the restaurant one night, a family that had been coming in to eat asked me if I knew of anyone looking for a house to buy. They had theirs up for sale as they would be moving to Bemidji. I was waiting on them and let them know that we were in the process of looking for a house to buy. They gave me their number, and I called them the very next day and got the details.

It turned out that they were looking for a trailer house because they're moving to Bemidji for the mom to go to school there. They had three kids just like us, and before we knew it, they offered to take our trailer house for the downpayment on their home that we would buy. It would make it much easier for us to get a loan. We already had some downpayment saved, and the trailer house was paid for, so we had an asset to put on paper.

When we went to look at the house, I couldn't believe we could afford it. It was so beautiful and spacious. It was on a dead-end street and had a cul- de-sac.

We moved in in early 1987, and they moved our trailer house to Bemidji, Minnesota. Everyone was so happy that it all worked out for two families just by word of mouth. It also had an empty lot that we purchased later on right next to it. God's path for us was never-ending.

After four and a half years in the trailer park, we now get to move to a big, nice house. It had a large kitchen, three bedrooms, a beautiful living room, and a ramp off the large deck in the back. I didn't think we would use that very much, but the kids loved running up and down it and even went sledding down it when it snowed. The deck was right off the kitchen with three large patio doors, which offered a lot of sunlight each morning. Our split-level house was so perfect and even had an attached garage, so I didn't have to go out in the weather anymore. I haven't had a garage since we lived in Thief River Falls. The yard here was huge, and we put a big swing set with a fort out there with a sandbox underneath. The kids spent hours playing there. It had been so worth it finally saving enough money and budgeting to have our new home. Now if we could just sell our house in Thief River, we could pay more on this house. We would be working on that soon, I was sure.

CHAPTER 25

Fitting In and Taking on Respite Care

My job with WDC was going well. This year, I was at the school almost all day instead of the house across the street. By the way, they called this house the Happy House because the kids were always smiling. I was getting to know a lot of the coworkers, and now I'd been asked to play softball in a league. It was so much fun and turned out I really liked sports. I also played "wolleyball" with the same group. It's like volleyball, but you can use the wall as a player. It's great fun. I loved getting out and getting exercise and having a girls' night out; at the same time I either got a babysitter, or else Ralph got up for two hours before he went to work at 11:00 p.m. and watched the kids. He liked working nights and always has. We didn't see much of each other, but he's a good friend and provider. He still worked his daytime job at R&L Fiberglass and two weeknights and weekends at Bell Hill. It did get lonely and put a lot of responsibility on me, but I was getting used to it. Ralph bought our first computer, and he's getting hooked on it. He could do his accounting there for the business and who knew what else. I knew nothing about computers and grew up using just calculators and typewriters. It's hard for me to believe he could sit on it for hours. It's like he's married to it. Ugh!

We still made time to go camping and visit our relatives on both sides. We had had a lot of weddings these past few years. We made time for family whenever we could.

We were also getting involved with respite care. It is basically taking care of children in your home that are handicapped so the parents can have a rest or a break. I worked with these kids at school as a paraprofessional, so I got asked to do this. I usually did two weekends a month, and the pay was just crazy. I just loved having them around, and my kids loved these kids also. I felt it's a privilege to learn about them and their disabilities. It came naturally to me probably because my dad was so disabled. I also felt it's a calling, and we all should help our fellow man. Since we're doing respite care, we also got asked to get relicensed for foster care.

Our first client was a young eight-year-old boy (Keith) who had recently lost his father. He had spina bifida and needed a lot of encouragement and help with his routine and care. He has a great sense of humor, and Joey, Amy, and Ryan loved to entertain him. Of course, the little guy loved all the attention too. It kept our household quite busy and always on our toes. He was in a wheelchair but could get around quite easily. Ryan rode on the back of his chair.

Another client was a little girl I took care of at school with cerebral palsy. She was also in a wheelchair but was nonverbal. That didn't stop her though as she was able to acquire a Touch Talker, which helped her with communication. Every other weekend and weeks in the summer, we would care for these children. It worked well with my schedule since I had summers off, and that's when these parents needed the most help. That ramp off the deck sure was coming in handy now. It's like God knew what we needed. Little did I know, I would be doing this for many years with two or three clients some weekends and weeks in the summer.

COVID Update, December 2020

During Christmas of 2020, we could not have large crowds of more than three families even in your home.

Many of us just stayed home and had a few of the kids join us. The pandemic is slightly better, and they are working on a vaccine. Many schools are closed and no sports right now and doing distance learning yet. We are still wearing masks and social- distancing.

Restaurants are still closed, but you can do curbside pickup. So we call in our orders, and they deliver to our car, or we pick up at door. Most want you to pay with a credit card so as not to have to handle one another's coins or paper money. We try to order out one or two times a week to help the economy and keep it going.

January and February of 2021, we still are seeing very little travel and going places. The gym opened up to walk on the track and work out, but you have to wear your mask. Machines are spread apart. We also came in one door and go out the back way to keep people separated.

They are also getting close to a vaccine. It's very exciting, and it gives us all hope. There is a process to this. The first to get the shot will be frontline workers like doctors and nurses, big businesses, school personnel, and then the elderly along with caregivers being next. It will be a little while until we get it. It's now March 2021, and they have a vaccines called Pfizer and Moderna.

Third Report, COVID

When we go in for blood work or anything, you have to have an appointment scheduled, so there's hardly anyone close together. Then they take your temperature, require a mask, and use sanitizer going in and out of the facility. You can also get tested easily now for COVID if you suspect you have it.

At first that was a real problem but has been fixed. Rick has had a test as he had to have a procedure done. It was negative. I have not had a test. We called to check on getting vaccinated, and we got an appointment April 4, 2021.

We went to the clinic parking lot in Staples and rolled up our sleeves and held our arm out the window of the car. We got the shot. Then two weeks later, we got the second shot. We had no reaction to the first shot, but the second shot we both had the chills, fever, fatigue, and appetite loss. I felt icky for eight to ten hours, and Rick felt bad for twenty-four hours. Now we're good and glad we're immunized.

More and more are getting the shot. They have sites set up at the armory, clinics, community center, and pharmacies. It's quite available now. It has slowed the virus down, but people are still dying.

We just had another neighbor get it and is pretty sick, but she will be okay. We can now go out to restaurants and movie theaters as long as we sanitize and wear masks and take precautions. Flying has opened up, but bus tours have not. We are still sitting home a lot. But it's almost May 2021, and we have flowerbeds and gardening to get started soon. We also have some projects around the farm to get done. It will keep up with the COVID pandemic progress.

Now let's go back to my story

CHAPTER 26

Busy Life

I was in the busiest part of our lives. The fact that we're back in Minnesota made life so much easier. We got to see our grandparents more and our parents and brothers and sisters. Our lives had changed a lot since being gone for three years to Williston, North Dakota.

Ralph had gotten so content to work day and nights and sleep the other hours. It's hard to get days off at Bell Hill if we had a wedding, reunion, or graduation, but that was getting few and far between that he joined us. Many times I just went with the kids myself. I was getting used to being a single mom, or at least that's what it felt like. I felt he got used to working so much out in the oil fields and just continued now to be a workaholic. I felt bad for him because he was missing out a lot of time with the family.

Something had definitely changed, but we would keep trying to figure it out. We are Catholic and go to St. Ann's church each Sunday. He did not join us for that either because of his work schedule.

Our kids had all finished first communion and been confirmed. God is good.

We have really nice neighbors, Joann and Gordy King. They're older but very good neighbors. Also Becky and Jim Bowen were such good friends; they were foster parents too. We went over there for football, BB games on TV, and just time to spend together.

The kids were now getting into a lot of sports and were on teams with Becky's kids. We spent a lot of times going to sports events. That's a whole 'nother family when you got into sports. I loved it, but Ralph didn't include himself in any of this. I guess it's his loss. I figured maybe things would get better when the kids left home.

Joey was now in high school and had such good friends. He had met people through work at Hardee's and also sports. Joey loved to go to the outdoor pool in Wadena. He rode his bike there and met friends there.

It's so great having an outdoor pool for the kids to grow up by. He also liked to skateboard. Amy was in seventh or eighth grade now. She loved volleyball, BB, and track. She was a very busy girl. I also likely loved watching the kids compete. Amy had had a lot of ear infections and struggled to hear clearly, but that didn't stop her at all. Joey was now getting his license, and boy, that made a parent realize they were growing up. It's a great part of their life but kinda scary. He was pretty responsible, and you just trust we'd raised him properly. It made me realize it was the first step of letting go.

It was so much fun to see them grow up. Ralph worked days and four or more nights at Bell Hill. His burial vault business was going well, but he had to work at Bell Hill nights to make ends meet.

I was full-time at the school, but with insurance costs for the family, I got a lot of deductions off my paycheck. We had to have insurance though!

Ralph loved the computer and did a lot of his business things on it. I knew nothing about computers; glad he could figure them out. He seemed to really like it as he was on it any free moment he had. He liked the game systems with the boys also. Even in school in the late eighties, we didn't have much for computers, but it's starting to grow. They now have them in the libraries, businesses, and homes. I feel they're quite complicated and expensive. We also had to make a computer room as you need a desk for the monitor, keyboard, printer, modem, and speakers. So we put it downstairs by the furnace room. That way it didn't interfere with the TV and music in the living room.

We were so lucky our kids all had their own room. We

still had extra rooms. I loved this house. We did build a double-car garage on the lot next to us, which was ours now. That's really nice as we only had a single-car garage attached to the house. I loved that I could just step into the garage and load and unload things without getting rained or snowed on.

Being it was a split entry, there's lots of groceries to haul up and down the stairs. We had to have a gate at the top because of the safety of the foster and respite kids we took care of.

CHAPTER 27

Kids' Teen Years

Loving the Teen Years

Joey's first car with a 1977 light-blue Plymouth Fury. He said it had a special motor, so it would go fast. Just what a mom wanted to hear: trust, trust, trust. He was very good to help pick up Amy and Ryan if I needed him to. That helped me out a lot. He seemed to be a good driver, and I hoped that continued.

Ryan was getting into Boy Scouts now and loved to go swimming at the pool. Ralph did help with Ryan's troop when he could. Amy was also in Girl Scouts, and I was a leader for their troop. Their activities kept everyone hopping. The kids all had good friends and close families to spend time with. We were so blessed.

It's Joey's senior year, and he would be graduating in May of 1992. He was taking classes at the college right by the high school to get some of his generals done. He could walk back and forth to his classes. He was thinking of an electrician career.

Joey also got to have a foreign exchange student his senior year. We got a call on a guy named Uli that was at another home, but it wasn't working out. We said sure, why not? We already took in a lot of different kids, and we're loving it. Uli was from Germany and such a fun fellow. He would be a senior alongside Joey and graduate with him in this spring. The boys hit it off right from the start and joined track and cross-country together. Uli was a tall, lanky fellow and could run like a deer. He even set some records. It was such a rewarding experience, and we learned so much about

SURVIVING LIFE AND
C☾VID-19

his country and family. He loved our large family and got along with Amy and Ryan and all the handicapped kids as well. Prom was a must, and they made memories together. Graduation pictures were so much fun and turned out great.

We had a big graduation party for the two of them, and Uli's parents showed up from Germany. What a wonderful memory. Many of our friends and relatives showed up and made it a festive affair. He got lots of money and presents, which made his day.

One good time while he was living with us was when we went to Canada on a trip with their class. We were one of the couples that were chaperones. The boys who were being boys had taken off in the middle of the night and went drinking. The drinking age in Canada was eighteen years old. We did not know that. They were caught and brought home, but I'm sure they'd remember it for the rest of their life. It was legal and all, but they weren't following the class trip rules. Ralph thought it was quite funny and quite daring. I think he wished he could have been with them.

Joey was still working at Hardee's but made the decision to go to Grand Forks to school. He could stay at Sonja and Bruce's; one of our foster kids lived eight miles from Grand Forks. They offered to put him up and see how things went. He was there several months but chose to come back to Wadena and enroll in Wadena Technical College. He went for six months for electrical classes, but it wasn't his cup of tea. He then chose to do accounting in computer programming. He really liked that and found something he was comfortable with.

Amy was now in tenth grade and played varsity volleyball and basketball. She kept us real busy with her extracurricular activities. It was so exciting and so much fun. Ralph didn't make it to very many of her games as he worked days and four or more nights at Bell Hill. I was full-time at the school and had full insurance coverage with hefty deductions coming out of my check. I knew we had to have insurance.

Joey loved being back in Wadena and working at Hardee's while getting through school. He had had some girlfriends but seemed pretty committed to this special one. Autumn was a real sweetie, and they spent a lot of time with each other. They seemed so happy together. I guess time would tell.

Amy had a lot of friends also but was so busy with practices and games. She had little free time in her busy schedule. Thank goodness we had such great neighbors and friends, like Becky and Jim, as we helped with carpooling and game nights. They had kids just as involved and sometimes on the same team as ours. Amy had so much fun and memories made with Steph and Jenny. What great neighbors we had.

Ryan was in track and cross-country in junior high. He tried basketball but was hard running and sweating with thick glasses. He couldn't keep up and figured it just wasn't for him. He was a very good runner. His friends kept him quite busy.

Joey worked at Hardee's and was going to school for computers and accounting. He tried electrical for a few months, but it wasn't what he wanted.

Amy worked at an animal shelter that a good friend of mine ran. She helped care for the animals and fed, watered, and sold them. What a great first job. Amy also wanted a monkey. I said no, and so did her dad. We told her they need *not* be in captivity. So that wasn't going to happen. She did get a tiny puppy from there, and it fell in a four-inch square hole on the deck. He got hurt pretty bad. Things happen when you have animals. We did end up putting it, Chip, down. We felt bad, but it was a pure accident. She also mows lawns for people and was showing Ryan the ropes. Amy now had a job at Super Valu in Wadena.

Summers were so busy. I did respite and foster care more

now as I was off from school until September.

Amy had had quite a few ear surgeries. She had chronic ear infections and now went to the Mayo for repairs. They took a skin graft off her thigh and put in her ear as they were so broken down and deteriorating. She had significant hearing loss, but you would never know it. It didn't slow her down at all, and I'm pretty sure she read lips.

CHAPTER 28

Grandbabies

Joey and Autumn just announced they were expecting. We were going to be grandparents. Wow! Oh my goodness, I was only thirty-nine years old, and Ralph was forty-three. It's 1993, and the baby was due January 1994. We're all excited especially Amy and Ryan. Amy was a junior and was working at the Henning Nursing Home. She really liked it.

Ryan was in eighth grade and still helped us at home a lot. I did miss the older two with them working out so much, but they had learned life skills and were good with money management. Taught them a lot of responsibilities.

Joey and Autumn were excited too, but they were both so young. Forrest was born January 15, 1994, but it didn't go as planned. His lungs were not fully developed, so he was rushed to Fargo, North Dakota. He was okay, but it was so scary for everyone. They rented a house in Wadena and lived together for six months or so. They kept trying, but being so young, it didn't go well. This was their story, so I will only write how it affected our lives.

We all tried to help as much as we could, but with all our busy schedules, it was whoever and wherever we all as a family could pitch in.

Amy helped with Forrest a lot with babysitting and just being an auntie.

CHAPTER 29

Amy—Another Graduation

It's Amy's senior year, 1995. She was keeping up with it all. Between work, school, and sports, she juggled it all quite well.

She also got to have a foreign exchange student this year too. She picked Anne from France. She was just a gem. She would live with us for the year as a senior even though she's only sixteen years old. She had fit right in and loved it here. She had a twin sister living in another state as a foreign student. It didn't go as well for her with her family. We learned some about the French culture. Her family came to the States for the girls' graduation ceremony and party at the house. Now I have another addition to my bucket list, and that's to visit them in France someday.

Here again it was fun for all of us to learn about the French culture. She made us French dishes that were so good. What a wonderful experience for all of us.

CHAPTER 30

Custody Issues

We were loving our beautiful little grandbaby. He was such a sweet soul. Who knew being grandparents would be so grand. Joey and Autumn had been trying so hard to live together and raise him. It was not going very well. She got another apartment now, and they were sharing Forrest's care as best they could. A lot had happened, and I didn't feel right putting the details in my story as it's their life story. It doesn't matter what details there are or why things happened. It is what it is. Things just didn't work out. So a long story short, they were in a custody battle. Now there's court dates, money for lawyers, retainers, and many dates to fit into everyone's busy schedules. He's not even two years old, and the grandparents and kids were trying to do the best for Forrest.

It was solely up to the judge for the final decision. The judge ruled that Ralph and I would raise him. We weren't expecting that as Joey and Autumn just needed some guidance. But we openly accepted the decision until at some point the two of them could decide in agreement for one to raise him. We all adjusted quite easily as we had foster kids in and out all the time. This was different though as he's our grandbaby. We had to arrange daycare. We had a good neighbor with a daycare on our block, and she took him in, which was a heaven-sent. It was on my way to work, and I adapted to packing the bag and dropping him off each day.

I felt bad for Joey and Autumn as I really think either of them could have raised him with some parent classes and counseling.

Ralph couldn't help much because of his day and night jobs. So we made schedules for the kids, and we all learned

SURVIVING LIFE AND
C◉VID-19

to live with the newness of the situation. We tried to be as flexible as we could be. It was pretty crazy at first, but everyone adjusted. Joey, of course, saw him more as he could come over to our house anytime.

Grandma Deb helped out a lot too. It really does take a village to raise a child. Forrest slept and ate good, so that was a blessing. He did get infections and had respiratory problems from when he was born. He got shingles and had such a high fever with cold baths and compresses.

I remember Joey holding Forrest to his chest, and it turned red from Forrest's temperature. It was probably one of the darkest times for all of us. His fever finally broke. Believe me, he didn't like cold baths, but that's what the doctor told us to do. It was a very rough week, and he was back to his pleasant self.

It was 1996 and had been a very busy year. One day, Ralph's dad, Leo, and Phyllis, his stepmom, called us home to Sandstone, Minnesota. Phyllis and Dad sat us at their kitchen table, and she apologized to Ralph for the way she had treated them as children. She felt she had to make things right, but Ralph just sat there stone-faced. He never accepted her apology, and I know why. There was just too much damage for too many years.

His brother Orville and I had planned to write a book of their life. Orville passed away before we got to it. Now it will have to be another member's story. Believe me, it affected us all. Her apology was sincere, and I forgave her, but Ralph had no emotion whatsoever through it all. Never talked about it again. "God forgives us all," I told him, but I don't think he believed that.

CHAPTER 31

Ryan Graduation 1998

Kids Move On

Joey worked and was going to college. He had a new girlfriend. It's 1997 now, and things seemed pretty good. We found out they were engaged, and Joey seemed real happy. They planned to get married. They got married in June.

Amy was done at Brainerd College as she had decided to go to Wadena college to get her two-year degree in early childhood. She did well in school. Ryan was a senior 1997 to 1998 and had done well too. He planned on going to Staples for diesel mechanic next year. Before he went on to college, he chose to go to Germany and France and visit those families that we hosted over the years.

Anne's dad was an optician and had offered to evaluate Ryan's vision while over there. We were excited that maybe more could be done with his eyes, but either way, it's a trip of a lifetime. So off he flew for a month after he graduated. Well, it turned out he had a great time, but Anne's dad felt there was nothing more that could be done without some very high risk of not seeing as much as he did now. Well, he was okay with that, and we all hoped someday new technology would hopefully help him.

Amy had met Jon from Wisconsin, and they planned to get married. Joey was married and now had two girls, M'Cayla and Alyssa. They were so sweet, so we're up to three grandkids now. It was such a blessing.

Joe lived in Fargo now and finished school there. He's into IT stuff. Forrest saw him when he could and loved to go there. I was just so glad they're all on a road to make their own lives. I prayed they all had the tools to go through whatever life threw their way. It's a hard feeling to not be able to tell them what's best anymore. Their decisions would be theirs and theirs alone. Of course, we could offer advice, but they could lose or use that. I just have to trust they'd been raised with a good education, values, and morals.

CHAPTER 32

Life Changes

We were empty nesters now! With the exception of Forrest. It's our turn to have more time together and maybe make more time for one another. It's 1999 now, and my youngest sister Audrey and Rick needed a place to stay with the family of three boys. They had a handicapped son (Dustin), so with the ramp and all the updates for disabled kids, we were the likely choice. They were moving back to Minnesota from Florida. It's for a month or so until they could find a place. They loved being back in Minnesota, and it went so well.

We'd go to work, and they had the house to themselves all day. She and Rick had leads on work right away, but it all took time. Well, just when I was thinking life couldn't get better, some truths started to come out.

I came home from school one day, and Audrey said, "I have to talk to you alone." So we went out for a diet pop and conversation. Little did I know I was about to hear a bombshell. She said, "I heard the phone ring, so I went to pick it up, and Ralph picked up downstairs at the same time." She said she couldn't believe what she heard. It was some lady talking pretty explicit things. She knew all about me being at work and that they could talk now. He was just as involved in the conversation. I couldn't believe it but definitely knew my sister wasn't lying. I didn't know what to do or say. So from that day on, I started paying attention to the phone calls, his work schedule, etc.

Audrey and Rick found a lake place and now were moving out. So we were now back to just foster kids and respite kids when they're here. I decided to start checking the phone bill first. I did find some numbers that were not familiar. He would say they were for work. Well, I called some of them, and whoever I'd reach were not willing to give out information of who they were or how we knew them. So I got nowhere there. So my next plan was to pop home on my lunch break. So I did. He would always be in the computer room on different sites. He'd be kinda surprised I was there for lunch. I just said it's nice to eat at home sometimes. Around the third or fourth time, I came home for lunch he was on a site that I couldn't believe.

It was something with other people and talking flirtations with each other. I did not know there even was such sites on there. So I confronted him about the phone call Audrey had intercepted. He said it was some lady from Bell Hill just goofing off. Yeah right! So I asked him about the computer shit I saw. He just said I just need to consider joining his group. I said, "Over my dead body." That's sick and gross. I said, "What's wrong with you?" He just insisted it was harmless.

I knew right then why he didn't need me anymore, and in my heart, it was the beginning of the end of our marriage. I did ask him after a few weeks if he'd go to counseling. He said, "What for? That's just people taking your money." So that was out. I confided in one of his brothers, and he had told me a lot of their family abuse. He felt it was due to that. I didn't care the reason, but it helped me understand his denial of right and wrong.

It amazes me how childhood trauma can affect a person so many years later. I kept trying to talk him into getting help. He wouldn't hear of it. So I was already working on a plan but had to put it off for a while as Amy and Jon were getting married in May in Wisconsin. I didn't want to ruin their day. Ralph and I walked her down the aisle together.

So we got through the wedding and acted like nothing was wrong. That was easy as he was never lovey-dovey! I do realize now I had a friendship marriage. I'm just thankful we had three beautiful kids out of the life we had. He was a good provider, and we had a lot together. So that summer, I told him I was leaving.

He thought I should keep the big house. I said no, it would be too much for me to take care of. I said I'd get a small house close to school so Forrest and the foster kids could walk to school if necessary.

So we started looking and found a three-bedroom with a nice yard four blocks from work, and it was nice and at a good price. The bank had gotten it back, so were really ready to sell. So January of 2001, I moved in. We had filed for divorce on grounds of irreconcilable differences. We had divided everything equally—money, IRAs, cars, etc.—so it was just paperwork for the lawyers from there. It was a very civil divorce, so that helped. My kids still don't know all the details as it was Ralph and my problems, not theirs.

They had all left home, but they were surprised. Put it this way, I will take some things to my grave.

Ralph never asked me to not leave, which surprised me. So in 2001, I moved to my little house with Forrest and the foster girl we had then. I loved it, but it was an adjustment. Ralph was being helpful with the loan and building me a deck off the back of the house, which was great. He also helped me move things there.

9/11 Story

I was forty-seven years old and starting over but knew it's what I had to do. We agreed on everything as far as the divorce. I was still doing respite care but took less kids at a time. When you make a life decision like that, you really find out who your friends are. Most of my friends were supportive, but a few didn't understand. But you know what, I never looked back.

I moved forward. I got a seasonal lake lot for the next

few years at Twin Lakes by Menahga, Minnesota. We had an old motor home I could drive and park there. It was so much fun and very good adventure. The kids loved it. I remember one bad incident though. Forrest was walking to the lake, which was, oh, maybe a block from the camper, and he stepped in a hole. It was a wasp nest. The poor kid was stung many times. We had to go get something at the clinic for the swelling, but he was okay. That was very scary. We had a lot of memories, fishing, swimming, and floating at the resort. I also did craft shows every November in Wadena. I made hats and scarves and fleece blankets. I love to sew and made some extra money through the years.

On Tuesday, September 11, 2001, I was at school one morning. I was working in the work room running off a math test, and all at once on the small TV that was there had an emergency report. It said the World Trade Center had been hit by a plane in Manhattan, New York. At first a lot of people thought it was an accident. But is soon became clear that two America airliners had been hijacked and were responsible for the strike. It was coordinated by Wahhabi Islamist terrorist group Al-Qaeda. The death toll was 2,996 people along with nineteen Al-Qaeda. Sixty-four innocent people were on the first plane along with six crew members and the terrorists.

American Airlines Flight 77 was out of Washington DC. A third plane hit the Pentagon. It was 9:37 a.m. ET. The hijackers crashed into the west side of the Pentagon. Many witnessed the crash. News media were there in minutes. This was one of four attacks that day.

Two planes were flown into World Trade Center and the other in a field in Turney, Pennsylvania, after passengers did try to take it over.

The cleanup was a massive operation. It cost hundreds of millions of dollars. The health concerns rose in Manhattan as the air quality was greatly reduced and caused respiratory illnesses. There were several deaths due to the dust clouds. About 18,000 people have suffered from the effects. The motive for the attacks were stated before and after the attacks.

Osama bin Laden had declared a holy war against the United States.

In 2002, bin Laden said their motives were to include Western support for attacking Muslims in Somalia, to support Russians against Muslims, and to support the Indian oppression against Muslims and the presence of US troops in Saudi Arabia due to sanctions against Iraq.

The US took the position that terrorist attacked the US because they hate us for our freedoms and government—the right of religion, speech, voting, and assemblies.

God bless America!

Fourth COVID Update

Wow, the state is now opening up in May 2021. We do not have to wear masks as of May 10 in most places. We still have to wear masks to the clinic, hospitals, and nursing homes to protect ourselves and others. It feels really weird to not put them on. I feel like I'm forgetting something. I guess we really did get used to them. We need to wear masks for flying and bus lines that are going now.

Our cousins planned a bus tour trip for July, and it was canceled because part of it went into Canada to see Niagara Falls, and they are not letting people into Canada yet. So Rick and I are planning to go on a bus trip to Tennessee if it's all opened up in the fall.

It has really limited our retirement plans, but life is life. I would not want to go if it's not safe. So this summer we are planning on camping trips so far. I feel so sorry for the families that have lost loved ones through this terrible pandemic. The cases have greatly improved. There are less and less almost everywhere. There are still people dying from COVID-19, but with the vaccines being administered, it has greatly slowed it down. In Wadena County, May 18 had only twenty-five cases and through it all twenty-two deaths. In Todd County, May 18 had eighteen cases and overall deaths eighty. In May, Otter Tail County, they had thirty-eight cases and seventy-eight deaths overall. Wadena is 38 percent vaccinated. Todd is 31 percent vaccinated and Ottertail 42 percent. There are some that do not want to be vaccinated. The states and counties have now started an incentive program by giving out gift certificates, gas cards, money, and groceries to reach these people. The more people that get the shots, the better the chances of COVID-19 not spreading. There are new variants popping up in some areas. People need to realize that this is a pandemic, just like polio, smallpox, 1918 Spanish flu, and more. I hope and pray they all get on board. Bless all of you who have helped to save yourself and others.

CHAPTER 33

My Soulmate

On April 2, 2003, Forrest was invited to a birthday party. It was a swimming party at the American Inn in Wadena for a good friend's son. So I took Forrest to it, and it was a life-changing moment I didn't ever expect or look for. There were other kids there and a lot of parents standing around watching the kids swim. My friend who had the party started introducing all of us to one another.

Well, I met Rick that day. He had brought Vernon to the party. He seemed nice, and I guess I caught his eye. A few days later, he called and asked me out. I guess he had asked my friend who I was and if I was single and got my number. She told him all about me, and when he called, I said yes to a date. So we went to the circus in Wadena with Forrest and Vernon. We had a blast.

Rick had been divorced a couple years before me, I found out later. Now this guy was quite big, but like a big teddy bear; that's how I described him to my kids when they asked what he was like. He told me later it took him a couple days to work up the courage to call me. I thought that was funny. We have been together ever since. Vernon and Forrest get along great, and we do so much together. We went to fairs, movies, camping, all of us. We had Vernon on weekends, and Forrest was still going back and forth between his mom and dad.

Joey got divorced and was dating Kim now. She had three kids also. Forrest loved to go there because of all the things they did. Joey bought Ralph's and my house after a few years of me moving out.

All at once he had a family of six kids at their house. Katie, her oldest, is Forrest's age, then Orly is a year or so younger, but they really get along well. Then Gracie is her other daughter. So between them, there's a lot of things to do.

Rick did construction for a living. He built garages, pole shed, houses, just about anything anyone wants. He lived out on his family farm six miles North of Verndale, Minnesota. That's ten miles from Wadena, where I lived in my little gray house. He did some farming but rented out the irrigated land. It was very beautiful out there. It's a peaceful tiny house though.

Since I had been married for thirty years, I really had no intentions of ever doing that again. So I went into this dating and having a lot of fun. It sure was nice having someone to go out to eat with and go to the movies. We went to fairs and farm shows too. He had been married two times before but not for very long to each of them. He has a daughter named Shona, and she is eighteen years older than Vernon, his son. Vernon was six when I met Rick. Forrest and Vernon did a lot with us together.

The church I go to was right out by Rick's house. Hope Chapel is a small country church, and I had only been going there a little while. He doesn't go to church, but I don't judge others. He lived in a very small house that's got a trailer connected for the kitchen. It's old! He had a big shop that's nicer than the house. There's a lot of sheds and a big red barn. So it had been a whirlwind the first year of dating. We both fell into the relationship quite fast. We didn't want to be apart. We planned our days, nights, and weekends around the kids' schedules.

I met his family over the holidays, and we all seemed to get along great. He has two sisters and two brothers. None lived around here. He had met my brothers and sisters. Also we loved going and doing things together. I was not used to all this attention, but I loved every minute of it. After four years of living alone, I did like his company, and he seemed to like mine. We both loved to camp, and we walked almost every day together.

At Christmas time in 2004, we were at his sister Dorla and Carl's house. We went for a walk. He said, "What would you say if I asked you to marry me?" I knew it was coming, but not sure if the time was right. I said yes.

So we got engaged but waited another year to get married. Through all this, Forrest was really getting close to Joey and Kim and family. So we talked as adults and decided that it was now that time for him to be with them. He was excited, but it was hard for him to leave after several years with me.

We also had to okay it with his mom as that was the agreement the judge had made. She was all for it. Then it would be Forrest just going to visit with her on weekends.

It was very hard for me because I had grown to love him in a different role than just grandma. But he could come see me as needed, which was hard because of all the other kids. It turned out between all the birthdays, weddings, holidays, and reunions, we saw each other plenty. There was an emptiness though for a very long time. My heart was heavy. The imprint was still there.

My best friend and neighbor passed away that year too. Joanne was a sweet person, and we did a lot together. I missed her so much. She was Forrest's cookie grandma as he called her. She was our neighbor when I was married to Ralph.

During this time now, Amy and Jon were raising two boys. So I had more grandsons. Also, Ryan married in 2004 to a lady with two kids. So we had another grandson and granddaughter. Then for another surprise, Joey and Kim were expecting next June 2005.

So I was up to eleven grandchildren. They were all so sweet, and we had made many good memories. I still struggled with my decision to let Forrest live with them, but I knew in my heart from doing foster care and raising three children of my own that it's best for children to be raised by their parents if at all possible.

They did a good job looking back on the situation. It takes a village to raise children, and this was a perfect example. He turned out great and was a typical teenager.

I started making scrapbooks for each of the grandkids. It was such a fun hobby. They all got them when they graduated. They loved to page through them when we're together. Pictures are so precious.

In 2004, I had to go to school to keep my job. They had a paraprofessional certificate we needed. So while I'm doing that, I also ended up having gall bladder surgery. With working full time, school and illness, it was a year to remember.

So now Rick and I are making lifelong plans. He had been told there was a surgery now that helped with weight loss. He's in late forties and had diabetes and was considered obese. The doctors said he was a candidate, and it could reverse his diabetes, help with blood pressure, and help him lose weight. He is five feet ten inches and 335 pounds. *He* wanted to keep healthy, so he had decided in spring of 2005 to go for the weight loss surgery. He has to go to classes before and after, but he didn't mind if it helped him get healthier. We were very supportive of each other, and to me it seemed like a no-brainer. So at the beginning of April 26, 2005, he had it done in Park Rapids, Minnesota. Wow, what a journey. He couldn't eat nothing but watermelon and light, soft foods. Mostly liquid. He was very weak and couldn't work for weeks. He was out of it for a long time. Many times he had to throw up even just a tiny bit of food. Rick turned fifty on May 2 and didn't get cake. But boy did he lose weight.

It was probably the worst summer of his life. I helped him as much as I could. We had plans to build a new house on the farm, so I put my house up for sale. I just posted a sign at my garage sale, and a daughter of an old friend of mine asked about it and wanted to buy it. I didn't even have to go through a realtor, just a purchase agreement with a realtor to make it legit. She only charged me $75 to write it up and told me the bank they go through could do the rest. So that was what I did. *It* took a while as this family had to clear up a loan or something, but I was assured it was moving along.

Rick had put a second bathroom in for me, and I had upgraded some. So I had bought it for $27,500 and sold it for $69,900. So I had money to put toward our new home too. Rick and I only wanted to borrow what we had to as we could do most of the labor. *It* is so exciting, and we both liked the A-frame style with a loft. So that worked out well. We walked around the farm and picked out a spot between the old farmhouse, which had to be taken down and the little shack he was living in. It was perfect. It has trees on three sides, a big yard, and the driveway in front. I remember Rick saying this was where the cows passed through all the time. No animals anymore, so it was only crop farming now with irrigation. We were good to go.

So we started building in September of 2005. Rick was somewhat better from his surgery but still losing weight. He got tired easily, but we weren't in a big hurry as long as we got it closed in by winter. It was so much fun. We are also planning our wedding. We decided to get married in Las Vegas, Nevada, in December.

My house sold finally in October, so I stayed with my youngest son Ryan and his wife mostly during the week because of work and with Rick on weekends.

I was there a lot to watch and help with the process of our new house. My stuff was in storage at the farm now. We also spent a lot of time in the summer at Twin Lakes, my seasonal.

So December 21, 2005, we flew to Vegas and had a wedding package deal. My friend Dorothy helped me book it all on the computer. She was so good at that, and I was not. I was just getting used to a nice cell phone. Still haven't got the hang of that. My grandkids know way more than I do. So I ask them or have them show me stuff on there. I just can't get over technology. I get some training in school, but that's even hard for me. I am getting better though!

So we got married at the Chapel of Love. It was a quaint little church, and you pick your flowers out right there. All paperwork was done for you.

The one thing Rick and I had to do was go to the courthouse and get our marriage license in Nevada. We stood under a trellis at the chapel, and the pastor's wife stood up for us. It was very beautiful and special. Since we both had been married before, it fit us perfectly. Then after our 2:00 p.m. wedding, we went on a limo ride and to the Stratosphere Casino & Restaurant. It was hundreds of feet high and had a revolving restaurant on the top. The name of it was On Top of the World. Believe me, it really felt like you were on top of the world. We had a five-course meal. It was so fancy. What a great memory. We were in Las Vegas for four days, so we got to see a lot. We had been there for a weekend when we were dating.

Rick and I didn't drink or gamble. He had been sobor many years. He had quit in his thirties, and that was one of the things that I loved about him. I've never been much of a drinker. It makes me sick, so I will occasionally have a wine cooler, but I can't even finish that. My drink of choice was Diet Pepsi. Rick's was Crystal Lite, and I liked that too. We both loved to go out for coffee, and our favorite outing was breakfast. We usually had omelets and sometimes split them as in this day and age restaurants had enormous- sized meals.

Rick was down to 215 pounds and looked so good. His health was better too. No diabetic meds, nothing since surgery. That was a real blessing. I hope it continues that way as there are no guarantees in life.

We flew home from Vegas and had Christmas with the kids the next week. That was always fun. Our kids didn't care that we celebrate together. They all seemed to get along. Shona had met a new guy, JJ. She brought him to our wedding reception on February 11, 2006. We had a party for friends and relatives at Ted & Gens, a quaint little place in Aldrich, Minnesota. It's close to home right on Highway 10. We had a great turnout. We had a buffet of three meats and all the salads and potatoes you could eat. We planned on 175 people but had to set up more tables as we served over two hundred. It was so nice. Rick's brothers and sisters met mine, and we had a dance with a DJ. What a perfect time together. A few relatives came out the next day to see how far we were on the house and helped us open our cards and gifts. Some of Ralph's relatives even came to our wedding party. They still treated me just like family after thirty years. They were such a cool family.

Ralph's mother had fifteen children with two husbands, so it was a large family. I could never forget any of them, whether I am divorced or not!

We didn't plan on a honeymoon yet, but Auntie Patty and Ray and some other relatives from my first marriage invited us to go with several of them to Alaska in June 2006. So Rick and I talked it over, and both of us wanted to go. We said yes!

It was a trip of a lifetime. By then we had moved in our new house, April 2, 2006. We needed a much-needed break. I'd say if you can build a house together, you can do anything together. With his construction expertise, it turned out beautiful!

Alaska Honeymoon Trip

We flew from Minneapolis to Vancouver, Canada. We boarded the *Diamond Princess* cruise ship. Saturday, June

10, we were heading for Ketchikan. There were ten of us. Auntie Patty and her sister Judy, Yoko, and Bob, a friend of all. Ralph and a guy friend I can't remember his name. Susie and Jim, another sister-in-law of Ralph's. Then Rick and me.

The ship was so fancy, and the service was grand. Our second day the crew had surprised us with balloons on our door and a sign that read "Happy honeymoon from *Princess* cruises."

We had so much fun and always had dinner with our group the same time each night. On a big ship, you really don't see one another so much unless you plan to because there's so much to do.

We had formal night and had to get dressed up in fancy clothes and all got pictures that night. You could also eat anywhere for breakfast, lunch, or dinner.

I think we tried just about everything, including caviar (yuck). They had pizza places, taco places, hamburger joints, and other restaurants to sit down and dine. This was all included in our package deal. Drinks too for some of those who liked that.

The next day we docked in Juneau and had so many hours to see that and a certain time to return to the ship. The trees and foliage and flowers were beautiful. Of course, on the ocean it was breath-taking. The water was a deep blue, and we saw whales jumping. That was incredible. We also had good weather the whole time.

We went on a tram on the thirteenth. Boy could you see everything from up above. It was a little unnerving as you are on a cable in a car looking over the city and mountains and ocean.

I couldn't even describe that feeling of being free in a world of beauty. The only negative thing was I got poison oak or ivy and had to see the ship doctor. He was Japanese or Chinese or something and didn't understand what I had. He finally gave me prednisone so I could start to heal. I am terribly allergic to sumac, ivy, and oak, so when I get it, I have to be treated right away, or it will spread like wildfire. Prednisone worked right away, so I didn't itch after that.

I probably got it on the bus that took us to the ship as the streets were lined with red oak trees, and the bus ride was very hot and sultry. *No air!*

We were now stopping at a port in Skagway on June 14. We saw waterfalls and caves and springs that day on a bus tour. We went by mountains and could walk in snow. We then went to Glacier Bay on the fifteenth, and oh, what a sight! The glaciers were like big mountains. They looked like fake Styrofoam. It was the most magnificent part of our trip. We got to watch them calve, which is when they start breaking up and falling into the ocean. It's like mountains of ice collapsing. The color was white with a light-blue tinge.

You have to see them to believe nature can be that beautiful. It by far was the best part of our trip. Then the next day on to Clouet Fjord. There we went shopping and went to like a Western-style town with old hotels called the Golden North Horse. We had our second formal night and were presented with a bottle of wine for the newest newlyweds on board *Diamond Princess*. We didn't drink, but it was still cool. I have it still in our cabinet for a good memory.

It was always fun to meet up at 7:00 p.m. with our group and talk about our excursions for the day and the things we purchased for souvenirs. Oh, and again, the food was out of this world. They had a dessert table about fifty- or sixty-foot long with just desserts and watermelons with carved pictures on them like gold miners and seals and trees. Someone was very creative.

On the sixteenth, we went to sea and were fortunate to see whales. They were enormous and very fun to watch. They seemed to put on a show for the cruise ships. We had great weather the whole trip.

June 17, we went on the Denali Express, a ten-and-a-half-hour train ride to Denali National Park. We saw two bears and a couple moose. When we arrived at the Denali Wilderness Lodge, we had a sit-down family style dinner theater. We were served ribs, corn on the cob, mashed potatoes, biscuits, and apple crisp. It was so good.

Our rooms there were very large. It was so huge and rustic, which Rick and I loved. The evening here was at our leisure, so we just hiked and looked a lot at nature on trails and the cabins. They had a place called the Savage Cabin Interpretation Center in which taught us about the Indian culture. It was very cool.

We had the morning at leisure and then went to a look out to see Mt. McKinley.

On the nineteenth, we went by coach to Anchorage, Alaska, and spent two days and one night there. We did a lot of shopping there and brought home gold nuggets and jewelry for the kids. It was definitely a tourist trap, but they could be fun too.

The twentieth of June at 10:00 p.m., we went from our hotel to the airport and had a straight flight home. Wow, a trip of a lifetime. I really hope our kids can someday enjoy this as we did along with the grandkids. You won't regret it, and it is a must-see!

CHAPTER 34

Settling In

I did give up my seasonal spot at Twin Lakes in Menahga. They just keep raising the fees. It was wonderful while it lasted. Now we go to other places like Wisconsin Dells with Vernon and Shona and Forrest. Also Valleyfair is always fun. New places make new memories. We also go to family get togethers at Long Lake by Itasca Park every year in July. It's my side of the family, but Rick fits right in. Then each August, we go to a new state park for Rick's cousins and brother and sisters and relatives. Always a great time. State Parks are pretty rustic and undisturbed. We do get water and electric if possible. I'm kinda spoiled.

We are now settling into our newly built house. I never thought I'd have a beautiful home that we created together, but it is a dream come true. We just love it.

I am having some health problems in the lady department. So I am having a partial hysterectomy on our first anniversary. Kinda bummer, but it needs to be done. So glad it went well, and I'm feeling so much more energy. I've been quite healthy all my life, but we all have a few issues. I also had surgery on my thumbs in St. Cloud. I couldn't even turn the car keys. My tendons had blown out. They reattached them, and I'm good to go. It was same day surgery and only off work for a week. It's amazing the medical advances we have. Other than that, I only have thyroid issues, but one little pill a day takes care of that.

Rick is still doing construction and is now working for JR Construction in 2007, 2008, and 2009. They build a lot of log homes, including a summer place by Mankato for Justin Morneau. He's a Minnesota Twins player, and Rick said that was really a great house to build. The log homes are beautiful. This keeps us busy with our jobs but seem to find time to have fun. I had a big surprise at school one day. Our foreign exchange student Uli, from Germany, and his family were on the playground when I came out to be on duty. I was just so shocked and couldn't believe it.

It was Halloween time, October 2008, and his little girls had never experienced or heard of this event. So we invited them to join that evening in our Halloween extravaganza. It's a party at the school with all kinds of games and treats for all. His little girls loved it. One of his girls was in second grade, so they spent a day in our second-grade classroom that I worked in. The teacher let them talk and teach about their country, and also they got in on another Halloween party in our room. It was so much fun. They were in the States for a few weeks but with us a few days. We had them out to our place for spaghetti and meatballs. What a memory for all of us. He was such a great guy to have in 1992 and as a host family to him. He fit right in, and he and Joey made many good times, some of which they think I don't know about (haha).

Amy and Ryan loved being a part of learning about Uli's family and his culture. What a great time for all. It was sad to see them leave again. I'm hoping someday to visit them in Germany. Just one of the things on my bucket list. Just hope it's not sixteen years between times.

In 2009, Rick is having a lot of kidney problems. He has stones and takes Flomax for that. He sees a specialist in Staples or St. Cloud. We take a day at a time. We also have now been licensed for foster care. With having built a new house, everything passed according to code. We now have a sixteen- year-old foster girl. Ashley is a sibling to Wayne we had in earlier years. She is a sweet, sweet girl. We enjoy having Ashley, and she's loving school and likes the peaceful environment out here on the farm. This is new for Rick, but he is doing good helping with her needs. She will be here until she graduates.

We went to Beaver Creek State Park in 2008 this year, and it was way south of us in Minnesota. We always have a blast.

In 2009, we all gathered at Itasca State Park. That's only an hour away for us, so it is really convenient. I have kept up with pictures and scrapbook them to take with us each trip. Everyone always loves to see them. Some of our fellow campers even help scrapbook a page or two at camp. It's fun to include all of us.

Our garden this year was great. We always plant green beans, tomatoes, and cucumbers along with squash and a few radishes. The only hard part is when school starts in September and I go back to work, it's canning time. I always seem to manage though!

This 2009 year has brought some changes. Rick was laid off from his job. He gets COBRA insurance for one and a half years, but it's not cheap. We always seem to manage, and he has some construction jobs lined up. The economy is slow this year and last year too. Recessions are not fun. Just not much work and can't find help. Rick also started on metformin for his diabetes again. He took this for a few months but had a lot of pain from it, so they switched him to Victoza, which seems to be better. Still having kidney problems, he has had stones removed surgically and has had them blasted also. He has a lot of back pain, so he is on oxycodone for that. He sees doctors a lot in St. Cloud as these issues need specialists. Thank goodness he gets unemployment now. That helps a lot financially. I have insurance through the school, so I'm covered. It's very expensive with a high deductible. Thank goodness I'm quite healthy, so I don't use insurance much.

It's 2010 now, and it's quite a year. Rick's health is not good. He has a lot of pain, and it's hard to work construction with a bad back and kidney problems. He tries so hard, but I think it's probably not going to get any better. We will pray that it does. We always seem to make it. God is good.

June 19, 2010, we had a tornado tear through Wadena. I was in town helping my boss from the motel. I clean on weekends for them. They were buying the wedding shop. I was helping them clean and get ready for the grand opening. It looked very gray outside, and a storm was brewing. They said, "You better get home," so I left, but I got to the car, and the door wouldn't open. There was like a vacuum and very still outside. It was quite creepy, so I went back inside. We all went to the basement, and that's when it hit. It was very loud, and a lot of sirens went off. The tornado took out the southwest residential area of Wadena. It also took the high school with it and damaged the tech school There was an all-school reunion being set up at the high school, but it was early afternoon, so the people in there either got out or got under things to a safe place. It was over within a half hour or so. My grandson (Tanner) was staying with us at the farm, so I called Rick, and they just got wind and hail. I ran home to be sure they were okay. They were happy I was all right.

That evening we went to see all the damage in Wadena. It was hard to believe what a tornado can do. It was an E4 with winds up to 170 mph. The damage was unbelievable. No lives were lost, but a lot of homes and devastation were left behind. Some of our friends lost their homes. The whole town came together as a community, and everyone helped everyone with cleanup and rebuilt the town and high school.

In 2008, it is the year my nephew Dustin passed away. He was my youngest sister's son (Audrey and Rick's). He was handicapped since birth. He suffered through many trials, and his family took the best care they knew how for him. He had a good life but is missed by all. He was only nineteen.

This summer we had our family reunion at Long Lake, like we do every year. My mom slept in our camper, but it's getting harder and harder for her to get up the steps. We love having her with us each year. She is so good and loving to all eight of us. We swim, kayak, and make fry bread and Uffda tacos every time.

On Rick's side this year, for the campout, we went to Gooseberry Falls by Duluth at North Shore Drive. It is such a beautiful area. We got lots of great scenic pictures with Vernon and family. He still loves to go with places. We love taking him. Shona and JJ and kids make it to some of these summer gatherings. They are all growing up fast. Shona and JJ got married in Fargo on September 25, 2010. We helped decorate the place, and it was just a beautiful outdoor wedding on the golf course.

Now back to school routine. It's so fun to have summers off and just side jobs during the summers keeps me busy, but it all helps.

We have canning done and no more mowing the grass.

CHAPTER 35

Losing My Mother

The holidays are coming soon. This Thanksgiving we are going to my mom's. It's always fun as she's a great cook. Living one hundred miles from us, we love to go see her. We have a great meal with as many of us that can make it home Then we play boardgames like Scrabble. She is a Scrabble queen. She has a Scrabble dictionary, which is kinda a cheat book but legal. Mom knows all these words we've never heard of, but they are in the book, so they count.

Shona and kids stopped by and got in on the game. Shona is only one I know of that challenged my mom. It was quite cute, but Mom proved the words. How funny was that! We all still laugh about it. We all told Shona to just let it go, so she did.

Christmas, we saw her again. I love this time of year. We went to Paul's farm for this and also made it to Paul and Deb's annual New Year's Eve party. Little did I know it would be the last New Year's Eve Mom would be able to attend. Early in January 2011, Mom got sick and was taken to Fargo by ambulance. She was hardly ever sick, but this time her kidneys shut down. They tried dialysis, but it was too hard on her. She didn't want to do it again and knew that meant she would die. We were all by her side until the end. The only thing she kept wanting was to go home to her own bed. She was too sick for that, so she passed away peacefully at the hospital. Then we had the funeral the next week.

She will be buried beside our Dad out in the country by Fosston. It's January, so the weather hasn't been very good. We've had two storms this week, but we are used to Minnesota winters.

Our mom was such sweet soul and will be missed a lot.

In February, we all agreed to go to her little house in Fosston and clean it out so it can be rented again.

We all showed up, and in seven or eight hours, we had it all gone through. We all needed nothing, but it was nice to have a few mementos from her life. No one fought over anything, and we all helped each other get through this. She had little money, but she had a houseful of love for all of us to share. What a blessing.

In Loving Memory of
Mary Motl
August 23, 1929–January 8, 2011

Those we hold
most dear
never truly leave us…
They live on
in the kindness
they showed,
the comfort
they shared,
and the love
they brought
into our lives.

In Loving Memory of Mary Bernice Motl

Mary Bernice Baustian was born on August 23, 1929, in Page, North Dakota, daughter of John and Theresa Baustian. She graduated from Fosston High School.

Mary was united in marriage to Glenn Marvel Curfman on June 26, 1948. Glenn and Mary farmed east of Lengby until Glenn's death in 1967. Eight children were born to this union.

Mary married Everett Motl, and they resided in the Thief River Falls, Minnesota, area. They returned to Fosston, Minnesota, where Mary owned and operated the Little Café for several years. Mary and Everett moved to Fisher, Minnesota, where she owned and operated the Fisher Café. Mary returned to Fosston, where she owned and operated Mary's Corner Closet until she retired.

Mary was a member of St. Mary's Catholic Church. She was also involved with many activities at the Embassy Center. Mary enjoyed spending time with her large family and especially enjoyed family reunions, where she could visit with extended family. Mary enjoyed camping, fishing, playing cards, wagon train rides, crocheting, and playing Scrabble with her entire family. Mary taught the art of doughnut making to her grandchildren. On Saturday, January 8, 2011, Mary passed away surrounded by family at Essentia Hospital in Fargo, North Dakota, at the age of eighty-one years.

Survivors include her children Alice (Beans) Wander, Waubun, Minnesota; Tim (Donna) Curfman, Alexandria, Minnesota; Ted (Jan) Curfman, Thief River Falls, Minnesota; Theresa (Marvin) Stark, Green River, Wyoming; Sharol (Rick) Mason, Verndale, Minnesota; Paul (Deb) Curfman, Fosston, Minnesota; Evelyn (Maurus) Karboviak, Finley, North Dakota; and Audrey (Rick) Simmons, Erskine, Minnesota. Mary is also survived by three brothers—Edward, Leo, and Jon Baustian; and one sister, Betty Leibnitz. In addition, Mary is survived by forty grandchildren, sixty-one great-grandchildren, five great-great-grandchildren, and many nieces, nephews, and cousins.

She was preceded in death by her husbands Glenn and Everett; parents, John and Theresa Baustian; her sister, Evelyn Baustian (Sister Karen); one grandchild, Dustin Simmons; and three great-grandchildren.

May her soul and the souls of all the faithful departed through the mercy of God. Rest in peace. Amen.

CHAPTER 36

Hard Times

Rick this summer June 2011 is working for a concrete company out of Grand Forks, North Dakota. He is on his third week there. It's a very hot and humid summer. Temp's up to 103 degrees. He ended up driving home from Grand Forks as he was sick. He had been sick the day before but still tried to work. It was a new job, so he felt he had to. Finally, the boss said, "You need to go home." It was over one hundred miles from home. His symptoms were dizziness, sweating, and severe weakness. He doesn't remember much of the drive. He got to Highway 71 by Park Rapids and needed to turn right to get home or left to go to the hospital in Park Rapids. He made the right choice and took himself to the hospital. I was at a family reunion forty-five miles away when I got the call from them. They said he needed to be transferred to Fargo as his kidneys were shutting down. He was on COBRA insurance at the time, and it was expensive with a big deductible. So I asked if I could take him to Fargo. They said it was okay, but I had to be there soon. So I drove there and picked him up. He was not in good shape, but I got him there.

He was in for four days. It took till the third day before his numbers for his kidney function started going up. Then things got better pretty fast. They said he was lucky it turned around for him. They said he had heat exhaustion and acute kidney failure. Oh, what a scare. From that time on, he just was weak and couldn't do much for work. His diabetes went crazy, and he was on insulin shots.

From this point on, he has a lot of kidney stones and back pain. Saw several doctors for this. We are now pursuing disability insurance as he really can't work. So I am doing the paperwork for that. A lot of the questions have to do with what he's not able to do anymore. I felt we had no choice at this point. He has been on oxycodone, and they just keep increasing that. Doesn't seem to help much but helps him sleep a lot. Between diabetes meds and pain meds, he can hardly function.

2012

In January of 2012, Rick had more kidney stones. It meant they had to be surgically removed in St. Cloud. He now has very good specialists there. In April of 2012, we were okayed for him to get disability. I can't believe all the paperwork was okayed, and he now gets money each month. Plus once you're on that, Medicare automatically qualifies you for medical insurance. Boy, what a big help. Sometimes you just know your prayers are answered. It was a very hard time for both of us. God is good.

CHAPTER 37

Moving Home

March of 2012, Vernon moved in with us full time. He called and wanted to live with us. He's fifteen, but we are so excited to have him. He will visit his Mom anytime he wants. So that changes our life also. Rick does not have to pay child support, which will help since he's on a limited income now with not being able to work. It has been so good for him having Vernon home as he is a great help to us. Talk about good timing for all. Prayer never ceases to amaze us. We count our blessings every day.

How exciting for Rick and me to have a teenager full-time in the house. Vernon is such a sweet soul. He brings friends home that are very respectful, and yes, some are girls. His friend Michael spends a lot of time here with him. He even hunts with us and has a deer stand. Vernon now is working on getting his license and goes to school his last two years in Verndale. That's where Rick graduated from, so he's proud Vernon can too. Vernon also plays football, so now we are back into the routine of running to all the games. It is so fun to watch, and they really are pretty good. They have Coach Mahlen, who was there when Rick and Wayne played football. Now he's Vernon's coach. He's been coaching since 1969, and he is good! Wow!

He and his friends keep really busy with riding four-wheelers and dirt bikes, snowmobiling, swimming, and camping with us. He also goes to Camp Jim and Camp Shaminah and learns a lot from them. He got his license now, and his first car is a 1995 Honda Civic. He thinks it's quite fast and also had to learn real fast how to drive a straight stick. He did good. He got a job at Russ Davis and has done real well and is saving money for college. He works in the mechanic shop on trucks. This is right up his alley as he likes to work on engines and plans to do machining.

We all went camping to Long Lake, our yearly camping reunion on my side. Sure do miss my mom, but we always have fun. This year we went to Lake Louise State Park for Rick's side of the family. It is always so fun to catch up on everyone's lives throughout the year.

Good Times and Sad Times

We had two grandkids graduate this year, Forrest and Kaitlen. It was very nice to see the relatives on both sides. A lot of Ralph's brothers and sisters were there at Joey and Kim's house. They still love and treat me as family even though Ralph and I are divorced. I feel the same way. When you know people for over thirty years, they are family forever. It did make me feel a tad bit older though.

It didn't seem that long ago that my own kids were graduating. Now their kids are. I gave them each some money and a scrapbook of their memories throughout their growing-up years. It's a keepsake made by Grandma!

This fall, September 18, 2012, my youngest sister, Audrey, passed away at her home at Lake Sara in Erskine, Minnesota. She was only fifty-two years old but had struggles since a teenager with type 1 diabetes. She died of complications of diabetes and obesity. She left behind her husband, Rick, sons David and Darren. She had lost Dustin in 2008. She is the first of us eight children to pass away. She was a very loving wife and mother. Her caretaking skills kept her family going even under many trials and some very tough times throughout her life. She was quite the trooper and will be missed by all of us. RIP, little sister.

CHAPTER 38

Diagnosis

In November of this year, I went to a health fair for women's night out, and they do some health tests there. My blood pressure was fine, but my blood sugar was elevated. So they recommended I go get an A1C done at the clinic. So I made an appointment but not until February. I wasn't too worried as I had gestational diabetes with all my kids when I was pregnant. They told me then I could eventually get type 2 diabetes. So I've known for years it was possible, and then you add in the family history of my dad with type 1, and it makes you realize you are at risk. I also have two sisters with type 1 diabetes. I have always been so fortunate to be healthy. I only take a small one-milligram pill for my thyroid since I was in my twenties. I know as my life goes on I may have to take some medicines to stay healthy but will cross that bridge when I come to it.

Typical Workday

I kept busy with work and fun. My typical day started at 5:30 a.m. when my alarm went off. I got up, took my thyroid pill, and needed to wait a half hour before I could eat. That gave me just enough time to get ready and go over my plans for the day. I left at six twenty and get on a bus at the school at 6:45. I had ridden bus for all the years I've worked at WDC school. I loved greeting each of the kids as they got on, and they were such good kids. Over the years, I had earned a lot of respect from them. It could entail just keeping them happy or cleaning up the puke, but that one hour a day paid for my health insurance each month, and I enjoyed it. Of course, I had to learn how to secure seat restraints and wheelchairs. Some years I did both the morning and after-school ride. I really learned to appreciate our dedicated bus drivers.

Then I would move from classroom to classroom, picking up several students at a time to take to our title 1 resource room. There we would break them up into smaller groups to teach them reading. These were students who just needed that repetition and more exposure to improve their reading skills. I would go to workshops in Staples, St. Cloud, and locally to be able to help them with the program. The type of program changed throughout the years.

We would learn what worked for each one together. It was always a good time with our title 1 team. As the day went on, I was scheduled to do playground and cafeteria duty. It was such a nice break as I got to go outside for one and a half hours, then lunchroom for the last group coming in to eat. It was so refreshing to have fresh air and break up the day. Then I would get my lunchbreak, which was half hour long. I usually had a protein shake that a lot of us made right in the breakroom. I never ate at school in all of my years as it was just too much food for me.

After lunch I would continue to pick up students and bring them to the title 1 resource room. Here we would work on math skills for them and do flashcards, worksheets, or games to learn about numbers. By far the hardest thing to teach them were story problems. Most would get confused with all the steps. Then for the last hour or so, I would go to their rooms, call each by name, and they would read the book or story we were working on to me. We would sit in the back of the room or go out in the hallway. They also could be tested on their comprehension for that book by going to the library and taking a test on the computer. Here they would earn prizes by earning points. Our school had a lot of incentives to keep on trying to be a better reader.

Then at 3:10 p.m. or so, we would load the buses and

send them home. Every day was pretty much the same routine except on holidays and programs throughout each year. Since I was cleaning two houses after school and the Pioneer Journal all on different days, it kept me going until 5:00 or 6:00 p.m., and then I headed home to catch up on things there and had evenings with Rick.

He had learned to cook supper as I bought him several cookbooks, and he had stepped up to learning how to make chili, soups, and hotdishes. He only knew how to make sloppy joes and goulash. Whatever that was. It had been so nice, and he needed to be needed too. Then we winded down each night with a walk and a few TV shows, then to bed and do it all over again.

2013 Happenings
Cancer Strikes

This year started off with one of my good friends learning they had cancer. First of all, Rita, a bowling buddy and good friend, kept having backaches a lot. She figured it was from her job as a mail carrier or from too much bowling. She finally went on to the doctor and found out it was cancer in more than one place. She did some treatments, but in the end, it took her life. RIP, Rita.

Then about the same time my good friends Alyn and Joanie found out Alyn has rectal cancer. I'd worked with Joanie at school for many years. Alyn belonged to the VA, so she would go there for his treatment. They were very aggressive in their approach and removed it, and now he lives with a bag. I loved his sense of humor through all this. He said I'd farmed for years and never lost my ass till now. He is doing good and has handled all the newness with grace. It has not slowed them two down. They still go to all the grandkids games and school events. They run way more that we do, including going to Texas in the winter. God bless their spirit!

Our camping this year went great at Long Lake reunion. We had a lots of people and spent a lot of time in the lake. The group did some fishing, and of course, we had lots of food. So much fun each year. My niece Brenda brought a large blow-up floatie that held ten to fifteen people. It always had to be repaired with leaks we caused. That was part of working together and many laughs along the fix.

This year on Rick's side, we went to another state park called Frontenac State Park. We had a great time, including some guitar tunes, swimming, campfires, and of course, yummy food. We all had our own camper and sites but tried to park close together. We had some that stayed in cabins or get motel rooms to go back and forth from the park. Always a fun time and time to catch up with one another's lives. Rick and I love to camp. Don't ever underestimate the great outdoors!

The grandkids had come out this summer to the farm to ride four- wheelers and swim in the river, and my kids camped down by the Leaf River at Camp Mason. It was beautiful with the oak trees and campfire rings. We also had Orly graduating this year, one of the grandkids. Joey and Kim always put on a nice spread. Many relatives and fun for all. Summers seemed to go by way too fast.

My friends Theresa, Ruth, and Diane got together like we do every year for our birthdays. We go out to eat and exchange birthday cards and gifts. Seems all our lives change quite a bit from year to year. A great tradition for many years, more to come too.

2014 News

This year starts out celebrating New Year's at my brother Paul and Deb's house out in the country by Fosston, Minnesota. It's always fun but just not the same since our mom was gone. Since Rick and I don't drink, we went for the food, games, and snow angels. Our mom always played Scrabble and any new game we brought to share. Still fun to bring in the new year together.

This spring I tossed around the idea of having a garage built close to the house. I asked Rick, "How about that Quonset building over there?" He said that was the loading barn for our pigs over the years and sheep and cows. They would put the animals in there and then load them into the truck. His dad would then drive them to St. Paul stockyards. There they would meet their demise! The more he thought about it, the better the idea was it might work. So he started the plans.

First we had to decide the best location. We settled on the northwest corner by the house. We had a drive around the house driveway, so now I would be able to back out into drive and just go out. I was really liking the idea as I was tired of walking a ways to the shop to warm up and get my car. It's not so bad in the spring or fall, but in the winter it was hard. I also didn't like when it was raining. So Rick got busy and poured a slab of cement for the floor in the spring. Then one day I drove into the driveway, and he had the building dangling from the forklift and was moving it to the slab. OMG, my heart almost stopped. I was thinking he would have a neighbor help guide him or something. Oh, know when he put his mind to it he thought he could do anything all by himself. He did have me watch so it didn't scrape or get too close to the northside of the house. It was close, but there's always someone watching over him.

He set it down with perfect precision onto the slab. Voilà,

I now had a garage. I just needed electricity to be put in. Well, we happened to have a savvy brother-in-law (Maurey) who was willing to help and guide that undertaking. So I now had plugins, lights, and an automatic garage door. I absolutely loved it. My car did too!

So now onto planning a graduation party for Vernon. He graduates from Verndale High School this May. We were having his party right here at the farm. I love to host. We would set up everything in the garage as it's all cleaned up and ready to use. We served ham and buns, salads, chips, cake, bars, lemonade and pop, and coffee. Oh, and baked beans. It went so good. We had lots of relatives, friends, classmates, and neighbors show up. He got a lot of cash and gifts from all. What a great day.

This year we spent the Mason campout at Crow Wing State Park. Shona and JJ and kids made it. Oh, how fun to spend time camping, swimming, and grilling. Amber and Vernon were able to come. Amber was Vernon's' girlfriend. She's a sweetie.

Moving Forward 2015

We were starting to think more toward retirement. Rick had been home several years due to his disability. We were planning on downsizing a bit. We didn't need 230 acres of farmland and hunting land. We found a good financial person to help with decisions. We would take some time to think about what's best for us.

My brother Tim called to let us know there was a lake lot on Lake Victoria in Alexandria, Minnesota. They had a lot and thought we might want first dibs on getting this one that's available by them. I guess we hadn't thought about it lately, but I do remember loving my seasonal by Menahga back in 2003. All we'd have to do was pay the seasonal fees and move a camper or trailer on it.

So we opted to go ahead and see how we liked it. We loved it and went as often as we could, usually leaving Thursday and staying until Sunday. We rode Rick's Harley a lot of time but needed a car to go shopping and garage sales too. So sometimes he would ride the bike, and I would drive the car.

I was working summer school and cleaning houses and business yet, so we were limited which days to go, but that's okay. We had animals at home to take care of too and lawn to mow and garden to water and weed. It worked well to go between them. Tim and Donna had introduced us to Bernie and Lorraine, the landlords. He did all the upkeep so we went there just to relax and have fun. We also met Hal and Teri, Mary and Don, Rosemary and Curt, Troy and Diane, which we got together often for picnics, pontoons, and just visiting. What a great bunch of lake friends.

We bought a pontoon from Tim and Donna's good friends and neighbor LeRoy and Sharon. They gave us a great deal, so it was easy to say yes. Rick and I also bought two kayaks. I learned to really love doing that each weekend.

The group always planned a Fourth of July pot luck, and that was so yummy. Great times together.

Vernon was going to school in Bemidji since fall of 2014 for engine machining. He really liked it. He found a room in a house that five guys shared the common area. Seemed to be going well. Along with school, he worked at a towing company and delivered pizza. We missed him here at home, but all of them had to move on.

We did decide to sell some acreage, the irrigated land, as the irrigators were aging like us! Rick couldn't do much to help keep them going. We also got offered a price that was hard to refuse. We always said Tiny, Rick's dad, would be flipping in his grave knowing what he paid per acre and what we got for each acre. Our tax guy had them write a check in

2015 for half of sale and then another check in 2016 for the other half so that we wouldn't have so much income in one year. It saved us thousands of dollars due to capital gain. We also agreed with our financial advisor to invest most of it for three years with them, and after that, we would get a return for the rest of our lives. This worked out perfect as I planned on retiring fall of 2018. If we died early, all of it that we invested that's left would go to the kids. It seemed like a good plan, and time would tell. We also paid off our debts, so we could save for retirement fun. Life is good! Oh, Gracie, a granddaughter, graduated this year also.

CHAPTER 39

Century Farm 2016

A century farm is a farm that has been in the same family for one hundred years or more.

We did not go to Paul and Debs for New Year's this year. It's one hundred miles, and it made me miss my mom so much that it's not fun.

We still went back and forth to Lake Victoria. It's only an hour from us, so it was close. I had been fishing a lot this year, and my brother Tim had shown me how to clean the fish. He is legally blind and still cleaned faster and better than me. But I was not going to give up. We were loving our pontoon also. The lake life is so serene and peaceful.

I had been planning on a century farm party here at the Mason farm. Planning on around 150 people or so and serving a nice meal again in my garage. It's June 5, so I rented a one-hundred-by-two-hundred-foot canopy. It was yellow and white striped. We invited the relatives, neighbors, and friends. If it's hot, we were covered or in case of rain.

I had a quilted family tree made for the Mason families that grew up here. I gave them to the oldest of each sibling. It was pretty cool, featuring a branch on a tree with each family's name on a quilted bird. So Dorla got for Vernie's family, Randy for Hilda's family, and to Laurel in Anna Mae's family. That was fun putting each correct name, birthdate, and deaths for some.

We also planted birch trees in our front yard. One for each sibling's family and a fourth for Rick and myself. They were about five feet tall and three or four gimels on each, which meant they each had three or four stems, which would be the trunk of the tree. Everyone pitched in from each family to help pay for them as they were a little expensive. We also released one hundred helium balloons as the grand finale. Wow, what a beautiful tribute to his family.

Rick and I also had a century farm sign made by Sign & Designs in Wadena, Minnesota. Julia is the best sign maker around. She made it about three feet by five feet with a 1961 Allis Chalmers on it. It also has a field with hay bales and a barn in the background. Rick displayed it by putting it between two posts, and it sat right as you come in our driveway.

Vernon moved home and was taking some time off from school to work and make some money. It was so nice to have him here. He worked for a machining place called O'Landers by Staples, Minnesota. He pitched in and helped Rick with a lot of things. He also had our large shop to work in so him and his friends worked on cars, trailers, four-wheelers, or anything that needed some work.

We had three graduation parties this year. Two kids I knew from work and our granddaughter M'Cayla. Wow, there were growing up fast.

Our camping trips on each side of our families were really fun. We went to Sakahta State Park on Rick's side. It did rain a lot this trip, so we were under tarp and canopies even to eat together. A little cozy, but oh so fun! We make do!

My friend Theresa moved to St. Cloud. She will be truly missed. We've worked at school together and have taken many walks over the years. My sister Evelyn and Maury from Finley, North Dakota, are moved back to Minnesota also. Their son Ricky got married June 4 to Jenny. What a beautiful wedding. He is in his thirties and getting married for the first time. This was all such a wonderful time until my sister Evelyn called and said three days after the wedding Jenny had died. None of us could believe it. It was a very sad time for all of us. Jenny had a disease called NFI, which is neurofibromatosis type 1. It didn't slow her down as she graduated from Mayville State University with an AA degree in early childhood and loved teaching little children.

She met Rick while he was employed at Mayville State. Her happiest days on this earth, as stated in her obituary, was her wedding and the three days spent with Ricky as husband and wife.

Never take life for granted as none of us know how long we have on this earth. These two lived and loved life together to its fullest. RIP, dear Jenny!

This summer we also bought a Polaris side by side. We're thinking it might be a little easier on our backs as we get older. It definitely was much easier, and we were covered for rain and wind as we rode together. It had a winch also to help pull brush and trees up the inclines. We also could pull a little trailer behind to give kids rides or bring wood up to the house. Should have bought it years ago. Live and learn!

My nephew Matt worked at Polaris in Roseau, Minnesota, and got us a great deal as his friend needed a bigger one with a back seat as his family had grown. We didn't need a big one, so it worked perfect to buy his. It was only one and a half years old and hardly been used with few miles. Also if we needed parts, Matt could get for us too.

Vernon was in second year now of machining in Bemidji. Amber was living with him and working at a hair salon there.

They had a trailer house to rent.

We found another use for the pig shed, another small building on the farm. It had been used to protect the mama pigs and her babies when she had them. It's ten by fourteen and was now a really nice hunting shack. Rick is so amazing at building and repurposing what we can. It is now such a nice retreat during our hunting adventures in November. We have a couch bed built in and a private small bathroom with a chemical toilet to use. Also benches, a table, lights, and lanterns. We use a battery for lights but tend to use the kerosene or lanterns most of the time. To top it off, we have a little barrel stove to heat if needed. We usually have to open the door though as it cooks us out, but oh so warm to come in to eat or warm up! It's pine inside and cedar on the outside. I feel like such a lucky person to have such conveniences.

Guess what, I am now a great-grandma. Alyssa had a baby boy. She named him Henry. He is so precious. My life just gets better and better!

2017 Memories

Rick's back pain had gotten a lot worse these past years. I felt bad for him, and pain pills didn't seem to help much. We were not riding motorcycle anymore as it's just too hard. It even bothered my back, so it's time to be done. It was a great ride while it lasted. We did let go of the bike and use the side by side a lot more. It was a good trade-off.

My youngest sister, Audrey's husband Rick, passed away this year too. She died in 2012 at fifty-one years old, and he was only sixty-four years old. It made us more aware of how precious our time on earth was.

Since I planned on retiring next year, we had planned a few bus trips. We mainly needed to know if we liked to travel that way or not. Our first trip by bus, I planned in a

SHAROL MASON

trip through Todd Wadena Electric Company. They took a bus from Wadena to Garrison, North Dakota. It was a three-day, two-night motel stay. It was to show and teach us where our electricity came from and how it's transported to us. We saw an open coal mine and a museum also. We both really liked the bus ride. It was so nice to have our days and nights planned for us. Rick really enjoyed it as it was geared toward a guy's likes. I liked it for the learning also but mostly to be able to spend quality time with each other. We had no worries or decisions to make, just sat back and enjoyed the ride. I had PTO days to use up, so I had the time off in the spring. A great trip.

We spent a lot of time at Lake Victoria again this summer. I caught a lot of fish and was getting better at cleaning. I loved a good fish fry. It's just so much better fresh. We had made and spent many days with our good friends there. My brother Tim and Donna were so fun to live by and enjoy each other's company.

We went to Tettegouche State Park this year for Rick's family campout. His sister Nancy came to this one from Georgia. She was so much fun, and we all got to catch up. It's easy to lose track of one another's lives when we lived so far apart. We kept in touch with texts and cards. She is married to Jerry.

We had over forty in attendance, but we truly missed Joylynn and Terry at the campout. She had something that affected her frontal lobe and made her unable to participate anymore. It's a lot like dementia, I guess. She and Terry were the rock of this event and had kept it going for many ears. Her twin sister JoGene and Terry now carried on for all of us. We missed her and commended her husband for taking care of her through her journey. We prayed every day that they got through each and every day together as long as they could. God had guided them to do what they had to do. God bless you both.

SURVIVING LIFE AND
C🦠VID-19

We had another granddaughter, Alyssa, graduate this year from Sebeka, Minnesota. Seemed every year we had some parties for that. It's always fun to see everyone and celebrate their milestones. Hunter graduated from Wisconsin. These grandkids kept us busy.

We planned another bus trip for Branson, Missouri. Randy and Ruth were going with us. It's a Christmas theme. Christmas in Branson, Missouri.

Rick did choose to have a revision surgery on his stomach. He was having problems with scar tissue and other issues. He was having it done with the same Dr. Smith in Park Rapids. It's Thanksgiving time, so he would be in the hospital for a few days. Our good friends Tim and Brenda lived by Park Rapids and asked me to join them Thanksgiving day. It was turkey and all the trimmings. It was such a nice break from sitting at the hospital and very much appreciated. He was doing good but on pretty much a liquid diet for a while. He had some pain but had a pretty high tolerance. Such a trooper.

We were now ready to go on our trip to Branson. His cousin Randy and Ruth were driving to Alexandria with us. We left from the Perkins parking lot to get on the bus. The bus stopped at other locations to pick a few people up here and there. We got breaks every two to three hours mostly to get a coffee break or bathroom break. Well, on our way the first day, we were stopped at a cheese shop in a little town, and to our surprise, we ran into my brother Tim and his wife, Donna. They were on their way home from Branson and had stopped there. So we got a really nice picture of the four of us. What a crazy coincidence. They were traveling with a different bus company but timed it perfectly.

While at Branson, we saw four or five great shows. The *Dudley* was a spectacular family show. We saw a few country shows along with one that was about Noah with a story from the Bible. They had real camels and donkeys, which made it all come to seem like real life back then. It was very touching and emotional. The characters dressed the part so perfectly that made it very moving along with very strong sound effects. We had many good meals together and such good company.

We saw a Christmas light show that made this trip so special. Having another couple to visit and eat with us was extra nice. We will never forget this bus trip.

This year we also had a Baustian family reunion at Uncle Paul and Deb's farm by Fosston. Every two or three years, he hosts a big campout at his place. We have anywhere from fifty to one hundred shows each time. Of course, Paul does so much of it, and we have a silent auction to help Paul with the expenses. We have karaoke and bonfires and so much food it's crazy. Sometimes we go to Lengley Lake, which is the place we went as kids to swim almost every day in the summer. This year my niece Laura and her husband Matt surprised us and showed up from New Jersey. It was so nice to catch up with them. She is my oldest sister Alice's oldest daughter. We don't get to see them much as they live so far away. A time to remember.

2018 Memories

This is a milestone year for me. I am retiring in the fall September 8, 2018. That's my birthday. I will be done working as of June, but officially can't collect SS until September. It's kinda bittersweet. I have loved my job at WDC schools for thirty-four years. It will be quite different to not go to work each day. I started working at age fifteen and have loved all my jobs. That works out to be fifty years of job security. I guess when I look at it that way, it's time to plan trips and outings and create a different chapter in my life. Rick and I will now have many more hours and days to spend together. I will still have my cleaning jobs. I will have sometime away each week. That way it won't feel like cold turkey leaving my dream job!

This has been a very busy year. I started off going with my best friend Joanie and her church ladies to Mission Central in Iowa in March. It is a place for anyone but mostly missionaries to have a place to stay while serving the Lord. It consists of all volunteers, and they have no budget. It was all built on a farmstead in Iowa using all the buildings to provide for anyone in need. The farm ladies who live nearby make sure all are fed and taken care of. They served fifty-nine different groups of people just in this year.

The food pantry is supplied by donations, and the meat is from various farmers, so there is no cost. We had so much fun touring this wonderful place. We slept like in big rooms with lots of bunk beds just like a dorm. We giggled half the night away and ate good meals. We also had some music and programs to enjoy.

This spring, our dear cousin Paulette passed away from cancer. She was only sixty-eight years old. She was one of our cousins that all camped together at Long Lake every year. We all enjoyed being together there and any family events. Through the years, we have all been at weddings, graduations, funerals, and reunions. She will be missed by many. RIP, sweetie!

Wadena Deer Creek School gave another coworker and me a fantastic farewell retirement party. It was in May, and they had it at the Elks Club. We had a great meal and program. My kids were there with a lot of the grandkids. *It* was so nice, and I got a lot of cards and gifts. It really has been a great place to work with wonderful friends for coworkers. I will truly miss my job.

In June, as soon as school was out, we put our seasonal camper and spot up for sale. I had a call like in two days. A lady from St. Cloud wanted to buy it. It's by Alexandria, Minnesota, so only an hour away. I showed it to her, and she will get back to me. Rick and I decided since I'm retiring, we want to go to other lakes and campsites. When you own one for four or five years, you realize you feel you have to go there because it's paid for all year around. So we hardly ever went anywhere else. When we did, we felt guilty for not making use of it. Well, the lady took it and didn't blink an eye at the price. She had the check ready and was so happy to get it. We will miss it, but we will see a lot of new adventures on our new journey.

In July, we spent time with my side of family again at Long Lake. We went kayaking a lot this year as this lake is so clear, and that's where it gets its name, Clearwater Lake. You can look over the edge of canoes and kayaks and see the weeds and algae plain as can be. Even when you are swimming or fishing, it is clear enough to see the fish coming to our hook That is why we go there the last thirty to forty years. There is no water crafts allowed except fishing boats and no water skiing or jet skis. I'm sure that is why it stays so pristine.

Also in July, I planned a trip with two of our grandkids, River and Isaiah. We went to the Twins game. We drove to Big Lake just past St. Cloud, Minnesota, parked our car, and took a bus to the field. It was so much fun, and the grandboys loved it. Mostly because we won, and we got lots of good food even though hot dogs were $5 and a bucket of cookies was $15. I love being a grandma!

The end of August, we got together with Rick's side of the family and went to yet another state park. Lindberg State Park. It was so natural, and they had beautiful campsites with an old rock building. We had a good crowd and great food and fun.

The next weekend, Joanie and I took a bus to the Minnesota State Fair. It's always a good day trip. We went to music shows all day long and ate fair food along with everyone else. Joanie had a deep-fried pickle. I couldn't quite go that far, but she loved it. I stuck with a greasy, fatty, deep-fried corndog!

Vernon and Amber are moving to Bell Plain, Minnesota, this year for work. He got a machining job, and she got into a great hair salon. They are very busy but have a real nice duplex house to rent. It's a lot farther to go see them but a fun trip too. I'm kinda starting to enjoy this retirement phase of life.

In September, I went on another bus trip with my neighbor and good friend, Norma. We went to see Maggie Mae. She is a homegrown country singer and Nashville recording artist. She has performed at Branson and Oxford, Wisconsin. She has entertained crowds with her country music and yodeling. In fact, the show we saw, you could wave a hand towel while she's performing. It said, "Warning! Waving this towel may cause Maggie Mae to yodel." Believe me, she did. She is a wonderful entertainer. We could sing along or dance. We were served a sit-down, home-style dinner. We stayed in a motel that night and went on a riverboat cruise the next day. It was on the La Crosse Queen, which is a replica of the old riverboat that used to run on the Mississippi River in the 1800s. It has a 150-passenger capacity and was built in La Crosse, Wisconsin.

Norma and I got our picture taken with the river in the background. It turned out so nice and was a beautiful warm day. We had so much fun together, and Rick didn't enjoy country, so he stayed home. It was a win- win for me.

Rick and I were planning a bus trip this October. It's through Eutopia Tours out of Alexandria. We're planning a six-day tour to Kentucky and Tennessee. Rick was excited as he lived in Tennessee when he got out of construction school. Well, just as we got it all paid ahead, Rick got sick ten days before the trip with Kidney stones. He had to have them extracted in St. Cloud and had a stint in. So there was no way we could go and sadly had to cancel. Little did we know how hard it would be to get our money refunded. I called them right away and told them, and it was eight or nine days before the trip so according to when we booked it, we just needed to give them a seven-day window before trip to be able to cancel. Well, in the fine print, unless you take out insurance, you only get 60 percent back. What a rip-off. Also we had another couple that could take our place. They didn't care about that.

So the fun began. They tried to tell me I hadn't called in time to cancel. Then they said they had told me about having insurance, which they didn't. So I got all my phone records and made two or three trips to Alexandria to prove to them I had followed their protocol. Well, in the end, they gave us back 60 percent with a $200 rebate for our next bus trip. What a joke, I thought, but we learned a very important lesson to carry insurance for any trip we book. Since Rick has health issues, I know now that's the only option.

In November, we had a nice Thanksgiving with Ryan and family. Amy and Jon and family and Vernon and Amber were here. We had turkey and all the fixings. Amy brought buttered shrimp, which was so good. Of course, we had pumpkin and apple pie for dessert.

Christmas was pretty much the same crew with Rick's brother Wayne coming to join us. Oh, and I made lefse for the first time. Turned out pretty good and one more thing to enjoy in retirement and off my bucket list.

2019 Happenings

This new year with retirement brought me to a stage where I was wanting to clean everything. I had hit all the closets and made donations to Goodwill, thrift stores, and church. It's like I finally had time to organize everything. I am really liking it. I'm also loving being able to join Alliance

Women and actually help with making homemade rugs by cutting up old blue jeans. We also do a lot of projects for the prolife pregnancy groups We do a collection of money in baby bottles to donate to crisis pregnancy group. Also *gallons of happiness* for kids in Mexico. They do not have even a lot of the basics like soap, toothbrushes, combs, toothpaste, crayons, paper, etc. That is so fun to hear back from the mission areas over there how much happiness it brings to them. In return, the missionaries that come visit us each year from there bring us blankets and honey and vanilla that's all made by them.

I also joined the community center in Wadena, another perk of Medicare. It's so nice when I can't walk anymore on the farm because of snow and ice! Rick had gone a few times, but he preferred the outdoors.

We also now have a senior group that meets the first Tuesday of each month in Verndale. I'm getting to know a lot more of our neighbors now in a different way. So with all my groups and luncheons with my coworkers and friends, time does go by fast. I still miss my job though, but I am adjusting.

In May, my brother Ted had some heart issues, so he ended up having surgery. He decided to go home a little earlier than doctors preferred. A few hours after he got home, he sat in his recliner and passed away. I think he knew and wanted to be at home to die. We will miss him a lot.

So as you can see, he did enjoy a beautiful and fulfilling life especially in his last twelve years with Jan. RIP, big brother!

This year my daughter Amy's Tanner graduates in Wisconsin. It's always fun to go visit, and this event we got to see so many relatives and share Tanner's accomplishments. What great grandkids we have. He got his memory book that I scrapbooked for him like all the others. It's from birth to graduation. They love the memories and all their sports and vacations they were in. It was so fun to watch their milestones and how different each of them are. I love their uniqueness.

Camp News

Long Lake reunion was another great weekend. We had our Uffda tacos on Friday night and potluck Saturday night with a super bonfire. It's always so fun for all of us. We went to Flaundrau State Park this year for Rick's side. It was so beautiful and rustic there. We kayaked and some swam, and we all took walks together

Vacation

The end of August, Rick and I went to Niagara Falls and Mackinac Island. Wow, I can't begin to describe the Falls. It was gigantic and just breathtaking. The bus trip was for eight days, and on the sixth day at Mackinac Island, we went on a horse and buggy ride. It was fun, but the buggy made Rick's back start to spasm, and he was in a lot of pain. We still had two days left, so I thought about renting a car to go home, but by the time I would drive home, the bus would be back too. He was so done that our trip was over for us. We did make it home. He ended up on more pain meds, and those seemed so addicting. He wanted me to monitor and give them out to him. I had been, and all we did was bicker or fight about when he got them. I had made up my mind that when this trip was over, he was on his own to manage his own pain. His doctor had asked me to help him but didn't know it was going to create a problem between us. He gets a limited supply per month, but at this point, it's way too many in my opinion. He now is not taking the right number of pills per day and runs out each month, then goes through withdrawal for a few days till he gets new prescription.

I went with him to the doctor, and she asked how many pills he had left, and he only had ninety out of 180, which he should have had lots more left. He was taking too many. She immediately reduced how many he could have. He was not happy when I told her I couldn't manage them as he insisted taking extras. I will not do that again unless he has no access to his meds. I can't believe how addictive opioids are. There is an opioid crisis, and he is in it. Doctors and hospitals are tightening the reins. I can see why they were handing them out like candy and now realize that the more you take, the more your brain craves them. That's crazy, but I can tell you that it is the truth!

He went from 5 mg (oxy) twice a day to 10 mg four times a day, and it was never enough. I am so glad I'm very sensitive to pain meds, so I have hardly ever taken them and have never been on for any length of time. Rick has been on them since 2005 and more since he started having kidney stones in 2008 working at J. R. Construction. It's really hard to see how normal people can get caught up in a crisis like this. It does happen. Trust me.

We had another cousin pass away this fall. Delvin will be missed especially at our Long Lake weekend. He was one of the fishermen of the crew. Larry and Dean and Delvin would go out and catch a lot of trout as that's what is abundant in Long Lake. They would take a boat or two and early morning and catch a bunch. Most of the rest of us would fish off the large dock that's available. Theresa and Delvin live by Morris, Minnesota, which is south of Alexandria, Minnesota. He got lung cancer and died at home as comfortable as they could make it. He had such a big heart and will be missed by so many of us. RIP, cousin!

Surgeries' Red Flags

It's now October of 2019, and Rick had been dealing with so much back pain. He went to a neurosurgeon in St. Cloud with Dr. Samadonoi, a back surgeon. She said he needed a few surgeries, and we would start at the top of his spine. So the first surgery, the end of October, was an incision through the front of his neck to reach the back and fix the disk there and remove the bone spurs. When she showed us the x-ray of his back and MRI, it literally looked like he had an extra spine. There was like a whole row of bone spurs running alongside his spine. She also said there's arthritis too. He got through that surgery, and he was so strong and healed well.

She scheduled a second back surgery for December 26 this same year. This time the lower back to fix discs, bone spurs, and two broken bones. This would require repair with plates and screws. We did not know he had broken bones till she did the surgery. This time he took a lot longer to heal and feel better. We had it done in St. Cloud and the same doctor, but on the third day, they let us go home.

But little did I know it would be one of the worse days of our lives. First of all, there was a bad blizzard going on outside. I thought, "Well, this is crazy." It was about 4:30 p.m., so it was getting dark pretty soon. So we tried to get him in the car, and that was excruciating for him, so we went back into the lobby. I know now that was our first red flag. I took one look at the predicament we were in and called back to his nurses at the surgical unit, and they politely gave me a number for the Gorecki house, which is about a block away across the street.

I called them, and thankfully they had one room left but on the second floor. So we talked it over as best we could with Rick as he was in a lot of pain and on meds, which made him think he was Superman or had powers. That's my second red flag.

At this point, I felt so alone and abandoned, but my survival for both of us kicked in. So now the car was parked again, and we needed to walk over to this house. I picked Rick up in the lobby, where I left him, and off we went. Now it sounds easy but believe me this was bordering on a disaster. He could barely move let alone walk. They gave us no walker or assistance, so we hobbled over to the house. He had no cane, nothing but me to lean on. We were in the middle of blowing snow and ice, but we did make it.

Now we need to get him up the stairs.

Next red flag. There was no one around for help, so I helped him up the stairs, straining my back in the process. I finally got him to our room. This house was just a midpoint like a motel for patients that couldn't get home. I had thought of a motel but remembered he couldn't bend to get in the car. Just when I thought things couldn't get worse, he had to pee like right as we got in the room. So I tried to get him to the bathroom, but oops, too late. Now I have an invalid that's cold, wet, and out of it.

Now I was thinking he needed help, and so did I.

My first priority was to get him settled in bed. It's now about supper time also. We had no food or water at this point. He did not have a change of clothes either. So I got him out of the wet clothes from the storm and soiling himself and put him under the covers. He was just moaning at this point. About the time I was expecting him to crash, he had to go to the bathroom again. I did try to get him there but again, oops, too slow. So I cleaned him and the floor up and wrapped a towel around him like a diaper and got him back to bed.

Now I stopped to access our situation. I got on my phone and called Domino's to get a delivery so we'd have food. I ordered, and they got the address. I got through. Wow, something went right. About ten minutes later, they called back and said they couldn't deliver there because it's across the bridge in St. Cloud. I said, "You're only five or six blocks from here." They apologized but refused. Well, I do have a car, and we needed water and dry clothes for Rick, so I left him against my better judgment and went to get supplies all the while hoping he didn't try to get up and fall while I was gone. Sometimes you just gotta do what you gotta do. So now I was thinking, do I have the whole picture of what we need to get through the night?

I realized he needed a urinal container so he didn't have to get up to go to the bathroom. So I ran to Walmart and picked up everything and on the way back grabbed the pizza at Domino's. I got back, and he was still in bed and resting. He slept for about a half hour, then woke up in a lot of pian.

I had picked up Advil and Tylenol as I knew he had no painkillers till we got home. So I dosed him up with those, and he used the urinal I had gotten him on the way home at the hospital. If I knew now what I learned from this mess, none of this would have happened. He did try to eat a piece of pizza and got some down. This was hopefully going to carry us through the night. Well, to put it bluntly, it was one of the worst nights of our lives. I did try to communicate to Rick all that was happening. I found out later he doesn't even remember leaving the hospital. So now we made it to morning. There are a few more people around from other rooms, and they were concerned.

First, I had to check outside. Well, Mother Nature had dropped eighteen inches of snow and ice on us. The red flags just kept coming, and the shades of red were getting darker!

It's cold out, and I had no boots, but a nice guy helped me shovel off the car and around it. His wife told me they had a wheelchair somewhere on the first floor to use. She went to get it for us. Rick was waiting in the room, and after letting them know some of my situation, they offered to help get him down the stair and into the car.

Others were cleaning off the sidewalk and making a path in the parking lot. I was hoping the main roads were plowed by now.

We finally got him in the car with three people helping

me. It was so cold, windy, and slippery, and he's not in a good mood because of the pain from back surgery. Before all this, I had called around home to see what we were looking at when we got there. It turned out our driveway was totally blown in.

First reaction, I had to find someone to plow a path. I knew Vernon was now living in Bell Plains and couldn't help. So I called a few neighbors and didn't reach anyone. I finally was so desperate I called our eighty-some- year-old neighbor (Roger), and he said sure he could have it done before we got home. We had a one-and-a-half-hour drive. He did, and believe me, it was just enough to get us to the back door.

I was so thankful to him as at his age, he had to put effort into a request like that. It was so nice to have a caring neighbor. Roger will never be forgotten for his kindness. I worked at WDC with his wife, Doris, for many years.

He lost her to shingles in her brain. She was the sweetest lady and one of the kindest, caring teachers I had the privilege to know and work with. She is missed by many. RIP, Doris.

We finally landed at our house through the snow, sleet, and ice. I'd never been so thankful to be home. I had to shovel out the back door while Rick waited in the car. Finally, we're going in, but I couldn't hold him up, and he fell backward. He luckily fell into the snowbank, which cushioned his fall. I was so sore from all the commotion through the night and this morning's drive home. I knew I had to muster up enough energy to pull him up. My adrenaline kicked in, and we made it in the house. We did it, and I ran to get the walker. He did use it as it gave him the stability he needed to move around. Not to mention a break for myself. We're hoping the new year would bring us some better days soon.

We found out later that Rick's back surgeon had left right after the surgery. The new doctor had okayed his release based on a number or something. He obviously didn't have common sense about sending us out headed for home in a snowstorm. I called it a blizzard.

I did let them know later that we were not happy. I found out later I could have refused their decision. Then they would have seventy-two hours to reevaluate and more staff giving input to the situation. Boy did I learn through this devastating experience. It will for sure never ever happen again. I am more knowledgeable and much stronger from it.

CHAPTER 40

Devastation

Wow, it's 2020 now. We were blessed to see a new year and hope it brought good things our way. We were planning to take more trips and have good health. Oh no, it's much more than that as you will see.

Rick was healing with a long, long road ahead. Rick still needed the bone spurs and disk fixed in the middle of his back, but for now, he was healing from the last two surgeries.

It was the spring of 2020. We were now living right smack-dab in a worldwide pandemic. When I started my story, I explained what it was and the procedures to follow. Now I will fill you in with day-to-day changes and how it affected our life personally. This was a terrible, devastating event in our life. It's happening, whether we like it or not.

One new thing for us was that Amber and Vernon were moving back to the area. Amber came in April, and he would follow after he finished his machining job there in Bell Plain. Her salon had to shut down due to the pandemic, and they were ready to be closer to home. They bought a camper from Brenda (my niece) and parked it by our shop. They would have all the hookups there and their own space. We were so excited to help the kids out and glad they're back. Rick repaired part of the floor in the camper and built a nice landing and steps to get into it. Amber has a job in Wadena to do hair when things opened up again.

Our grandson, Isaiah, graduated this spring also. It was quite different. They got their diplomas in the parking lot of the school as a drive-through. There was no ceremony as you couldn't have large group gatherings. So no party to celebrate either. It was upsetting to all of us and so different and sad. He moved on and got his own apartment though to make new memories. So all we could do was wish him good luck in his future and told him how proud we were of his accomplishment.

Our kids and grandkids all seemed to do fine. I had a lot of confidence in all of them since I left home at fifteen. I knew it just made you stronger and more determined even if there's bumps in the road to success.

This summer was pretty low-key, and I had hours and hours to write.

In September, Vernon and Amber found a five-acre hobby farm, and they bought it. We are so happy for them. It's by Wadena a little way out in the country. I love their wraparound porch. It has so much character. I'm sure they will have a few projects and hope we can help. It has birch and pine trees that are just beautiful. I'm sure their memories will be endless. Happy, happy!

Now to some bad news, which was mentioned in the pandemic updates but needed to be put in the month of my autobiography story.

First was the car accident and death of my brother-in-law (Beans, eighty- two years old) on November 7, 2020. They did have a simple gathering for immediate family. We didn't go to this one. Then Evy, my sixty-four-year- old younger sister, passed away November 17, 2020, of diabetic complications. It still haunts me that we couldn't be there for her final day. Typically, before COVID, the whole family would gather as she took her last breath. So sad for her and us too!

This fall, I have not felt really good either. Overnight my blood sugars jumped up, so I started taking extra walks and thought that would help. It made it worse. So I called my doctor in November and got appointment in December. Well, overnight my blood sugars really went up even though I wasn't eating for ten to twelve hours. What? Well, there's a thing called dawn phenomenon. It's a syndrome when your liver gives it a signal to have the energy to even get out of bed. It then spews sugar out, and that raises your blood sugars. The same thing can happen if you exercise too much. This was hard to believe, but I know it's not from eating too much. My A1C was 7.5; it had gone up. My doctor put me on a diabetic pill called metformin. I'm hoping it helps. Time will tell. I have lost eight pounds even before meds, and that's another sign of diabetes getting worse. Since I've been able to control it with diet and exercise these past eight to ten years, it is hard to believe it can just change like that. I always knew it could, but it was still an adjustment when it happened.

My doctor said we would check my A1C in three months. So now I have to check my blood sugars three times day or when I get up before meals or two hours after eating and at bedtime. She wants to be sure I don't go low. So I keep this regimen up each day and take a 500 mg metformin at breakfast and lunch and increase in six weeks to a 750 mg at breakfast and bedtime as my numbers are highest overnight.

The stress of deaths in the family, Rick's surgeries and illnesses, and the pandemic limits, it is not surprising. Since retiring, I've also had to work hard at keeping my blood sugars in check naturally. I've taken natural supplements that have helped that include cinnamon, chromium, and other great remedies to keep me borderline. Right now, they are not working, and I've had to switch two or three times throughout this pandemic because products are not readily available.

A lot can change when the world is disrupted.

We are now in the start of 2021, and the pandemic has closed businesses, and several ships are stuck at sea and not able to get to port. So products are stuck until the COVID cases subside.

There was an attack on the US, our capital in Washington, DC. Many supporters have stormed it in response to Donald

Trump losing the election, Biden becoming president, and the fact a lot of the country felt the election was rigged and he cheated. They hoped to overturn the victory of Biden and as joint sessions of congress was assembled to count electoral votes that would prove Biden had won or not. During this, Trump supporters rioted and assaulted police officers, vandalized property, and occupied the building for several hours. Five people died before, during, or after following this event. Many people were injured, including thirteen police officers. Four officers who responded to the attack died by suicide within several months of this. It all started with the Stop the Steal rally, where many protesters were around the capital. It lasted twenty-one hours. So there were reporters on the hill as all this unfolded. The people in session and all others were evacuated from the capital out the back door before the riot started in the front with pushing through barriers, breaking windows, and trash everywhere. The rioters now were desecrating the people's house. This is something our country will never forget.

It has been a long winter this year, but we can see warmer temperatures each week. I had my A1C level taken end of April, and it dropped to 9.1, so I am happy about that. The bad news is I'm losing more weight without trying. I had lost eight pounds before any meds, and now I'm down another seven pounds. I'm trying to reach my doctor, but it seems we are playing phone tag. The 850 mg of metformin has definitely upset my stomach and bowels. When I finally reach my doctor, she says we'll check it in July. To me it was a long time to wait. Finally, I asked her if I could see a dietician to see if there was more I could do with my eating. So I met with her, and she felt I needed to let my doctor know of my weight loss and stomach issues.

During this pandemic, it has been hard to get my medical issues under control. So I kept calling, and they do not want me to come in because of the high rate of COVID. So we

SURVIVING LIFE AND
C☼VID-19

do as much over the phone and drawing labs. My numbers kept creeping up, and by the time my blood draw in July happened, I was at 9.3. My doctor put me on glyburide along with extended-release metformin to see how that would work. The extended form is less mg and not so harsh on my system. I guess we'll know at next check and over time. It's very hard for me to wait three months or more. I am also doing a strengthening class at the MAS community center to help my osteoporosis. I love exercising, and we have a great group of ladies. I go at 9:00 a.m. Tuesdays and Thursdays. We move to really cool music. Some of its songs were from the seventies and eighties. So relaxing. I then go upstairs and do a couple of machines for ten minutes each and walk the track for a mile or one and a half miles. Twelve times around is a mile. So it's easy to figure how far you've gone. Joanie, my friend, comes when she can. It's really a fun time. I feel pretty good on this plan for my diabetes. Masks are required.

In May, Ace, our dog, died. He was eight-years-old, and we found him dead in the ditch. We don't know what happened, but there was no blood or broken bones. He looked like he had a heart attack. We will miss him a lot.

On June 5, Maury, Jacke, Filip, and their kids had a celebration of life for my sister Evy. It was so nice to finally be able to get together with family. There were many relatives and friends that came to grieve the loss of such a sweet soul. Some still wore masks as it was a large group, and that's what we are supposed to do. We did go to her grave site and saw where she was buried and the beautiful marker they had created. We all gathered at Maury and Evy's house and watched a nice collection of memory picture on a big screen in the garage. All her brothers and sisters were given a beautiful candle with Evy's picture by her favorite yellow roses on two sides were a cardinal, her favorite bird. Then a nice poem about how God knows when you're tired and the pain is over and that he only takes the best. So fitting as she fought a lot of medical battles throughout her life.

Kailee, our granddaughter, also graduated. One more on her way to adulthood. She's getting her own apartment also, and we are so proud of all her accomplishments. Ryan and Tena raised some sweet kids. We love it when they come out to the farm.

The birthdays, graduations, Christmases, and campouts are so precious.

The memories just keep on a coming.

July, Long Lake reunion was really fun. This year we did superheroes. We had Batman and Batwoman; that was me. Lots of fun characters. It's so nice to see the creativity we all came up with. It also gives the littles a chance to show their fun side. Rick's back pain has not improved much. He is on a fentanyl patch now but doesn't seem to do much. Time will tell. He has tried medical cannabis also. He doesn't like the vaping with that as it's like smoking. He doesn't smoke, so he only takes it occasionally. It also comes in tincture form. That's where you put it in under your tongue, and it goes into your bloodstream. It gives him a little relief. At this point, he is so sick of chronic pain and chose to go to the reunion and set the camper up for me. Then he went home to his own bed and came and got me the last night of camping. So he only spent one night, but that's enough. He knows how much I love camping, so did that for me. He is so loving. My teddy bear!

This summer 2021 has been so great. We are in a drought, and because of that, some places are having wildfires. The worst are in California. There is also one up north of us in Ely, Minnesota. Many thousands of acres have burned. One good thing from the drought is we have no mosquitos. They need water to multiply, and obviously we don't have enough for them to hatch. What a treat to not have to use pesticides and repellant. Much healthier for all of us.

The COVID-19 pandemic is still very real. There are

some schools that are distant learning early on this year because of a high number of cases. It is getting better in our area, but in the big city, it's always much worse. Most people are getting vaccinated. Rick and I didn't hesitate at all to get the shots. We are at higher risk because of our age and diabetes and heart and other health issues. Some people, of course, are refusing to get vaccinated. So the government and state reps and big businesses are giving incentives. Some of them being a $100 cash, gas cars, restaurant gift cards, etc. The idea being, the more people that get the vaccine, the more the spread is controlled.

The unemployment freebie is going to stop soon for most. That should help the businesses. Right now so many people just don't want to work.

There are Help Wanted signs all over in every city. It's just crazy. The housing market has gone bonkers also. Houses are way overpriced, and people are buying anyway. Part of this is due to the fact people have learned to work from home and can move and live anywhere they want. In all my years I have never seen anything like this. The interests rates are the lowest in history.

In July, we got a notice from my cousins Larry and Veronica that somehow through ancestry.com we now have a new cousin. His name is Russ, and he has a family out east in Massachusetts. So we all met them at Larry's July 9 for a gathering to meet them. His wife and two daughters were with them and their boyfriends. Rick and I stayed at Ponce De Terre, a county park in Morris, Minnesota. It was like only a mile or two from the get together. Paul and Deb stayed also with their camper. We had so much fun, and his family fit right in with several of ours. What a blessing to have additions to the family. It was too bad our annual Long Lake campout was two weeks later because they could have met so many more there. Although we had a lot less there because of COVID this year. So it worked out well. Some wore masks to this.

Rick and I went to the Itasca Tractor show again this year. We love the parade of many kinds of tractors. We also love the fresh lefse and delicious fry bread. There's also a lot of buildings with antiques and old engines and tools of the past. It's only an hour from us, so we go every year. We also went to Sibley State Park this year with Rick's cousins and brothers and sisters. It rained some but would clear up just enough to have picnics together and go for walks. Grandkids came to stay in August early from Fargo. Emma got stung by bees playing by the playhouse. She survived even though she's dramatic. We also went to the Dalton Farm Tractor Show. There again lots to browsing around and antiques to look at. We ran into a few old friends and watched the tractor pull. I took pictures for Norma, my neighbor, as her granddaughter was pulling for the first time. She did really good, and I gave the pictures to Norma to cherish.

In September for my birthday, we camped two nights at Itasca State Park. It was fall, and the maple trees in the park were spectacular. We were glad we went because of the drought we had no color anywhere else. Driving through its park, it felt like we were under a canopy of red, yellow, and orange leaves. I took a lot of pictures, but the best ones were imprinted in my mind. It reminded me just how beautiful mother nature is. God is so good.

In October, we rented a cabin at Stoney Point resort by Cass Lake. We had cabin 8. It was so cute and cozy. We were celebrating Rick's sobriety of thirty-four years. He quit drinking all on his own that many years ago. He said he knew he had to so his life would be better. I'm so very proud of him. I didn't know him at that time, but I know I wouldn't have wanted to if he drank. So this was a cozy little cabin. It had a lot of pine walls and a loft, like our house. It was fully equipped with a full kitchen, a living area, and a nice bathroom. We just had to bring our food and towels. It was right on the shores of Cass Lake, and this time of year it was so serene and private. This is the same resort we rent a condo for our family reunion each year in January, the dead of winter.

There's a casino nearby in Cass Lake, so we went and ate there. Brenda, my niece, had said how good their prime rib was, so we thought we'd check it out. We got there, and it was about average. But we probably won't go back.

First of all, we sat there for about a half hour before we got water and a menu. Then another twenty minutes to come get our order. Very nice waitress, but we think she was the only one serving people. This is how it is right now with the pandemic. No one wants to work, and many places just can't get help. Everywhere you go there's Help Wanted signs lining the streets of businesses. She did bring us our salads and said how sorry she was it was taking so long. Well, another hour went by, and here came our well-done prime for Rick and my meal for me. It was mooing, that's how rare it was. Blood was oozing out, and we absolutely could not eat it. Not to mention that our appetites were ruined. So we told her to package it up, and we'd take it home to the cabin and cook it. So that's what we did. When she brought the ticket, she said it's on the house as you should not have had to wait and then for it to be not cooked correctly. We went back to cabin 8 after leaving that poor waitress a nice tip. This was Friday night, so Saturday my brother Paul and his wife Deb called, and we had dinner with them at a smokehouse BBQ in Bemidji. It was so good. That sure made up for last night's disaster. We all went shopping and for a nice walk at a park there. All in all, it turned out to be a great weekend. There's nothing better than spending time together.

I also had another adventure with a group of old friends. Linda and Shirley, Jan, and Nancy are friends from when our husbands all worked at NL McCullough oil field group in the 1980s. We decided to meet at Hankinson, North Dakota, as it was located in the middle of most of us. There is a casino there. I don't gamble much, but some of them do, and we could get cheaper rooms if you go in the middle of the week. So we went Tuesday to Thursday. We got some free money for the casino and one free meal a day. Pretty nice deal. We all ate dinner together each night at the Twin Buffalo Grill at the motel. Shirley made us all buttons to wear from 1980s from when we all partied together. They were so funny to see ourselves from forty years ago. But so fun to be together and reminisce about the good old times. Some sure could remember more than the rest. Nancy and Ransome came all the way from West Virginia to be a part of this week. They made a vacation to other places like Wyoming, where they used to live. It had been forty years since we saw her. Oh, how we could all just pick up like it was yesterday is beyond comprehension. We thought Ransom would be bored, but he was a hoot and fit right in even though he was the only guy there. It was great getting to know him. We were all sad that Linda O. couldn't make it to stay over but was going to try to come with her son for a few hours one of the days.

Linda G, Linda O., Jan, and Shirley have met a few times at Applebee's in Fergus Falls. We went there as Linda O. has cancer and getting treatments so it's a lot easier for her to come to lunch. She had lost most her hair last spring but was hopeful the chemo was working. She did feel pretty good at that time. Now with this trip, we're not so sure. We had so much fun, and there was a deli place there which was large, and we met there and put tables together to play board and card games. It definitely was a time to remember. Linda O. did not make it though, but we plan on going to see her later this fall.

Wyoming Trip

It has definitely been a little better year to get out and get to go places. COVID is still around but manageable. The key is if you're sick at all, stay home. So when my brother Paul and Deb called about driving to Wyoming, I said yes. My sister Theresa's husband, Marv, from Wyoming, passed away. He was eighty-two years old and had health issues.

It's October 15, 2021, and I am starting out by picking Jon, my nephew, from his place eight miles away. We are heading to Paul and Deb's house by Fosston, Minnesota. That's one hundred miles from here but always a good drive. Rick can't make the trip as he isn't well enough, and we would have to stop way to often because of his stomach issues. He's glad to stay home and take care of the animals and hold the fort down so to speak.

I always invite him, but he chooses to be a homebody. We found out Marv's service isn't till Tuesday the nineteenth, so we have four days to drive to Green River, Wyoming. It's nice we are retired, so there's no set schedule. Paul is planning to see sites on the way out and on the way back. Our first day we left from Fosston, but before we left town, Deb and I stopped at the public library and checked out twenty or thirty magazines and a few books for our trip. We knew we would have reading time in the car. Then we proceeded to Trent and Kelsey's in Mandan, North Dakota. We spent the night there. We all went out for dinner at a grill and sports bar. Kelsey is Paul and Deb's daughter. They are such good hosts.

We got up early and left 6:00 a.m. We stopped at Hardee's drive through and got egg sandwiches and coffee. Then we headed to Devils Tower national Monument on the South Dakota–Wyoming border. We stopped at Theodore National Park entrance at a rest stop. Got a lot of cool pictures from the overlook. Deb saw a sign for Medicine Rock State park close by, so of course, we had to stop. It was very sweet and interesting. The rocks were supposedly of medicinal properties in early years. When we got closer to them, they were like soft sandstone that could be carved. Many people had carved hearts and their initials into what looked like rock but was very unique sand. They were formed when a glacier cut through the area many years before. We might have carved some too. These were so amazing and something we had never seen before. The only downfall was the snow was melting there and our shoes got a little yucky. We cleaned them off as best we could with sticks and other snow patches.

Now we are entering into Wyoming, and we stopped to eat a little gas/food/gift shop and had lunch. They had picnic tables outside, and even though it was only thirty-five or forty degrees, we chose to eat on one. We moved it into the sun, which helped a lot. We made ourselves ham and turkey sandwiches on buns or bread, chips, and trail mix to boot.

We now were one hour from Devils Tower. On our way following the signs, we encountered a herd of one hundred or more cows. They were quite a fun road block to watch. It slowed us down, but again we're in no hurry. Then some four-wheelers and trucks helped herd them across the highway. It had stopped quite a few cars, but oh, what a fun sight to witness. It was very cool. I love these experiences imprinted in my mind. We are so thankful for good weather and roads.

Devil's Tower

Devils Tower is located part of the Black Hills in the northeastern part of Wyoming. It stands 1,267 feet above the Belle Fourch River. It was established September 24, 1906. Its name originated in 1875 during an expedition by Colonel Dodge when his interpreter reportedly misinterpreted a native name to mean Bad Gods Tower, later to be named Devils Tower. It is also the first national monument erected in the United States by President Teddy Roosevelt. It was not visible for millions of years, but as water and wind slowly eroded the landscape, the igneous rock could emerge. The top of the tower is covered in rocks, grass, cactus, wild flowers, and surprisingly sagebrush, which is uncommon in the Black Hills. Devils Tower has several hiking trails. We took the 1.3-mile trail, which started in the visitor parking lot. It wrapped around the massive rock, which looked more like a small mountain. The trail was icy in many areas as the trees kept it from melting. It gave us a good workout, and my brother Paul loves to walk as it's the best therapy for his blood clot in his leg.

Deb, Jon, and I all like to hike too. We spent a little while at the gift shop at the visitor center. We were required to wear masks there. Wyoming has a higher rate of COVID at present. We didn't mind as it's been the norm for one and a half years. Now we were headed to Gillette, Wyoming, to a motel an hour away. We'd sleep good tonight. We all stayed in the same room. It helped keep the cost down, and all we did was sleep and got on the road again early. I got a bed to myself. Deb and Paul got a bed, and Jon blew up an air mattress and took a spot on the floor. Worked well. We googled places to eat and went to a place called the coop. Yes, it was a chicken place. Pretty good but nothing special. We got a good night's sleep and got up at 6:00 a.m. again to be on the road. We would be to Theresa's Sunday night, which was two days before the service for Marv. We had a great breakfast before we left the motel. Paul stopped for gas and coffee, and we were on our way to Casper, Wyoming, to go to a park and waterfall.

We googled things to do en route our trip. There were hiking trails picnic areas and rest stops. We made it to Rotary Park and got our goodies from the cooler and bags. We had sandwiches again, chips, doughnuts, and rolls. We set out after that to check out a two-mile hike. The trails were snowy and slippery. We found out from area hikers with us that this area had been hit with twenty to thirty inches of snow this week. We missed it, and places were just getting plowed out. There were some highways closed, power lines down, etc. The waterfalls were beautifully nested in the winding trail routes. It was one of the most beautiful sites. Snow all around us but waterfalls cascading down the slopes. We took a lot of great pictures. And kinda hated to leave. We hesitatingly did leave and made it to Theresa's' house by evening.

She was quite distraught the first night we were there. We all understood completely. She wasn't very well herself and had a lot of health issuers, which required medication. She did show us to our rooms, and we all had supper together. Paul is a great cook and soon took inventory to go grocery shopping. We planned on eating at Theresa's house as we're already sick of road food. We shopped on Monday and bought stuff for three or four days. So he made spaghetti tonight and toasted garlic bread. Hmm, good!

We also checked out a hiking trail at a park close to the house along with some sights. Theresa rode along but didn't get out much. She needed a walker for balance. We checked out where the cemetery was also, where Marv would be buried.

It's Tuesday and the day of Marv's grave site service. Marv was in the Navy, and they gave him a beautiful military honor. It was very touching as they played Taps and thanked him for his service. They had a gun salute and presented my sister Theresa with the American flag after they folded it with the utmost respect. Some of their friends put a potluck luncheon on at the American Legion. We prepared some of the food for that. We met some of their friends and visited for a couple hours as we celebrated his life. RIP, Marv!

Wednesday, we got up early and headed to the Grand Tetons by Jackson Hole.

We were now back on the road finding our way home. We hiked a trail called Jenny Lake loop. We thought it was two miles, but oops, it was seven miles. I had forgot to bring a snack in case my blood sugars dropped. Well, they did go low and thank God we met some other hikers who had bars and candy in their backpacks. They were so kind and gladly gave me a protein bar and candy. It's nice to know that a total stranger could come to your rescue. I had done that for others in the past. It was so welcomed to have the gesture in return. We made it back to the car and continued to see the Grand Teton Mountains. They are part of the Rocky Mountains in North America. They extend forty miles into a north-and-south direction through the state of Wyoming and east of the Idaho state line. This is so amazing it should be on everyone's bucket list. We took lots of pictures, but they really didn't do it justice.

We stopped a lot of overlooks to get the breathtaking views and, of course, pictures of all of us. We stopped at a park and had our favorite traveling road meal. Sandwiches, chips, and pop. We saw a moose at the entrance, and as we drove on, the tall mountains ran into the skyline and clouds. You would have to see that to believe that picture. It's in my mind forever. On our way hiking to a waterfall, we saw buffalo and wild horses.

It's now 5:00 p.m., and we checked into our motel room at a Super 8. This was in Jackson Hole, Wyoming, and right in the midst of bars, restaurants, and shops. Oh boy, maybe we'd get some shopping in! We started out by going to the Million-Dollar Cowboy Bar and Grill. It was open in 1933 but had improved by adding music, games, and literally genuine saddles to sit on as barstools. They were purchases in 1973 for $97 each. The owners were known as the Texans. The next thirty years, two couples owned it but sold to a hotel owner in 2018. They kept on improving the place and had booked artists like the Bellamy Brothers, Moe Brandy, Midland, Toby Keith, Diamond Rio, Oakridge Boys, Hank Williams, Randy Owens, and many more. We had the best burgers we've ever had, made from great bison meat with fries. What a neat, neat place.

Most places were open well into the evening, so we took a lot of selfies and pictures to put on Facebook. We wouldn't stay up too late as we got up early to get on the road by 6:00 a.m. We would be starting our new adventure tomorrow in Yellowstone National Park. We'd all been there, but it never got old.

It's Thursday the twenty-first, and we had a good night's sleep. We went to breakfast in the motel, and they served fruit and protein bars and, of course, coffee. We all loved our coffee this early in the morning. We were now headed to Yellowstone. We barely got a few miles done, and we ran into a roadblock. It was not our typical block. It was a herd of buffalo crossing the highway in a very slow-moving fashion. Cars were stopped for twenty to thirty minutes until the feisty buffalo stopped fighting one another. It was quite a show. We were several cars from the front so we got out to take pictures. There were park rangers trying to encourage them to cross, but that didn't seem to change their demeanor. When we finally were able to pass through that area, the sun was shining brightly, and the sunrise on the Tetons was gorgeous. It was a priceless picture when the sun just kept rising up and over the stretch of miles of mountains.

We stopped at West Thumb Geyser Basin. The geysers magically spewed out of the ground and out of a lake. It was absolutely breathtaking. My nephew Jon had never seen them before, so that was a new experience for him. Paul, Deb, and I had seen the ones at Old Faithful, but they were different than these. We drove a bit farther to see Old Faithful. We had googled the times, and the one was going off at 1:05 p.m. We got there at 1:00 p.m., so it was perfect timing. There were other geysers and times going off throughout the day. Grand Geyser was awesome too. Deb felt we should stay and watch Castle Geyser at 2:30 or 3:00 p.m. So we did, but it never went off. The basin predicts this one, but they aren't always right. Mother Nature definitely rules and has a mind of her own. God sure made a beautiful world as we stopped at the Paint and Pots Fountain. It had colors running together in the waterflow. Yellowstone has 2 million acres to explore.

Gibbon Falls was next on our to do list. We stopped at Canyon Village at the lower falls overlook. There was a trail, but it was closed, so we pulled off at all the overlooks we found. We all took some amazing pictures and had to pull into turnouts, as they're called, to let crazy speedy people by us. We spent the whole day just catching the views and enjoying the ride. We had tried to book a motel room, but in the park, there was no reception for our cell phones. As we drove out of the park, we finally got a room but had to drive a little farther, and now we're in Montana. We settled in around 9:00 p.m., but we were all pretty hungry. We found a place at the Grand Hotel in the downtown area. We had fish and chips and a lava pecan chocolate cake with cream and caramel sauce. We all shared it and could barely finish the rich dessert.

It's October 22, Friday, and we were up early and back on the road again. We were heading to Kelsey and Trent's from Montana to Bismarck, North Dakota. We would stay the night and head for home tomorrow. I talked to Rick each day, and I could tell he was anxious for me to get home. I was getting ready to be home too.

But one last sightseeing excursion. Deb had heard Trent telling her about the "enchanted highway." So of course, we could not drive by that sign. It was a thirty-five-mile trek with metal sculptures of birds, deer, grasshoppers, fish, insects, cowboys, and farmers ranging from thirty-to- forty-foot high or long. The only problem was each sculpture was four or five miles apart. The road was hilly and slow, but we got to the last one anyway. Paul figured we could cut across country and get back on the main road, but no. There was no way around without going way farther out of the way. The only alternative was to back track from the highway we came from to get to Bismarck. Most of us were not sure if this detour was worth it. But all in all, our trip was bittersweet.

We finally arrived at Kelsey and Trent's, my niece. They are such good hostesses in their new house in Mandan, North Dakota. They ordered Papa Murphy pizza and salad, and it was waiting for us when we arrived. It was so good and appreciated. I love all my nieces and nephews. They had been raised to be such wonderful, caring, and loving people.

We left early Saturday morning after breakfast, of course. We made it to Deb and Paul's house around 3:30 p.m. and quickly unloaded all our goodies and luggage and headed to Verndale. We traveled over 2,700 miles is all and made many forever memories. Thanks, Paul and Deb!

This week, Rick and I got back to our routine. We take a walk together each day, one or two miles. The nice part of being home is I actually get real home-cooked meals again. We both cook and bake, but Rick's still a crockpot, one-pan cooker. Love that we still have dates like breakfast at the Spot Café in Staples. Our favorite is still the spot omelet that we share. It's huge. This week we went to the cozy theater and saw a movie. That's always fun to have theater popcorn and candy. Now I'm getting ready this week for deer hunting.

CHAPTER 41

The Deer Hunt

I didn't start hunting until I was in my fifties. When Rick and I got married, we hunted on the farm a few years together. When Vernon and his friends took gun training, they joined us in the hunt. We even have names for our deer stands. There's Rick's stand, Vernon's stand, Michael's stand, which were named by each of them using that particular one the most. Of course, Rick built me one, which was called the Mama's mansion as it's the best with a deck to sit and watch from. It didn't get any better than that. The views were spectacular as it's on the Leaf River Bank and was surrounded with a tree line. You couldn't paint pictures like that. My first deer was my second year of hunting. There was a herd of five or six that stepped out of the woods onto the field. My adrenaline kicked in, and I got so excited I just shot at the biggest one. I hit a small doe standing beside the big one I wanted. I definitely needed some practice to make a better shot. I was just so glad to get one this particular season.

The next few years were spent teaching the kids the ropes and watching their excitement when they shot their first deer. It was an experience for all of us each time and many pictures and memories made. Some years were ridiculously warm, and others were just downright cold. We have buddy heaters to keep us warm in most of the stands and roofs on most of them They're very durable and cozy. I didn't always get a deer, and there were years we didn't even see any. For the most part we'd get one or two between the hunters to harvest. The funny part was Rick and I didn't even like or eat venison. Ryan was the best hunter with the most patience. He had poor vision and wore thick glasses to see. He relied on his other senses. He bow- hunted out here in 2013 and bagged a four-point buck with a bow and arrow. That one was on his wall. He said he heard it and just waited till it was close enough. He makes me so proud. Some years we take five or ten pounds of meat and make into venison jerky sticks. Those I really liked. Rick does not hunt anymore, but Ryan, myself, and different grandkids each year come out for their turn at learning. In 2017, Isaiah got his first deer and helped gut it and all. He was so proud, and it's fun to watch their excitement through the process.

Rick made the old pig pen, a ten-by-eighteen building into a cozy fun hunting shack. It had four windows, a porta potty, woodstove, built-in couch bed, and a table and chairs to warm up whenever we needed to. I loved it, and sometimes we just vegged there and watch for the deer. What a heaven-sent. There had been years we should have been more diligent for the hunt, but time together was also so important.

Kailee, CC, Isaiah, Kirsten, and Conrad, the grandkids, never complained if we just sat around enjoying snacks, pop, Chex mix, reading, doing homework, listening to music, and making the best memories ever.

Michael and Vernon were more serious about hunting, but they also didn't come out much after the shack was built. Most of them left their signatures in one or more of the stands, but of course, the mansion had a lot more. I loved seeing them every year along with hearts on their very own creative drawings. They for sure left their marks on the walls and my heart. There's a special place in my heart for all my grandkids. Love all of you!

I have a lot more stories but will fill you in on a few that really stand out.

In 2017, I shot a small doe and hit it in the front knee. It dropped but crawled to the woods. I had to go follow its blood trail. I felt so bad and had to finish it off. It made me cry because it was the first time I missed the heart or lung shot. I know it suffered till I got there, but as hunters, you just do what you have to do. I got over it and continue hunting the next day. Ryan and I hung it up and were glad to get one that year. The next year, I shot one off the mansion stand, but it ran to the swamp, and we never found it. They seem to always run toward the Leaf River. I retired the winter of 2018–2019 and was so excited for the week of hunting. My first year without working around a schedule of all the luck, we didn't see a one this year. What a bummer that was. The last Saturday of hunting I was in the hunting shack, and I heard a noise on the deck.

This may be my best deer story yet! When I looked out the window of the door, there was a big doe standing on the other side. She was right on the deck looking back at me. My adrenaline kicked in, but I was at a loss as what to do. If I opened the door, she'd be gone. I also couldn't shoot through the door. So I did the next best thing and enjoyed watching her through the window. It must have been five or ten minutes, and by then I had my gun in hand but knew there wasn't much hope for a shot. I decided to open the door slowly, but of course, she sprang off the deck and walked down the lane. I had no shot as her butt was all I got a view of. This is why I hunt. The beauty of nature is so incredible.

In 2020, I shot a button buck right in the field behind the house. He ran into the grove by the house. I shot him twice, but he just staggered and fell about a quarter of a mile from my first shot. That poor guy just kept on breathing. Ryan caught up with us and finished him off. It was right at dusk, so not much fun to skin and gut. Ryan with his poor eyesight always came through though. We were quite the team even in the dark. He parked his truck with the headlights shining on us to help while I held the legs so he could gut it. We do work well together. He was always told if he wants to do something, go for it, and he has never held back. I don't know how he has accomplished so much, but I do know his other senses seem to kick in. It's fun to watch him feel his way through the fur and flesh to get the job done. He finds the bone that needs to be cut. It's like he could do it blindfolded. I am so proud of him.

We have taken so many beautiful pictures of the landscapes around the deer stands. We especially love as the sun sets each night. The river makes a pretty exquisite background for group pictures and just watching and listening to the water flowing down the river with all of us in our orange gear.

In 2021, we saw a lot of deer. Seems like every time we went out, there they were. My shots would be too far, but it's the beauty I love. The first morning we saw one on the trail on the way out but was gone before we got our guns off our shoulders.

We saw two in the south field at 10:00 a.m. but just watched them move on into the brush and woods.

Sunday early morning, Ryan followed two does and a buck, and he just kept following them.

He just couldn't get close enough to shoot. I saw a small doe by the mansion but let him graze, waiting for the big one. We saw two bucks in the back swamp off Michael's stand. Then at 3:40 p.m., I had a perfect shot in the field off Rick's stand. It was a ten- or twelve-point buck. So I pulled up and shot, but my magazine jammed. I couldn't believe it, but I kept my cool and took the clip off and reloaded it that way with two bullets. Now ready with my reload, I watched that beauty walking into the grove. It was worth it though. That's the closest. Thirty yards that I'd ever been to a buck with a rack like that. At the same time, it was heartbreaking 'cause I'd probably never get that chance again. We could truthfully say the bucks were in rut during the season this year! I would be getting my clip checked as this has happened a couple times now. It didn't want to release the bullets into the chamber. By the way, my gun is a 7 mm '08 Remington with a nice scope. This year was the most deer we'd seen in a very long time. It sure made you want to get out there and hunt.

The weather has been great too. Not too warm and not much snow. Monday we hunted into the afternoon and didn't get any shots off. Tuesday we were out by noon. About 4:20 p.m., I was in Rick's stand, and I heard branches breaking and noises from east of his stand. I waited patiently, and I couldn't believe it. He turned back through the trees and came out on the south field. He was headed right toward my stand. I waited until I had a good shot in my crosshairs of my scope and boom. I shot. It ran fast toward the woods, so I really thought I must have missed him. I didn't get a second shot off. I texted Ryan and told him I felt I really took a good shot. He said to just wait five or ten minutes in case there's a buck following as he had heard noises also. I waited, but nothing showed up. For some reason, my gut feeling kept telling me to go check, where it had ran. Ryan texted and said, "Yes, go look, you never know." So I got down from my stand and went out into the field, where I shot it. I couldn't find any blood, but I continued following his hoof tracks. He had dug into the dirt and was easy to follow. Still no blood, but I was still able to see his path he took. I followed his steps for about a quarter of a mile, and there he was. I had shot him through the lungs, and he didn't bleed out. Voilà, I finally got a six- point buck. I was so excited as I had thought it was a doe. I texted Ryan, and he came and got some great pictures of my deer and me. Then we gutted him, which took us pretty close to dark. The process took a while as I had to go back to the house and get Ryan's truck and the tag from the shack. When I got back to where I had left Ryan, they were gone. Here he had dragged the deer out into the field as his truck would not fit on the trail where the deer was.

He met me on one end of trail, and we drove around to load the deer up on the other end. Then we had to go back into the woods, as dark as it was, and find Ryan's sunglasses, knife, case, coat, and water. We found it right away. So we tagged him and couldn't wait to get to the house to show Rick. He was pretty impressed. I was so proud of my very first buck. Then Ryan took him to Wadena and hung him in his garage. He took care of calling it into the DNR also. I am so honored to hunt with my boy. We make quite a team and work well together. I couldn't hunt without him. Ryan was going to have the head mounted for me. That would be so nice, and I couldn't wait. We hunted on Saturday again, and I shot another buck, but we followed blood trail until he crossed Highway 23 and stopped at that point. We have plenty of memories from this year and plan to hunt a few more years. I love the hunt!

This was a long week and kinda sad. My good friend from when we lived in Williston back in the eighties was dying of cancer. We had known for a while, but now she had just days. I felt I better go see her before the holidays. She lived only seventy-five miles from us. Three of us got together and went to see her to say our goodbyes. She was in a hospital bed in her cozy living room with her own boy's home taking care of her in her last days. If I had my choice, I would die at home too. She was still able to eat a little but mostly water and liquids. We all visited about our time together in the oil fields and caught up on where and what all our kids have done. It was so bittersweet, but it's what you all do. We were one of the loose ends that needed to be tied up. Her boys were taking such good care of her in her final cancer days. She was so ready to let go, we could tell. She would always be in our hearts till we meet again. We went out to lunch after our visit before heading home. Linda G. came from Mayville, North Dakota, Shirley from Grand Forks. Such a sad day for all. I am so glad we got to say our goodbyes.

CHAPTER 42

Priceless Vacation 2021

Wow. It all started with Rick and I going on a Branson vacation with Randy and Ruth four years earlier. But this year, Ruth had planned one with Donna, a good church friend of mine. It was the same Christmas tour leaving from Alexandria on a chartered bus. November 17, 2021.

They had planned it for months, and I was so happy they could go. Donna had never been on one before, so Ruth had offered to go with her. Well, as the time grew closer, Ruth found out her cancer was back. She had beat it for ten years or so. She now had to endure five weeks of every weekday radiation at the Mayo Clinic in Rochester. Randy and Ruth stayed during the week at a comfort house near the hospital, then drove home each weekend. It was a five- or six-hour drive.

The third week of treatment, it was going good, but symptoms started to surface. She became too sick to go on the trip with Donna. Ruth called me up and asked if I could go in her place on the trip. I was so sad she couldn't go but felt guilty that I could. So I said of course, but I would pay you for it. She's said, "Oh no, I won't hear of it." She was so glad because Donna would not go by herself. So here I was taking an unexpected priceless vacation. It was a six-day trip, and I was dedicating this chapter to our cousin Ruth. Hopefully she would enjoy reading about our adventures and journey down the road. What a great friend. I am so blessed.

Our first day was a very long day. We got up at 5:00 a.m., and Donna picked me up here at the farm at 5:30 a.m. It's Wednesday morning, and we were heading to Parkers Prairie forty-five miles away to meet the Hart bus line. We were one of the first ones to get there, which was good as we got the pick of which seat and where on the bus.

We both thought the middle would be good on this fifty-six-passenger coach. It was great. Usually on bus trips, they make you move back a seat each day so everyone gets different views. Because of the COVID, they left us in our same seats the whole trip. We ended up stopping every two hours or so to have a break or pick up guests along the way. For lunch we stopped at a mall, which had a food court and plaza. There was a lot to pick from. I had Subway. Then for coffee break, we went to a Kwik Trip. We were both loving that these bus trips, knowing the routes and all the hot spots to take in.

We arrived at Fairview Suites at 6:30 p.m. Donna and I got settled in our room with a queen bed for each of us. Then we walked across the street to cracker barrel and met our bus friends. We sat with Harlan and Rita, and they were from Detroit Lakes, Minnesota. That's only an hour from our homes. They also lived just two blocks from my oldest siter, Alice. What a small world. They did not know her though. We had such a nice visit with them. Donna and I ate light as it's already 7:30 p.m., and we didn't need a heavy meal. So we ordered off the kids/senior menu and had chicken strips with tater tots and corn bread muffins with butter and honey. It was only a $5 meal but way more than we could finish. As the waitress gave us our bill, Harlen grabbed both of ours and said, "I'm getting theirs." We said no, we got our own, but he insisted. We thanked him, and he remarked it's just like paying for the grandkids. That made us both feel pretty young!

On our way out, there was a gift shop, and I found a Coca-Cola bottle opener for Ruth as a souvenir. She collects anything to do with Coke. Her house is decorated with many items and so quaint.

We were drained after a long bus ride and went back to our room. We put our swimsuits on and headed to the jacuzzi for a half hour or so. It was very relaxing and an end to a wonderful day. We had set our alarms for 6:30 a.m. but woke up at 6:10 a.m. and got ready for the day. Our luggage had to be out in the hall by 7:00 a.m. We were ahead of schedule but went down for breakfast. We had a waffle and eggs and bacon with coffee and juice. It was included with our stay, and now we boarded the bus to head to Branson.

We stopped midmorning at a cheese shop in Osceola, Missouri. I bought several chubs of cheese to bring home for us and Randy and Ruth. I got a garden vegetable, pepper jack, farmers, horseradish, and mozzarella. That's my favorite. I also picked up a gourmet sample of pecan chocolate. Everything was made fresh, and oh so good. I also bought myself a pair of PJ shorts. The PJs I brought with were too warm last night. We were now headed to Bob Evans for lunch with a menu of five choices. So many of the meals were included in our bus trip price. We're loving that! We could pick two of the five choices.

Our tour guide was the mom of Hart travel and her name is Georgia. Her husband Ernie is the assistant and sits in the back of the bus by the bathroom. Their son, Rick, is our driver. It's definitely a family business. They are so warm and welcoming. We also did not have to wear masks. They made it optional, and some did wear them the whole trip. They kept us entertained with stories, games, and trivia. Made the ride go fast.

We were now heading down the road again. It's the driver Ricky's birthday tomorrow, so we were passing a card around and signing it. We could put money in if we want. We did. Donna and I had saved our giant cookie for our snack from our lunch.

Today would have been homemakers back home. I have a great vice president that takes over for me when things like this happen. I did have to juggle a few things to take a trip like this spur of the moment. Nancy had to come over to my house and pick up the food and supplies. She knew how to run a meeting, so I felt very good about being gone. Then I got a call from another member, and she and her husband had COVID. So there would be less people at homemakers. The meeting was supposed to be at her house. So Nancy rearranged and called all the members to change it to the Alliance Church in Verndale. It's so nice to trust a friend and neighbor to take care of things. She definitely stepped up to the plate and called me later and reassured me it all went well.

Right now, COVID was ramping up again in our town and neighborhoods. We were back to social distancing, and many restaurants did only drive-through. No indoor eating. It's a new strain called the Delta variant in our community now. Last Sunday at church we only had eight people. We were hoping and praying it would pass soon and no one die from it. It's a big uncertainty for all.

Now back to our journey. This afternoon we went to a theater. We saw Daniel O'Donnell. He was a very talented singer and comedian. He originated from Ireland but was now an American citizen. We had a very nice buffet supper and left there to another theater. Our driver took a detour to a very grand light show all about Christmas. We then went to enjoy a country singer and comedian, Neil McCoy, which took us out and about until 11:00 p.m. It was a very long but beautiful day. As we settled in for the night, I got a text message from my McCullough Williston friends that Linda O. had passed away. It was sad but also a blessing to know she's not suffering any longer. She was in hospice with pancreatic cancer, which we knew when we all visited her a week or so ago. May you RIP, my dear friend. It was so fitting that at both shows we saw today they sang "How Great Thou Art." I know as I fell asleep that was all for her.

Her boys were having a celebration of life when this COVID got under control. It would probably be next summer.

This virus kept us all from doing traditional services and just being there for one another.

I knew now how a day could be so great and sad all at the same time. I definitely lived my life the way it came to us and to the fullest.

It's Friday, and we got up at 6:40 a.m. and put our bags out and headed to breakfast at our motel. We boarded the bus and were on a grand tour of Branson, the city. We stopped at a trout fishery, where these were literally millions of stocked fish, then an overlook where Andy Williams used to live down below. Wow, the mansions we saw were spectacular. We were going to see the college of the Ozarks. It's where students worked to pay their tuition. I liked that concept.

Then we spent two hours downtown Branson. They had gift shops, cafés, and five-and-ten store. We opted to eat at a burger place called the Clockers Café. It had clocks everywhere. We had a burger and chips, which were excellent. We realized we were running out of bottled water for us on the bus. We started watching for that. We ran into an Amish shop along the street, and they had fifty-cent bottled water. We got eight each. Most places were $3 a bottle at all the shows and theaters, uffda!

We were now going to see the Duttons' Christmas show. They featured violins, guitars, and almost any instrument you could think of. It consists of a family with all members being so very talented. They danced, sang, tap- danced, and put on a heartwarming Christmas show. After the show, we went to the fudge place. The Duttons made their own homemade fudge. Of course, Donna and I had to taste test and buy some to take home to Rick and friends. For supper tonight, we went to Charlie's Steak and Ribs and Ale House. It was one of our best meals so far.

It's Saturday morning, and we just finished breakfast at our motel. It's so nice to know breakfast was always ready for us. We had gotten to know a lot of people on our bus. We took turns to talk about where we were from, family, how many trips we took, etc. They passed the mic around, and we each took a turn to talk about ourselves also. It's really fun to hear where everyone was from. Donna and I had been eating and hanging out with what I call our sistas. Jenny, Carolyn, Cindy, Kim, and Julie were a group of friends that went on this bus tour together. We just hit it off and had so much in common. They were from Princeton, Norwood, Young America, Ely, Chaska, and that area of Minnesota. We had such a good time. We even exchanged emails and cell numbers. They really liked when I told the bus how I got to go on this trip. They loved that I was writing a book and they would be mentioned in it. I got permission from them. I'm hoping I get to reconnect again with them someday. Maybe another bus trip, who knows. If not, it was still a memory I'll treasure knowing them. I will miss my sistas.

We're heading to a mall this morning. I found my sons-in-law each a shirt. They would get it in their stockings for Christmas. Jon said, "The only time I get lucky is when I find my car in the parking lot!" JJ said, "We couldn't wait to grow up. What in the hell were we thinking?!" Donna and I also got Branson sweatshirts. Now we were official tourists, right!

We found the Grand Village. It had many novelty shops We also needed to eat and found the Hard Luck Café nestle among them all.

All the waiters and waitresses took turns singing with a microphone live the whole while we ordered and ate. It was like an old-fashioned malt shop with music from the sixties and seventies. Of course, I remembered the words and, like others, couldn't help but sing along. It was so sweet and just took us back in time. I hope someday my kids and grandkids find this place. It was like a diamond in the rough. What great food and memory. I still have those songs from Garth Books, Elvis, Johnny Cash, Journey, etc. playing in my head. Wow. The food was phenomenal.

We continued finding more Christmas gifts for the kids and grandkids. One of our best days ever was not until we attended the Jesus Sound and Light Show. It was so real with real donkeys, horses, sheep, and birds. People flying like angels set back in biblical times as angels and Jesus. You could feel the thunder and lightning sound effects through your whole body. It was so touching many people were in tears. They showed Jesus as he hung on the cross and everything. It was three hours long but the most moving production I've ever seen. Donna loved it too.

But guess what, our day was not over yet. We went to a chicken and steak buffet with so much food you couldn't believe it. Then we loaded the bus for a Hughes Brothers Christmas show at 8:00 p.m. It was great also. Each show was so different and unique. This was another family talented great show. We got back to motel at 11:00 p.m. I called Rick, and he was doing fine but missed me now. Boy were we tired tonight, so we didn't talk to late. I was missing him and my own bed.

It was Sunday and our last day in Branson. We headed to Iowa to spend the night. We stopped at a museum on our way there. It's so cute the way we exited the bus. Each stop we took turns. One stop its door side first, then next stop its driver's side to get off. We were like a bunch of little kids as to whose turn it was next. The driver kept track, and he ruled. Thank goodness for him.

We stopped at Golden Coral for lunch and that was another buffet, which was excellent. Way too much food, but oh, so good. The Steamboat Arabia in Kansas City, Missouri, was also awesome.

The Steamboat sank in 1856 and not found until 1985 by a family seeking adventures. When found, there were still dishes, canned goods, weapons, clothes, and shoes. A lot of the finds were from rich people who were going to sell the wares and goods to settlers coming to America. It all went down in the Missouri River from hitting stumps and roots and downed trees hiding under the water.

They were preserved in this museum. We were headed to Des Moines, Iowa, to our motel for the night. It's been a ten-hour bus ride today.

We stopped at Cracker Barrel for supper. I had shrimp and tater tots. Couldn't eat it all. There were a few drawbacks because of the COVID pandemic. Most places did not have enough help. Almost all restaurants and motels had Help Wanted signs up and were hiring. We had to be patient as this took time to get service sometimes. The poor waitresses that were working were worked to a frazzle. They got frustrated, so we just tipped them very well. We appreciated these essential workers.

It's been this way the past six months even in our little towns of Verndale and Wadena.

We were used to seeing the mess that these places were experiencing. I was heading to the hot hub and then made my phone call to Rick for the night. It's Monday morning, and we had breakfast with our newfound sistas. They came up with that name for all of us. Thought it was pretty special. They were all so nice. Harlen and Rita gave me their number also on the bus this morning. These are people I may never see again, but who knows if our paths will cross in the future. I hope so.

Georgia had a handout about the twelve days of Christmas and about the candy cane, how it came about. I am including these in my book. I loved learning about them and hope my readers do too.

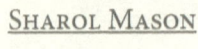

Twelve Days of Xmas

What in the world do leaping lords, French hens, swimming swans, and especially that partridge who won't come out of the pear tree have to do with Christmas?

From 1558 until 1829, Roman Catholics in England were not allowed to practice their faith openly. Someone during that era wrote this carol as a catechism song for young Catholics. It has two levels of meaning: the surface meaning plus a hidden meaning known only to members of their church. Each element in the carol has a code word for a religious reality, which the children could remember.

The partridge in a pear tree was Jesus Christ. Two turtle doves were the Old and New Testaments. Three French hens stood for faith, hope, and love. The four calling birds were the four gospels of Matthew, Mark, Luke, and John. The five golden rings recalled the Torah or aw, the first five books of the Old Testament. The six geese a-laying stood for the six days of creation. Seven swans a-swimmin' represented the sevenfold gifts of the Holy Spirit: prophesy, serving, teaching, exhortation, contribution, leadership, and mercy. The eight maids a-milking were the eight beatitudes. Nine ladies dancing were the nine fruits of the Holy Spirit: love, joy, peace, patience, kindness, goodness, faithfulness, gentleness, self-control. The ten lords a- leaping were the ten commandments. Eleven pipers piping stood for the eleven faithful disciples. Twelve drummers drumming symbolized the twelve points of belief in the Apostles' Creed.

From Bethel Our Saviour's Lutheran Parish, Herman, Minnesota, newsletter:

Candy Cane
A CANDYMAKER'S WITNESS

A Candymaker in Indiana wanted to make a candy that would be a witness, so he made the Christmas Candy Cane. He incorporated several symbols for the birth, ministry, and death of Jesus Christ.

He began with a stick of pure white, hard candy. WHITE to symbolize the Virgin Birth and the sinless nature of Jesus, and HARD to symbolize the Solid Rock, the foundation of the church and firmness of the promises of GOD.

The candymaker made the candy in the form of a "J" to represent the precious name of JESUS, who came to earth as our Savior.

Thinking that the candy was somewhat plain, the candymaker stained it with RED STRIPES. He used three small stripes to show the scourging Jesus received by which we are healed. The LARGE RED STRIPE was for the blood shed by Christ on the cross so that we could have the promise of eternal life.

Unfortunately, the candy became known as a Candy-Cane a meaningless decoration seen at Christmas time. But the meaning is still there for those who have eyes to see and ears to hear.

I pray that this symbol will again be used to witness the wonder of Jesus and his great love that came down at Christmas and remains the ultimate force in the universe today.

On our way home on the bus, we had another opportunity to talk on the microphone. We were to tell of our favorite show or anything that stood out to us. I couldn't pick a favorite as they all had such substance and talent. I told them again that I had outlined our trip so my friend could read it later on. It's easy to forget how fun a trip like this can be. Now I'll have proof.

We stopped at a Russell Stover candy store. I bought several boxes of chocolates to give for gifts. Of course, they're for Ruth for her generosity in giving me this trip. I got some taffy for Rick as he really loves that. They had a variety of candy, not just chocolate.

We were starting to drop people off at their destinations now, only three so far, but next stop there would be ten getting off at St. Michael. Then my new sistas would be next. We had a great time getting to know them and hoped to keep in touch. I promised to call Cindy when my book got published. I didn't know how long this would take me. I did know I had a great start, and it's been a super experience to recall my life from birth to retirement and beyond.

My rough draft would hopefully be done by summer of 2022. I had several years to fill in but would get there. We dropped two more off in Clearwater and some in St. Joseph's. The bus s getting less and less. It would be an hour and half till we got to Parkers Prairie to get Donna's vehicle and go home to Verndale.

The Hart Travel people called ahead and had the car warming for us. What a bunch of truly nice people. It's only twenty degrees outside, so that would be so nice. We were about an hour ahead of schedule, so we would surprise Rick and be home for supper. I will end this chapter with a lot of great memories of a truly priceless trip to Branson, Missouri. Thank you, Ruth, from the bottom of my heart.

One of my favorite sayings is, "Life is not measured by the breaths we take but by the moments that take our breath away."

It's November 23, 2021. I just got home from my Branson bus trip. Jill from the Hart Travel bus service just called me this evening and informed that someone tested positive for

COVID-19 that was on our bus. So I now was quarantined until I could get tested. On Wednesday I called to see where I could get tested. When I called the clinic, they patched me over to the hospital COVID line. The nurse said yes, they could, but no results for two to three working days. Well, it's Thanksgiving tomorrow, so I was not going that route. I called around to Lakewood Health, and they did not do rapid tests either. I phoned a few pharmacies, and they weren't testing right now. I went to the Armory as that was where most get a rapid test, and it only took a few minutes, but they were closed until Monday. So that was what I was doing. I would quarantine until I found out. Rick was going with me too since he'd been in close proximity. I had no symptoms except we both had a bad headache on Wednesday. We felt fine otherwise, and I was quite tired after riding a bus and sleeping in different beds and using other pillows. I assumed my headache was from all that. Let's hope so.

It had been quite hard to just stay home. I had gone over to my good friend Norma's place. She was our neighbor, and we ran a few errands, so I now had to call her and tell her I was exposed. She wasn't too worried as anytime we went anywhere you could be by someone who had COVID or the Delta variant. I apologized to her anyway. Thank goodness she was the only person I'd been in contact with.

So now it's Thursday and Thanksgiving day. We had planned on going to my oldest son's house, Joey and Kim, as Ryan and Tena and kids would be there and a lot of the grandkids. I had to call them and tell them Rick and I couldn't make it. It's a repeat of last year as we couldn't gather more than six people with all being in the same family. So we stayed home then too. So Rick and I ended up going to St. Ann's Church drive-through to pick up our turkey dinners. It was very good. I also baked us a pumpkin pie to help feel more like a holiday. We had turkey, mashed potatoes, vegetable, gravy, cranberries, and a pumpkin bar. Oh, and a roll, but no stuffing, but that's okay. We had a good meal and feel blessed to get that. I also had a lot of time to work on my autobiography. They had you drive up in front of the church, and they handed you the Styrofoam boxed meal through the car window, and you handed them a donation. Easy peasy.

Rick and I had been going for walks as much as we could. He was limited to about one mile now as his pain was still quite intolerable at times. Like I told him, any walking was better than none. We both loved our time together when we took our walks with buddy and the cats. Yes, two cats or three sometimes came with and one dog. We loved it.

Just one day ago, a new variant of COVID surfaced in Southern Africa. It's called the Omicron variant. It spreads faster than the first two. But so far, it has not been detected in the US. It has been found in several other countries—the UK, Germany, Belgium, and more. Our CDC is already on top of it and working on a treatment while comparing if our shots we already have taken may help with the spread. It all takes time, and there's much to learn about each of them.

November 29, 2021, my older sister, Theresa, the one who just lost her husband out in Wyoming, was flying into the cities today. She was taking a shuttle from there to St. Cloud. From there my oldest sister, Alice, and her good friend Yonna were picking her up and bringing her to her apartment in the same building as Alice. She would be living in Detroit Lakes, Minnesota, now. That is only fifty-five miles from us, so we should be able to connect more. She had been in Wyoming twenty-eight years. A big change for her and a blessing for us.

Well, today Rick and I went in for our COVID testing. It only took about fifteen minutes to get through the Armory test site. First they had us take a picture on our cell phones of their app, then it downloaded a lot of questions to answer. Then we went to another table, and they verified our birthday and name. Then on to another table to verify who we were, and then they swabbed both nostrils, and poof, it's all done. We got results within half an hour. So meanwhile we ran a few errands like bank, gas, and post office. Then we got results right on our emails on our phones, and we were both negative. We had been vaccinated, myself two doses and Rick three, so we felt pretty safe that we didn't have it but now felt quite relieved to have proof. Boy, what an ordeal. I did not like quarantining for a week already. Hope we stayed healthy and avoid this virus and any new strains.

I just got my third Pfizer vaccine as I believed in prevention. It got really sore this time but only felt lousy for twenty-four hours. I had gotten really tired and lost my appetite; that's not so bad. After having been exposed now and quarantined, I really felt that the shots worked. The cases were mounting as many people refused vaccinations.

I just got a call from my oldest son, Joey. My children's dad, Ralph, my ex, was in the hospital in Wadena, and it didn't look good. He had lung cancer and melanoma cancer. The tumor was bigger, and he's probably not going to make it. It's a weird feeling, but he'd always been a good friend even through our divorce. I would pay my respects and pray he didn't have to suffer long. No one deserved that. Ralph passed away after five days in the hospital. They kept him comfortable and all the kids—Joey, Amy, Ryan, and Sonja, one of our foster children—made it home to say their goodbyes. What a blessing, no more suffering from cancer.

Rick and I would pay our respects once the celebration of life was planned.

The funeral was the eighteenth of December. The kids had planned it at Karvonen's funeral home. A lot of his brothers, sisters, and relatives came. Sonny, our foster daughter, wrote a nice tribute to him mentioning how safe and welcomed she was in our home. My daughter Amy gave a little speech also. I can't believe how strong all my kids are. It was closed with military honors, including the gun salute and taps. It was very touching. They presented my oldest son, Joey, with the flag. A nice lunch followed and time spent at the American Inn Motel with relatives. Then at 6:00 p.m., everyone met at the Mariachi Mexican restaurant to eat together. It was slow, but such good food. They were short on help due to the pandemic. Everyone was needing workers. My kids and their friends all pitched in, and Joey made drinks. Amy and Ryan and Tena helped set up extra tables as they were only expecting thirty, but fifty or more of us showed up. They also helped with water, chips and dip, and silverware. What a beautiful time for all of us. Their dad, Ralph, can rest in peace now.

We got a call that one of the cousins tested positive for COVID, so we're exposed again. We hadn't been by them, so we should be okay. My special niece Brenda texted me to tell me she had it. She picked it up at her school most likely. She had been right down in her bed for a week and couldn't eat and was very weak. She said she had no energy and had a really bad headache. Everyone had different symptoms. She couldn't be around anyone for ten days. That was very hard as she was an energetic person. Get better, Brenda!

It's December 27, 2021, today. We just got hit with eight inches of snow during the day today. It's beautiful, but we were snowed in for a while. So guess you know by now that I had time to write in my book. I've had a good breakfast with Rick consisting of scrambled eggs with bacon and onions, English muffin, and coffee. We almost always ate together as it was our time to converse about our day or week or special quality time. I love the saying, "The family that eats and prays together stays together." I do live by that and have believed that all my life. I was taught that as a child when all ten of us would gather at our table on the farm.

Our good neighbor, farmer Dan, as we called him, just passed away from COVID. He had been in the hospital for weeks and then had a heart attack, pneumonia, and strokes.

He never made it home and left four kids that he loved dearly. He was divorced, so their mom would raise them. We had now lost three neighbors to COVID.

Now he was a friendly sort of neighbor. He borrowed things back and forth and would stop in just to see how we were doing. Rick had known him for almost sixty years, and I'd known him for over forty years when he and his wife did foster care. Rick said when they moved here from the cities, they had real battery-operated toys, and Rick's sibling had tonka toys. His parents and sister had passed, and he had only one brother left. RIP, Dan.

January 22, 2022, Rick and I went to Tim and Donna's for his surprise birthday party. We were also picking up his recollection of when we were kids and years we were apart. We got there about two, and Missy, my niece, and Jeff were there also for Tim's birthday. He was turning seventy-two and was surprised with cupcakes and coffee. We had a great visit, but it was starting to snow, so we left early to get home before dark. The roads were pretty bad when I suddenly realized I had forgotten my phone on their table.

We were only ten miles out, so we turned around to retrieve it. They had all run uptown but the door was open, thank goodness.

We made it home safely, but the roads were bad, and it was dark and hard to see with the snow coming down good the last twenty-five miles. Then we made supper and watched some TV and went to bed. Rick was very tired and restless. He had a severe backache and couldn't sleep mainly because he had to pee quite often. He woke up in the morning feeling even worse. He could hardly walk across the living room. I told him we should go in as something wasn't right. We had been to St. Cloud Friday for an appointment with urology, and they were going to schedule surgery as he was having trouble with going to the bathroom. They were going to be calling next week. He didn't seem to have any problems after the tests Friday, but now we weren't so sure with these new symptoms. We were waiting for the doctor to come in right now as I did talk him into going in to get checked at Staples. It also could be a kidney stone or bladder infection. We'd been through this several times already. What a long day. It turned out he had a bad bladder/kidney infection. So we had another new experience while leaving the hospital. We asked where they were calling the antibiotic prescription into. She said, "We now have a vending machine for prescriptions."

I said, "What?"

She said, "Here's the code number to put in and follow the steps from there."

It asked his name, birthday, and code. Then the machine made some noises, like a pop machine, and out dropped his bottle of pills. Oh my goodness, how convenient was that. No waiting and wondering when to go get it at Walmart. It was labeled just like at the pharmacy and maybe took two minutes. I love technology like this, especially when it works so fast. Our world is definitely getting automated. Gotta love it!

Rick was feeling much better today and on the mend. It's been a week.

February 2022, he had bloodwork done. Things were improving, but his blood sugars were high, and his liver numbers were too high. He also couldn't get an appointment for six months for his discrepancy on his brain scan. It was July 15, 2022, or maybe sooner if someone canceled. He was on a waiting list. It was very hard to get into specialist without a long wait. Patience is a virtue.

CHAPTER 43

Long Lake Junior

We all gathered January 14 to 17, 2022, at Stoney Point Resort by Cass Lake, Minnesota. This was our second year to have a winter getaway. Rick did not choose to go to this as it's loud and too many people and commotion. He didn't mind that I go as it's my side of the family. He knows I truly love being with family. Friday night was Brenda, my niece, and Chrissy, another niece, and our meal plan. We chose pizza, salad, and dessert. Brenda called me Thursday night because she couldn't get the take and bake from Walmart as we planned. The pandemic had a surge in cases, and many stores were out of products due to workers and truckers not being able to deliver. Many shelves were empty. I told her I would get the eight to ten pizzas here at our Walmart. Problem solved, we thought. I had made three different salads to bring and left Friday morning about 11:00 a.m. I figured that would give me time to pick up the pizzas and still get there by early afternoon. When I got to Wadena Walmart, they were out also. On I went, thinking I'd find them along my one-hundred-mile trek to the resort. I did stop at the store in Sebeka, Menahga, and Park Rapids. These grocery stores, which have always had take-and-bake pizza in their delis, said they didn't do them anymore because products were too hard to come by. I did find eight frozen mediums only in Park Rapids. I could only get sausage/pepperoni there. Who knew I would have so many problems finding pizzas. Wow! Since I had emptied Park Rapids shelves, I knew that wouldn't be enough as they were not large ones. I stopped at a pizza shop place, but their large one were $20 a piece for a thirteen inches. We couldn't afford that, so I went to Domino's. They were outrageously high priced too.

I proceeded to Coburn's to their deli. I asked an employee, and she said, "We don't make them anymore due to lack of ingredients because of COVID-19 crisis." I then went to the freezer section as a last effort. I was hoping to find some supreme large or extra-large pizza there. I got lucky they did have the green mill brand homemade frozen to bake. They were two for $10.00 and extra-large supreme. Normally $9.99 apiece. They were a great deal, and I was thrilled to have found them. Brenda had gone to four places in Bemidji last night, and I had gone to seven different places to collect what I could find for forty people to eat supper. The great part was when I got there and we cooked them up, everyone was so hungry there were no complaints, and they loved them So we were done with our one meal prep for the weekend. Each family took a turn for a meal, and the rest sat back and enjoyed. The meals were always a surprise and oh so good.

The resort was a large lodge with two large kitchens and dining and living space. There was several bedrooms with two being on the main level for anyone with disabilities or special needs. The rest of bedrooms were upstairs with each side of the lodge having a common area by them.

We also had a nice pool to swim in. It included a hot tub, which held lots of us. That got the most business from all our crew. The kids had a kiddie pool with a bucket to dump water on them. They never knew when it's going to tip; the screams and squeals were worth the wait. There were many bathrooms within this large lodge.

Some of the family activities shared during the weekend were board games, puzzles, cards, and the littles sharing their special toys. We also went snowshoeing and sledding if weather permitted. The guys also had fish houses out on the lake if fishing was your forte. The little guests loved the outdoor activities whether it's cold or not. We were all Minnesota hearty. In the evening, the adults enjoyed a few beverages if they chose. We sat around and shared memories and stories of our family members who couldn't be with us. That might be because they've passed on, and we were all missing them or because COVID prevented others from attending. We also had creative people like Brenda and Chrissy who made Long Lake Jr. T-shirts and pillow cases and bags. Their cricket machines were priceless!

Thanks, girls. It was a wonderful time to spend with family in the dead of winter. We hope it continues and many more memories will be made.

Our good friend, neighbor, and Rick's cousin, Randy's wife, Ruth, lost her battle with the cancer bully. She had it ten years ago, and it came back. She was doctoring at Mayo Clinic, but they couldn't operate the tumor this time. So she came home and was on hospice until February 3, 2022. She was in our homemaker's group, so we are going to go get an arrangement tomorrow and take food over to the house. She was the friend and neighbor that gave me their trip to Branson last November because she couldn't go because of the cancer returning. That was her, always thinking of others and such a giving person. She will truly be missed but never forgotten. RIP, Ruthie!

ER Trip

February 16, Rick was supposed to have a procedure done at 11:30 a.m. in St. Cloud. Well, he woke up at 3:00 a.m. in the morning with groin, abdominal, and severe back pain. He was having trouble urinating also. So we called the St. Cloud urologist, and he cancelled that surgery and wanted us to go to Staples twenty miles away and get a CT scan, urinalysis, and culture. So I called Lakewood Health and talked to his care team there, and they would call back to get him set up. Well, about two hours after I called them, they got back to me, and he could get those tests done if his insurance gave the okay. I thought "Oh boy," so I asked how long that would take. The nurse said anywhere from a few minutes to hours to days. She promised she'd get back to us as soon as she got the okay. Well, it only took about a half hour, so that was good. We went in at 1:00 p.m., and he was in and out quickly. About 4:00 p.m., they called about results, which were sent to his doctor in St. Cloud. He has a large kidney stone that had to be removed but couldn't until they get the infection under control.

Urology from St. Cloud called and said we needed him to go to St. Cloud Hospital right away. So I grabbed a bag, and off we went. We got there at 6:00 p.m., and it took forever (two hours) in the ER. We were getting a little discouraged and figured we would be lucky to get an antibiotic at this rate. They finally called us back into an exam room. Boy did things start happening then. They hooked him up to an IV right away and started fluids, antibiotics, and pain meds. They told him he would be staying the night and having surgery either in the night or early morning.

I left around ten, and he wasn't in his own room yet. The nurse called at 11:30 p.m. to tell me they'd call me when he went to surgery. So I didn't sleep to well. I stayed at my brother-in-law's, so that's like ten minutes from the hospital. That was so nice to be close. They called about 5:00 a.m., and he was headed to surgery. The doctor called about six forty and said it went well, but they couldn't take stone out at this time. When he got a closer look, the stone was embedded with infection, and he needed a tube put in to drain that. Also a stint to help with urination. Rick had had stints before and would not be happy about that.

Dr. MaGee said he would remove the stone on the twenty-eighth of February if all this settled down. He had him set up for that already. He was very concerned that if this infection didn't get better soon, it could turn to sepsis, which was not a good thing. So we were hoping the draining would help while he's in the hospital. Not sure when he would get to go home. When I got to the hospital, he had 103 temp and was talking out of it. They told me things had gotten worse, and he now had E. coli infection in his blood. They had to figure out which antibiotic was best to give him. He would be in the hospital a while was all they said. Tonight for sure. I could stay till 8:00 p.m. tonight. Visitors' hours and people were limited because of COVID. He could only have visitor one, and it had to be the same person throughout his stay. Given that it would be me, I would stay at Maury's again tonight. I brought Rick some dark chocolate, and he ate a little. He was drinking lots of juice and water but not eating much yet. I also got him some word search books to do if he's here a while. It took several days to grow the bacteria in his culture in a petri dish. So they treated the infection with a broad antibiotic till then. Once they knew the results of what bacteria it was, they would know which antibiotic would be best to treat him. Didn't look like he'd get over this very fast. Praying he could fight it.

We were told today that two days before we got there, the hospital lifted visitation restriction. Until now I would not have even been able to be here to be with him. So we felt very lucky that I could spend time with him when he needed me the most. Visiting hours were from 8:00 a.m. to 8:00 p.m., and you get screened each day as you came in with COVID questions and no symptoms. If none, they gave you a name tag sticky to wear as you went inside and outside You had to wear a mask at all times. Today the internal medicine doctor came in and said he would be here another day and hoped the culture would be ready tomorrow for instructions of what to give him for the bacterial infection. He needed IV fluids and meds that way for now.

Rick was moving better today and used a walker twice to go for a short walk to bathroom and hallway with the OT and PT teams. He ate more for breakfast and lunch also. He had beef stroganoff and blueberry crisp for dessert. We didn't make noodles much at home, but they went good for him today. He still had a lot of pain when going pee and that stint and stone hurt when he went.

He was adjusting quite well to that. I spent the day with him from 9:30 a.m. to 5:00 p.m. and back to say good night at seven before closing time. I was going over to my niece Jackie and Filip's for supper. It would give me a little break.

I was staying at Evy (my sister) and Maury's house once again. I thought it would be upsetting because she's gone. I miss her so much. Instead, it was comforting as I could feel her presence throughout the house. The bathroom was decorated with her style of decor. The kitchen was like all the other times, just Maury doing stuff instead of her. Right down to the lap blankets she'd always offer as we would settle in for the night. All the family photos of her kids and grandkids made it like she was still there. I wasn't expecting to feel so good about it, but know I'd be there again to help myself grieve. Her heart and spirit live on forever.

So now I went back to the hospital and sat with Rick for another one and a half hours. Visiting hours were over at eight, but he was going for a walk, and the nurse said I could walk with him first.

I had told her we took walks together daily. Then she teased us that she might have to call security if someone else saw us as it was after eight. Then she broke out laughing. They were lighthearted at this hospital.

From there I went to Jackie's, and we watched *Sister Act 1*. That was so relaxing to just forget about the chaos right now. Then they put on another movie, but it was not so good, but we watched it anyway. We had sleepy time tea and nuts, candy, and cookies. What a blessing to have family close by. Then Maury and I went back to his house. It's going on 11:00 p.m. now and definitely time to rest.

Saturday morning, I got up about 6:30 a.m., and we went to Perkins for breakfast. I took a shower and got ready for another long day. Jackie and Filip met us there, and we had such a good big slam, which is three pancakes, two eggs, and two bacon. It was very good. We also had coffee, of course. The prices had really skyrocketed because of the pandemic. What used to cost $5 or $6 a meal now was more than doubled. I picked up the check as Maury had bought lunch the other day. It came to $30 for the two of us for breakfast. Wow. Inflation had hit once again.

Gas prices were going up, groceries were way up, and any extras had really skyrocketed. Coffee used to be free with a meal or $0.50 a cup, now it went from the last few years $1.50 to $3.00 a cup.

Rick and I didn't really get affected as we love to cook at home and don't eat out very often. It had taken a toll on businesses as restaurants were hardly even half full let alone full. Before I went to visit Rick this morning,

Vernon texted as he was checking on the status of our house and animals. Wow, just when you think your worries can't get worse, they do! He got there, and the back door had blown open, and the animals were in the house. It was only fifty-five degrees, Vernon said. To top it off, the fire alarms were all going off, and he could not find any heat source to cause that. He figured the batteries must have been low, so he fixed that issue. We have a wood stove in the living room, so he lit that to help the chill in the house to improve quicker.

Then he had to hunt for all the cats to figure out if they were hiding in the house. We had been letting them in the house with the dog this winter as the temperatures outside have been forty or fifty degrees below wind chills with negative thirty-five degrees actual. Buddy was also a good therapy dog for both of us. It's like having a kid around again. Vernon also jumped in the side by side that had a plow and removed the snow that had blown into our driveway and around the house. He is a heaven-sent. Rick told him to take some split wood from the pile for his place. They lived south of Wadena and Verndale and just got a wood stove in before winter. They didn't have time before the snow flew to collect any wood for themselves.

We shared a lot of things back and forth with them whenever possible.

Rick helped him put in the chimney pipes and stove. They loved it on these blustery cold days. Before Vernon left, he fed all the cats and dog outside and gave them water. Things should be fine now for a day or so. I let our church family know that Rick was here, and they could pray for him in church tomorrow. Prayers are powerful. Rick was still running a low fever now but did shower by himself, which was a good step toward going home. They were trying to figure out which antibiotic to send home till they got results of which bacteria was in his blood. His kidneys were functioning better as the doctor had said this morning. They were shutting down some from all the trauma. In the night, he had filled the one-liter pee jug thrice, which meant they were better. Rick said all he did all night long was use the urinal, which I guess was a good thing. Not much sleep though.

It's 1:00 p.m., and the medical doctor had not been here yet to see if he could get released this afternoon. We just got the word from internal medicine he could go home with antibiotics and a few changes to meds. So off we went.

We got home late afternoon and were greeted with a few obstacles. Rick asked the doctor before he left if he could get some Percocet for the ride home. He was very adamant that was a no. He felt it made him confused with all that's going in from antibiotics, kidney function, and meds. In fact, he told him he should hold off the oxy for a while till things got better. He only took two a day. Well, I knew that wouldn't happen, but that was Doc's opinion.

His primary doctor had always said, "You don't go off oxy as you will have withdrawal." In my opinion, I think he might have been having withdrawal for four days as that's one big symptom, being disorientated and confused. Only God knows these answers, and I guess it didn't matter as long as he's okay.

The last RN we had also made our day. It is a small world when she knew where Verndale was because they come up north to Bluffton to hunt with her husband's family. They bought their grandma's land, who was an old friend of mine. I bowled with her at Wadena Lanes for many years. She had passed away but was a lady you'd not forget. RIP, Jan Brewer.

So when we got home, there were lots to take care of since that storm came through. We had snow to remove by the house, some ice, and the house was cold from the door blowing open. We got the woodstove going, which still had a few coals from Vernon starting it, so that was nice. I was not good at fires, but it took off right away. Now I had to run to Walmart as they close a five at the pharmacy. I went to town and got his antibiotics for bladder, and kidney meds. I had five minutes to spare. I grabbed Subway, our usual. We shared a twelve-inch chicken teriyaki sub with his extras on his side and mine on mine. They had creamy potato bacon soup for Rick and a cheesy broccoli for me. We got a cup for each of us. *Mmm*, good! We settled into our cozy home and fire and went to bed.

Sunday was a new day, and I didn't feel I could leave him even for an hour with these circumstances to go to church. Our country church is only a mile away but still too far in case he needed help going to the bathroom or keeping hydrated. Then we got the forecast on the news that two storm systems were coming across Minnesota. We were in the thick of both. So now we had to get prepared for being stuck inside for two days, Monday and Tuesday. Well, I started off with hauling loads of wood in to fill the wood rack. Our woodpile was in the woodshed, which was sixty feet from the house, but the path needed shoveling.

I got that all done but took breaks between wagon loads. I also had to climb up the ladder to our house roof to clear away the snow and ice from the three skylights. This was something I had to do some years as it built up ice dams if I didn't make a path. There was at least two feet of solid snow up there, but I loved to go on the roof! Call me crazy! We noticed we were low on milk; it had spoiled while gone, and we needed Gatorade. So I made a quick grocery list and picked them up at Super One. Then later tonight, Vernon and Amber stopped by to see how Rick was doing or if we needed anything. We had a nice visit, and they were on call if we needed anything. The kids were all good to help us out.

One more thing that happened while we were in the hospital. Buddy, our dog, had ruffled through Rick's clothes and rug by his side of bed. It looked like he had made himself his own bed. He never went in our bedroom, but obviously he must have really missed Rick or knew he was sick. Dogs sense things!

Animals are such good therapy for us. I swear this one is half human. We love him.

It was a mess cleaning up all the dog hair. We love Buddy, and Rick and I agree. He brings joy and fun to us. He's like a therapy dog for Rick. This winter had been brutal for the animals. So we felt they needed to be warm. We might be quite the pushovers! We love you, Buddy!

It's Monday, and the snow just kept on a coming. The forecast was correct. We were doing fine and hoped nothing changed. He had a follow- up with Katie, his primary doctor, tomorrow morning, but we were pretty sure that we would have to cancel. A day at a time!

CHAPTER 44

COVID Update, February 2022

The pandemic is still going on with restrictions somewhat lifted. On the fourteenth of February, they started allowing one visitor per patient at St. Cloud Hospital. Before that it was no visitors unless the doctor okayed it if it would be necessary. So we got lucky there. I just had to answer several COVID questions and show my ID as being the only visitor on computer to see Rick.

The visiting hours were good from 8:00 a.m. to 8:00 p.m. I also had to wear a mask at all times, which had to be a clinical one. There is no more wearing homemade cloth masks in required public places like, clinics, hospitals, dentists, etc. Wadena County as of February 17, 2022, has had ninety-four cases weekly, positive rate 14.5 percent, fifty deaths, and only one admission to hospital. In Todd County the same week, they have 194 positive cases with a positivity rate of 14.59 percent and fifty-four deaths. A larger county next door, Ottertail, has 363 cases with a positivity rate of 16.18 percent. New admissions of nine people with 160 deaths. People are getting more and more vaccinated in each county. So as far as I can see, the pandemic has improved, but we still have a long way to go.

Most schools and churches are not making masks mandatory. Also restaurants do not either. The businesses are still hurting as people just don't go out to do everyday things like they used to; they are limiting themselves for their own safety. Traveling is still pretty strict, and borders to other countries are still not open due to pandemic. So we are not making any plans right now due to that but also Rick's health concerns at this time. Bummer!

Tuesday, February 21, 2022, Rick was supposed to

have a post-op with his primary doctor but got canceled. It stormed again, and we couldn't get out till it's over. Our driveway is so plugged again even though I plowed it with the side-by-side plow last evening. There is no way I can do it again as there's nowhere to put the snow. It will have to be snow-blown with the Skidster this next time. He made an appointment with Katie tomorrow, Wednesday afternoon, so hopefully we can get out by then. Mother Nature can get over this anytime now. I can't remember a winter like this on the farm. Not exactly a good time to have one more whammy thrown our way. He has to get a COVID test by Thursday, or his surgery will be canceled. So we are praying things start to fall into place.

CHAPTER 45

My Snow Angel

I woke up this morning and just felt plain crappy, and so did Rick. It's twenty-two degrees below zero, and he just couldn't work up enough energy to snow-blow the driveway to get out for appointment, so we kinda discussed it and came up with the best idea to use his 2012 four-wheel-drive Chevy Silverado. I thought he's crazy 'cause there's two feet of snowdrifts to go through. We knew as we checked it out yesterday. Not to mention the three-foot drift in front of garage his vehicle is in. So for now that's our only choice, and I just got busy with all the other chores I needed to do. We had a nice breakfast, egg scramble and toast, together. It's always better when you have a meal together. After breakfast, I went outside and cleaned out by the back door and uncovered the cat and dog food. I scraped the ice off the heated water bowl. Then I went and fed those cats. We have left the service door open all winter so they could get to their food and water in there. Sylvester and Yeller greeted me. So they got their dose of pets and hugs.

Now to my biggest job today. I needed to go up on the house roof for the third time this year to open up the skylight windows so the snow on top of them doesn't melt from heat from the house and make ice dams. As you know, I'm half monkey and love to go up there. Thank goodness, I'm not scared of heights, and if I slid off, there's four feet of snow all around the house. We were trying to think of some sort of see-through cover to keep the snow off the windows. Rick is so handy; he'll think of something. Most years everything just melts off, and there's no problem. Well, up I went, and when I got to the first of three windows, it's covered with a foot of snow. Instead of a shovel this time, I used a brisk

265

broom. That worked great.

So I moved on to the second skylight and did the same along with making a path for water to run off the roof this spring. There was at least two feet of snow on the west side of the roof and a foot on the east side. Time to move to the east side, where only one skylight resides. This one is easier as there's a little less snow to move. I also leave the best for last.

I also noticed when I crossed the peak that the ridge vent was not open along the hole peak line of the house. I had brought a hammer to help with ice and snow around windows. The hammerhead part fit perfectly in the groove on both sides of ridge vent. Oh my god, things were looking up! That was really lucky as I piggybacked the whole length of house. It felt real good to be done with this job.

Now if Mother Nature will cooperate, it would be nice. But for now, all is good up there.

It's now 11:00 a.m., and I'm ready to sit and relax with a hot cup of coffee. just as I get off all my winter gear, we noticed there was a Skidster snowblower cleaning out the south path up on the front field. We have had workers along County Road 23 for a long time replacing the electrical poles. They had been by our house for the past week clearing spots in the ditch and fields high ground. So they had been using the end of our driveway as a turnaround. We watched for about a half hour or so, and then they were gone.

I decided to go out there and see if they left a worse mess than the drifts had made. While I was there, I'd get the mail and take Buddy for a walk. I also could find out if the drifts were worse. When I got about to the shop, I was trekking through two-foot drifts instead of one-foot ones. Buddy didn't want to follow, but I got to the end of the driveway, and the Bobcat had cleaned out the whole end of the driveway and a few yards toward the house but had left another excess foot of blown snow on top of the two feet in three nice piles. I was thinking Rick could probably use the truck and plow through with the four-wheel drive. He's done that before to make our way out the driveway.

I got the mail and went to the house. I was pretty exhausted as I was no spring chicken anymore and a little out of shape. I had not gotten my walks in or gym time in with all the things going on with Rick and all the weather circumstances. When it rains, it pours. I thought when it snowed, it snowed a lot lately.

I went back in the house and got all my duds off. I was now ready for my hot cup of coffee again. Just then, I saw that the Bobcat blower was back and, believe it or not, coming down the driveway. I thought, "Oh my god, my prayers are being answered." I had said a little prayer for someone to help us clear this snow when I was praying for Rick to be able to plow through it with his truck. I have always believed in prayer, but this was answered so swiftly. I quick got dressed in some of my winter clothes and was headed out to see if he could do the whole driveway. He was about halfway up the main part of driveway when he stopped to talk to me. He first said as he opened his heated cab window by sliding it., "Hi, how's your day going? I was just so overwhelmed I started to cry. I blurted out through my tears and choking words that he was just such a heaven-sent. I told him about Rick's appointment and how we couldn't get out to go to it. I spilled my heart on this total stranger.

I told him about Rick's hospital stay and illness. I let him know Rick was in no shape to help with the situation. He said, "It's okay, ma'am. I saw your footsteps out by the end of the road and thought maybe you were not able to get out. I thought I would check to see if you were okay." I asked his name, and he said, "I'm Dusty, and I'm in the right place at the right time." He assured me he would get it all cleared out for us. It was quite a long driveway, but he didn't care.

My heart almost did some jumping jacks. He then asked

where we piled the snow and how wide to go. I explained we went all the way around the house and clear by the doghouses and my garage. With tears rolling down my cheeks, I was showing him where and what to do. He had the sweetest Bobcat I'd ever seen with a blower way bigger than ours and tracks on it to boot.

I went into the house to tell Rick. When I saw him, he had a shit-eating grin that no one could take away. He said, "How did you talk him into doing all that?" I said I was good and was brutally honest.

I also told Rick our prayers were definitely answered. He just kept grinning and was at a loss for words as we watched Dusty do the work. I really can't ever remember Rick having a reaction like that in all the nineteen years we've been together. I could tell he was very thankful too.

I decided I better go outside to watch and guide where he needed to plow. He got to the forty-foot path to the woodpile and pointed to it. I nodded, and he cleaned a nice wide path to the woodpile. He finished that, and now we're north of our home. There were obstacles like rock gardens by the house and landscape walls as he maneuvered around. It was like he could read me like a book with just hand and head gestures. He made at least five or six rounds around the house and driveway. He also made it all wider in case we got any more snowfalls.

I'm still running on adrenaline. I went inside, and Rick and I watched from the east and south windows as he went up and down our half-mile driveway back and forth, throwing the snow forty feet to the banks. One beautiful part of all this was that it was a clear, sunny day with no wind. That hardly ever happened anytime Rick had had to blow snow. He'd been here probably an hour or more already, and Rick and I felt we should pay him for his generosity. So I dressed up a little again to catch him as he came around the house by the back door. I went out and waved and he stopped to talk.

I thanked him from Rick and me. I told him we would like to give him some money for all this. He said, and I quote, "Absolutely not." I pleaded a little, but I knew he was doing a favor, and favors are not payable. I thanked him again and told him how blessed we felt. I also said good deeds never go unnoticed. He just smiled and said, "I'll do by the shop too before I leave." He truly was a special kind of snow angel. Our prayers were answered again.

This was such a pleasant surprise, and it's so touching to know there are still people in this world that help you survive. I felt he was a wonderful good Samaritan. Thank you, Dusty, and I hope someday you will read my book so you know just how grateful we were for your generosity.

Rick decided to take my car to his appointment, which wasn't a possibility this morning. I was hoping this week just got better and better.

This week had been way better. We're hoping his COVID-19 test was negative and infection was gone. That way on Monday it would be a go for his kidney stone removal and test to be done to figure out why he kept getting stones. We had many people praying for Rick.

We got word his COVID test was negative. They still had you get one before surgery as a precaution. Safety measure for everyone.

Well, it's Monday, and we're up at 4:30 a.m. and heading to St. Cloud. We got here at 6:30 a.m., and I stayed to get him checked in. Then I went to Perkins with Maury and family and had breakfast. They told me at check-in it would be around 10:00 a.m. or 11:00 a.m. they would call me. Then I could pick him up. They called me about 10:30 a.m. and I went and got him and headed home.

He had to stop a few times to use the bathroom because when you have a stint, you feel like you gotta go even when you don't. The first night home, Rick was pretty sore and up a lot. I slept pretty well. I was so tired from the early day yesterday. I have senior meeting at 12:30 p.m. today in Verndale. Jo and I are bringing the treats. She made peanut butter rice crispy bars and chocolate chip cookies. I made a cheese tray with three kinds of cheese and got a variety of party crackers. We took turns picking each other up as we're neighbors. She turned eighty-nine this week. You'd never know she's older. She got out and did things and spent a lot of time with her kids and grandkids. It had been so fun for me to get to know the neighbors by belonging to my different clubs.

Retirement had been so good that way. Instead of having to be to work, always on time, I could pick what I was interested in doing and if I could go or not. With Rick's medical issues, it had made my life so much easier to have an option. Today at our meeting at the community center in Verndale, we had two men presenting how they make pens. These were not just any pen; they are specialty, custom-made. They got them as kits and put them together using a lathe and their expertise skills. They made them with beautiful wood of many colors as the body. Then they personalized them with making them look like the flag or a hunting rifle and more. They actually used a fake bullet for the tip and end. They were high-end for executives and businessmen. They also would make great birthday or Christmas gifts for the hard-to-buy-for person. I ordered a camouflage one for Ryan, my son, for his birthday made as a rifle style since he's my hunting partner. I thought he would love it. They were quite expensive but so unique.

Last month while at a monthly senior meeting, the lady from the *Verndale Sun* took my picture with our knitting class, and I happened to be goofing off. So I was plastered over the front page of the *Verndale Sun*.

A bunch of friends this time brought me a few copies to keep. They all thought it was a hoot. I had held the yarn up to my head, and it looked like bunny ears. I didn't know she even took the picture until I was featured in the paper. It was cute.

Rick and I went to bed early, but he was so uncomfortable. He took the stint out tonight instead of early morning. It helped with a lot of the pain. We couldn't believe how long the stint was, about a foot. No wonder he was in pain every time he got up or sat down. So he definitely slept better then. Now he didn't have to go back until March 30. That was as long as there's no problems before then.

Today was Wednesday, and we were both very tired and just starting a new puzzle with a picture of kitties. It was so cute and only 750 pieces in case spring got here early. We didn't do puzzles once it's nice outside. We would have pizza for supper as that's our tradition every week on Wednesdays. That way we didn't have to think about one day a week what we would eat. We had done that for years. Rick also made French toast for our Saturday breakfast each week!

Rick was done with antibiotics March 4. So now we would see if the infection's gone. He still had some pain, but each day got a little better. It's the weekend now, and it's way below average temperature. We had had most the winter below average. Couldn't wait until spring. I was still hauling the wood in until Rick healed up. Buddy helped me and hung right close by. Usually, I was visited by two or three cats too. They loved to jump on the wagon of wood as I loaded it.

I went to church Sunday and prayed for Rick and all the other sick people in the world. Ukraine had over 2 million people flee their country. There's been a lot of innocent lives lost already. Poland has come to the rescue of most of them. The US and other countries are helping with food, clothes, and money. What a terrible time in our history. There is talk on the news that this could turn into World War III. We sure hope not. The refugees have to be so distraught and sad. Russia is showing no mercy as on the news last night, they said a church was bombed full of innocent women and children. They thought they were safe!

It's Monday, and I went to breakfast in Henning with my Deer Creek friends I worked with over the years. It's twenty-eight miles, and we meet each Monday. I usually only go one or two times a month. I may have to rethink that because gas prices are skyrocketing from the war in Ukraine. Groceries are getting very expensive also. So we are even watching what we used to buy or if we need it or not. For instance, potatoes have gone from $2.99 or less for ten pounds to $5.97 or $7.97 at Walmart. We can afford it, but we don't have to like it.

We are half done with our new kitty puzzle. It is so colorful and fun. Thursday, I went to lunch with my good friend Ruth. We hadn't connected for quite a while. It's so fun to catch up and share pictures of our grandkids. Then I picked up groceries and got three prescriptions for the next three months for me. Rick had only one this time. He was starting to complain about pain a lot again.

He's looking kinda sick again. He got gray looking. He took a bath to help relieve the stress. I was busy cleaning the house as my daughter Amy and Jon were coming from Wisconsin. The McQuiston side of family had planned way last summer to have their winter get together in Wadena. The idea being it would be easier for Ralph since he had cancer. This way he wouldn't have to drive so far. Well, that plan didn't work out since he passed away in December. They decided at the funeral they would still come to Wadena as planned in his honor. I thought that was very nice. I planned on going to see all of them and say hi! So I've known most of them since I was eighteen right before I married Ralph. They have always been family, and they always will be. They have gone through a lot since they lost John and Ralph (his brother) within two months of each other.

My daughter Amy and Jon got there around one thirty or

so. We all had such a good visit. I miss my daughter living six hours away. I would go visit them tonight at the American Inn along with others that were here for the reunion. The kids left around three, and like almost immediately Rick had such terrible pain. This time it was on his right side. I kept asking him, "Are you sure?" because the surgery eleven days ago was on the left. He said no, it's definitely on the right side, radiating around to the front. He kept asking for more blankets as he was shivering. So I put more blankets on him to help. He just kept getting worse. He was finally jerking and shaking so bad I thought he might be having a seizure. His mind was all over the place also. He'd ask for something like a drink and then would say, "Don't leave me alone." I knew something was wrong. I went into care taking mode. Like what to do first and what to do at all. I asked him if he needed an ambulance. He didn't want that. He could not get up out of his chair to use the bathroom, so we tried the urinal. That did not go well. I finally assessed the situation and decided he had to go to the hospital in Staples.

So I went with our plan of Vernon to come help get him into my car. First, I called the hospital and let them know we were coming to the ER. That way his records are pulled, and it saves time. They asked me all the usual questions and lastly about how long until we would get there. I said I was calling our son to help load him, so I wasn't sure. I said thirty minutes or more. Then secondly, I called Vernon. Luckily, he was working his Staples job and was on his way home. He got here in about twenty minutes. Bless his heart! He came in, and it took twenty more minutes just to get him up and out of the chair and to the car. He pretty much could lift Rick's weight, which I couldn't anymore. Well, I had already put his shoes and socks on. Thank goodness. I had his jacket ready, but he couldn't or wouldn't put it on. We just wrapped a throw blanket around him and got him to the car. Well, it took another twenty minutes to get him positioned in the seat. He couldn't bend his head to get in the car as the pain must have been taking over. So Vernon finally kept trying to get his butt farther on the car seat and his legs in front of him. Finally we got him in the car. I ran into the house and shut our Swiss steak supper off. I ran back to the car, and away we went. Before Vernon got here, I had warmed up the car and parked it by the closest door for him. That helped for his shivering. So twenty miles later we're in the ER at Staples. Visitors were still limited, so Vernon went home to wait to hear what was wrong. They got Rick some paper pants to wear and started collecting urine and blood for testing. This started all about five or so. I texted Shona and my kids to let them know. I always do that in case something were to go really wrong.

Now we're waiting. Time goes really slow when you have to wait. The doctor came in and said they needed a CAT scan. So they did that. It only took eight to ten minutes to do but a half hour or so to read results. It's now six thirty, and the doctor came back with not so good news. Rick has a 6 mm kidney stone on the right kidney, and it's pressing on the bladder. She said, "I'm sending you to St. Cloud Hospital right now by ambulance." Well, he wasn't fond of that idea. He kept insisting that I could transport him. She said, "Rick, you are too unstable and sick for Sharol to take you." He wanted to wait till morning, but she insisted he go now. So he was transported by ambulance and there by 8:30 p.m. He got some strong morphine for the trip but said it was still like a lumber wagon. I was so relieved; I didn't have to take him. It was the best decision and took the pressure off me. They would call me when he got there. So now I planned to go early in the morning because he couldn't have visitors until eight anyway. This gave me time to go home, pack, take care of the animals, etc. I let Maury know I might need a place to stay again. He was always so welcoming, and it's so nice for me not to have to get a motel room.

When I got home, I got everything planned for the next three or four days, I figured. The kids called from the reunion and asked me to come in town and visit. So I drove to Wadena ten miles away and had a good visit along with venting to them. I guess we all could use support. I definitely welcomed that tonight. I only stayed a little over an hour but got to see a lot of family.

I woke up at 6:00 a.m., and I had fed the animals, packed a cooler with water and juice, and left by 7:00 a.m. It was fifteen degrees out, but the sun was shining, which always helped the mood. Rick called on my cell phone and said surgery was scheduled for 10:00 a.m. I really couldn't go up to the hospital until they called that he's back in his room. Meanwhile, I made it to Maury and Evy's house. We had coffee, and then Jackie called. She is Evy's daughter. Emma was home from college. We told them I wouldn't be going to the hospital until they called me. Well, they were going to the St. Cloud Christian bookstore and asked me along. I went, and I found an angel visor clip that read, *"Never drive faster than your guardian angel can fly."* It also glowed in the dark. Emma had one, and now I had one too. I love *it*.

We then went to the crossroads mall to Macy's and Penny's and a few other stores. It was so nice to spend a few hours with them. I also found a Christmas springbok puzzle. They were the best-fitting puzzle pieces and our favorite brand. Then at Macy's I found some therapeutic coolant pillows. They were on sale for less than half price. I hoped I liked them as the pillow I had wasn't working for me. Time would tell. We really didn't have stores to shop around Wadena for stuff like that. So it was a lucky find. Around eleven fifteen, the doctor called me, and Rick was out of surgery, and he said it went well. They got the stone and some fragments from the last surgery too. Jackie and Emma dropped me off at Maury's, and I loaded my goodies in the trunk and headed one mile away to the hospital. I did stop on the way and got a Subway sandwich. I had to also take care of me and eat on time because of my diabetes.

When I got up to room N417, Rick was doing really good. They brought his lunch in, and he ate some of that. Their food got no prizes according to him. About 1:00 p.m., the RN came in and let us know he could go home today. Well, this was a first but so welcomed. We all knew you got a lot more sleep at home than in the hospital. Last time with stone removed, it was four days.

Now they were getting things ready for him to be released. I called Maury and told him the good news. We needed some of that right now. She said by two thirty everything should be ordered to take home with us. He needed at-home instructions, antibiotics, and pain meds. Well, another hour went by, and she had come into our room once more and said the pharmacy was running behind. I would say so. Finally at four, they suggested we go to the drive-through pharmacy. She said it might be faster.

We now realized we could have been home already if we would have gotten to leave at two thirty. We were one and a half hours from St. Cloud. So we got him loaded and went to the pharmacy on the other end of the building. The nice young pharmacist said it's going to be a wait. We must have looked exhausted or something. I politely asked how long. She said five to ten minutes. Phew! That's nothing after this long. We finally got his prescription. We made it home by six. We had supper, Swiss steak, from the night before. Boy was that good. Rick hadn't eaten a decent meal since Friday at noon. He was 95 percent improved and told me to go spend time with my kids Joey, Amy, and Ryan and the others at the Wadena motel. I was hesitant, but I did go into town and visited. I stayed about an hour and a half. It started snowing pretty heavy so that was my cue to get home. It was hard to see the road, but I drove slowly, and with the dims on, I could manage. It actually was less scary than on the way into Wadena. I had seen nine deer along the drive. They must have been out and about looking for food. It's common to see a few, but not nine.

Rick slept pretty well, but with the stint in, he felt like going but couldn't go much. I got up Sunday and went to church with my church family. There again, they are such good support system. We were all there for one another. It was such a blessing. We had soup for lunch and were waiting for Vernon and Amber to stop by this afternoon.

This was the way it went when problems arose with our health. I'm not going to go into detail like the last few months as it is an ongoing part of our lives. I felt compelled to journal day to day with issues to help everyone realize we will all have struggles at different times in our lives. With all our support systems in place, our kids, church family, and friends, it keeps us up beat and hopeful. I do keep quite busy in between appointments and hospital stays. I have always made time for myself even in the stressful times. The best part of all this is it brings us closer to one another each time a new issue arises. We are both so happy we have each other and can take care when needed. In sickness or in health, love prevails. I feel for people that have nobody to be with them, especially when they're sick.

It's March 22, 2022, and it's snowing out. This week will be below average again. It's been that way for many months. We did have a couple days of warmer to help the snowmelt. But there's a chance of snow two out of the next five days this week. We know it's spring though as the robins returned today. That is always a sure sign it's going to warm up. The forecast might be rain some of these days. Rick and I took the side by side out yesterday to try to plow the path to the river. It just rolled the two feet of snow up into a gunky ball and stopped us dead. So we raised the plow and just four-wheeled through it. It was so fun spinning and breaking through the wet, slushy, heavy snow. I thought sure a few times we would get stuck, but that four-wheel drive really pushed through. We had fun and couldn't wait to ride the trails through our fields and forests as it warmed up.

Today was a new day as I called it. So we finished the puzzle and baked cookies. We're still in the thirty to forty degrees and teens at night. I'm tired of winter and so looking forward to spring. It had not been very much like spring here. This last week in March had been awful. We've had two snowfalls and rain and sleet. We went to see a movie Saturday for date night. It had Sandra Bullock in it. She is one of my favorite actresses in *The Lost City*. I loved it, and Rick was okay with it. I love corny comedies with a twist of a love story. Like Hallmark is my channel, and Rick likes action flicks. Guess that's kinda typical in relationships. It creates a good balance. We have tried walking, but we have a foot of hard snow on our trail when we went this week. We kept breaking through, and it took a toll on our back issues. So I hadn't walked for a few days. My body said to take it easy, so I did.

It's April 1 today (April Fools), and I always tried to plan a joke on Rick. I just told him there's a deer in the yard. Of course, he did look and knew right away I was lying. Still fun every year to try. I was very believable as I really don't like lying ever.

Rick and I were going on a lunch date today with Sandy, Dorothy, and Jason to El Mariachi, a wonderful Mexican restaurant in Wadena. It's so hard to pick from the Mexican menu as it all looked so good. It was very good food. Then we were getting our weekly groceries at Walmart. Rick would shop for them while I got some pictures off the phone camera. I needed to add one more page to my grandson River's finished book (I thought). He went to Washington, DC, on a band/choir trip. River was one of the students to be picked to present a wreath in honor of the fallen soldiers. So of course, I got some pictures off my camera. Looks like they had a lot of good memories to cherish. It's so nice to be back to our normal everyday things.

It's the last week of March 2022 and very blustery. This spring is not a good spring. We've had snow in small amounts, which is not helping to melt the foot or so in some places around the farm. Our walking path is still covered with ice and snow. It continues to snow into April, but we know it will get nice sooner than later. We have two appointments for Rick in St. Cloud, so it's a good time as we can't do any yard work yet or flower gardens and all the spring fun stuff, things we both look forward to.

My friend Joanie called and asked me if I could go with five other Deer Creek friends to a dinner show at Chanhassen Theatre in the cities. I looked at my calendar, and it was clear that Wednesday so I got to go. I love spur- of-the-moment outings. She knew that. Another couple had to cancel, so she asked Barb and I from our breakfast group on Mondays. She was available too. Brian and Sandy are our chauffeurs with Alyn and Joanie along too.

It's April 6 and snowing out again. The roads are pretty slick especially in our yards. I drove to Joanie and Alyn's farm to catch my ride. Alyn and Brian took the front seat since they're the only guys along and like to guy- talk. Barb and I got the middle seat in the SUV. I get kinda claustrophobic in the back seat of any car, not sure why, but I feel closed in especially on longer trips. Thank goodness I have great friends that understand. So Sandy and Joanie sat back there. They're the rowdy ones, so they get along great, haha! I can't wait to see what's in store for us today.

It started out on a sad note because one of our good breakfast coffee club gals passed away unexpectedly in her home. Carol was eighty years old and such a sweet lady. She will be missed by all of us. So our first order of business was discussing getting her a bouquet of flowers from our group. Joanie offered to pick them up, and we all pitched in some money. The funeral is Friday, but I can't go as we have an appointment for Rick in St. Cloud for a heart procedure.

We all got belted up, and we're off! Our route started in Deer Creek and I- 94 right to the Chanhassen Theater. Oh my goodness, what a crew. We laughed, we cried, and told a lot of stories. You can't beat good company and good friends like them.

When arriving, we were escorted to our reserved seats. We got here about eleven fifteen and the dining table was beautiful with very comfortable chairs. We had several choices off the menu, which were included in our dinner ticket. I had the haddock with rice pilaf and seasoned sautéed fresh vegetables. Three in the group ordered that. Joanie opted for a large baked breast of chicken and the guys ordered chicken strips with French fries. Some had drinks, but I just had water and milk. The service was great, and we all loved this great food.

The show *Footloose* is now starting. It's a musical, and it was just so uplifting and wonderful. I would go see it again in a minute. I hope all my kids and grandkids can take this one in someday. The talent of these young and old performers was incredible. It was a great blessing to spend with good friends and good food. I love days like this.

Now we're heading home. We will take the same route. We were all getting hungry as it's five thirty or so when we got to Nelson. We stopped at a hamburger bar and grill. I had a turkey club with fries and some had cheeseburgers and fries and Reubens. Of course, we had to have an hors d'oeuvre, so Barb ordered a large order of onion rings. I could only eat half of my sandwich as I got full on the onion rings. We also hit happy hour, so some of our group got buy one, get one free drinks. Needless to say, the rest of the ride home was with a lot of laughter, which is good for the soul. Thanks to my friends for a great experience and memory.

It's Thursday, and I do have a day planned with my good

friend and neighbor Norma and her daughter Carla. We had gone out for Carla's birthday a while ago and had so much fun. Norma decided that's what she wanted to do too. This time instead of westward, we went south to Alexandria, which is one hour south of us. She wants to eat at either the Angelina's, an Italian restaurant, or the Depot, a steak for her birthday overlooking the water.

We started out by going to a couple thrift stores, and we found a few items. Then at noon we opted for the Italian place. It was really good. Now we were shopping at target. I hadn't been to that store in years. I found Rick a couple under armor shirts, his favorite. We checked out a new thrift shop, and it was so nice. I found a great plaque for our bathroom as I'm sick of the pictures that are in there. The new one says, "Life is not measured by the breaths you take but by the moments that take your breath away." I just love that saying, and now I get reminded each and every day. I am so lucky to find things like this and to try to live by them.

We are all drained, so we decided to buy dinner for Norma at the depot place. Since it's her birthday, she can pick anything off the menu for half price. What a great deal. She opted for a steak and the works. I had chicken wings with honey mustard sauce. Great choice, and Carla had a chicken salad. We are all enjoying the fact we can go to restaurants again. Two years of the pandemic was enough. We are all hoping the businesses can recoup some of what they lost with COVID. It's another memorable day with good friends and good food!

We went to St. Cloud for Rick's appointment. It went really fast. We called Maury up and met him for lunch at Jimmy's, an old Irish pub. He had eaten, but Rick and I had the fish special. Many places serve fish on Fridays during Lent. We had a good visit with him. Still missing my sister Evy so much, especially when you know she would have spent time with us today.

Rick and I have been trying to walk a short distance each day, but it's still not in the ideal conditions. We try to time it between rain, sleet, and snow and rough terrain. I had a dentist appointment and cleaning on Monday, and yes, I need another crown as my forty-year-old fillings are giving out. This one is cracked, and a piece is missing. It doesn't hurt or bother, so I will get it done in fall. We finished another 750-piece puzzle and now are refusing to do any more. We usually are done in February, but this winter just won't quit.

Easter has come and gone. We spent the day at home and made T-bone steak on the grill. You just can't beat that. Then a walk in the snow, coming down in just breathtaking flakes. This time of year, those snowflakes are bigger and wetter. Our path is still not clear, but we meander around it on the dry spots. Buddy is loving the river, which has opened up to its natural beauty. The first time he checked out the water, he yelped and ran back to us. It totally was a shock as he didn't expect it to be that cold. He has gotten used to it the last few days.

My good homemaker friends had their annual garage sale. Norma and I went to it, and we always find some good buys. They have the first sale of the year, and it's always in a heated garage as the weather is so unpredictable. It was cold this year.

Our grandson Isaiah and Tasha bought their first home by Wadena this week. I got the grand tour, and it is really a very nice home. We are so happy for them. It's Ryan's forty-second birthday this weekend, and he and Tena have been celebrating. I am definitely feeling older as my kids age, but we all know we have to expect that.

I am cleaning closets and drawers in preparation of our garage sale in June. I love doing sales and downsizing every year. Since I've lost weight from getting on diabetes meds, I have a lot of clothes that are too big for me. It's fun though 'cause I get new stuff in place of them.

Norma always helps me with the sale and puts a few goodies on it from her stash. She sells plants and has such a green thumb.

Rick and I went to the cozy theater Friday night for date night. We saw *Father Stu*, which I really liked. It was about a rebel guy who wants to turn his life around. He decided to become a priest, which presents a lot of obstacles in his way. It is based on a true story, which will touch your heart. A must-see.

My niece Brenda came to stay with us. We love having Brenda here with us. She is just like a daughter. She has stayed many times over the years. She goes to workshops and trainings in Staples for her teaching curriculum. I used to go with when I was working at WDC. It was always so fun and a good time to learn together. The last two years were canceled due to COVID-19, but now they are back on track. Gabi, her daughter, came to be with us for supper too. Also one of my favorites. We visit and reminisce and just catch up on everything. We may have stayed up past my bedtime, but it's so worth it. We always lose track of time when we're together, and I love that.

I got my haircut today and have been going to a girl in Verndale. She knows my hair now and cuts it so nice. I miss going to Amber, but she's working full-time somewhere else. I took my neighbor Norma to a spring tea on Thursday at the VFW. It was the home council for homemakers that put it on for all the homemaker groups. It was very nice with tea and brunch service to all of us. They had hired Erik for the entertainment. He is a local singer and band player. Norma and I love his music. He played a lot of oldies but goodies. The council had a short program for us also. What a fun day.

I love this time of year as the auctions sales have started. Rick and I went this Friday to look around to see what they had on the Verndale sale this year. I will go tomorrow to bid on anything we find of interest. We did find a couple park benches I want. They would look beautiful down by the river. They had a few piles of lumber, but not very much.

Now it's Saturday, April 30, and I'm heading to the Verndale auction. It is raining again and not supposed to let up all day. Our weather has not been springlike at all. We have not had any average temperature days for months. It's like ten degrees or more below what it should be. We know it has to get better as summer is around the corner. Let's hope anyway!

Well, everything is going quite high this year. The park benches I wanted went for $175 and $150. I can buy a new one for that. So I passed on them. Then I ran into Gabi and Austin again this year. So we visited and had lunch together. There's nothing better than auctions, hot dogs, and fries.

I also ran into Randy, Rick's cousin, and visited for a while. He caught me up on how David, another cousin, is doing. He is recovering from his strokes. It's slow progress but going forward. I also ran into Dylan and his sister. They had my great-grandbaby Emma with them. She is so cute and such a good baby. She was born in November, so this was her first auction sale. She loved the crowd. Alyssa, my granddaughter, wasn't with this time. It ended up I bid on a few items, but I did not come home with anything. First time ever!

I had church at 9:00 a.m., and there were only twenty people today. It's getting less and less in our little country church. I love Hope Chapel and hope it doesn't close. My week is pretty busy starting with Rick's birthday on Monday, May 2.

I went to breakfast in Henning, Minnesota, with my WDC retirees and brought an ooey, gooey, caramel roll fresh out of the oven home to Rick. We are going out for dinner with friends on Saturday for his birthday.

Tuesday is my Verndale senior meeting. I picked Jo up to ride to the meeting. We are ordering from the Galley, a new little café in Verndale. I got a California burger and french fries. It was good but not real warm. They had to bring twenty-five orders to the fire hall, where we meet. Pretty hard to keep it all hot. We had lunch, then our meeting. We made plans to go to a sculpture park in Vining, Minnesota, this month. Then we'll have lunch at a place in that town.

It's Wednesday, and Dorla and Carl are coming from Mankato, Minnesota, to visit us. They will spend a couple days in Wadena at the motel and coming out here for a few meals. I'm making sandwiches, fresh veggies, and angel food cake with strawberries for Rick's birthday, and Dorla brought four different kinds of salad. My favorite was the crab salad. We always have a great visit, and they like to go for walks on the farm. They are heading to Bemidji for a graduation ceremony.

Thursday this week, I have our last homemakers gathering. We are meeting at the Hub in Sebeka, Minnesota, for lunch. Then we end our year until September by heading to the Amish greenhouse by Sebeka. I get my geraniums there as they are so beautiful. Of course, I always find a few other flowers I can't pass up. I got a couple tomato plants there also.

Friday we just had steaks for supper and caught a movie on Netflix. Saturday I went to another auction a few miles from us. There weren't very many in attendance, but I spend a few hours and bid on a couple tractor seats. We plan on putting them down on some stump by the river. I got them really at a reasonable price, so I was quite thrilled! Then at 5:00 p.m., we jumped in the car and went to Hilltop in Hubbard for dinner with two other couples. Tim, Brenda, and Rick and Deb. We all got quite full, so we took Rick's birthday dessert home and had that later. The best caramel cheesecake ever! The only thing missing were Bill and Becky, who were our neighbors for several years. They moved back to Oregon a few years ago. Becky is Brenda's sister and reminds me of the good old times. Sure do miss them.

It's Sunday, and as you can see, our weeks keep us pretty busy. Mother's Day is always special. The kids all phone home to talk, including our foster kids from the past. It was so nice to hear from so many. Then Rick takes me to a greenhouse by Staples, Minnesota, Rosenthal's, to get our garden plants and flowers. This is one of my favorite outings. I am never disappointed. It also gets us moving to get our garden in, but it is getting harder and harder to do the tilling and marking the rows. Not to mention the digging and planting it all.

We are downsizing some, but as we planted, we both wanted some of everything. We went from thirty-six tomato plants in 2021 to twenty-four this year. Also twenty pepper plants to sixteen this year. It's a start. We got it done in two days and just in time for two to three days of a steady rain. What great timing. God is good!

I also went to some garage sales this week. I got a nice white bench from a good friend's sale. Rick had to sturdy it up and revamped it a little. It looks great by a big white birch tree facing the Leaf River in each direction. We definitely captured the beauty of nature from this spot. The eagles were flying over while the geese stood across the river staying safe. The swift rapidly flowing water gushed over the logs and rocks that had fallen prey to the river.

Rick and I went to Randall, Minnesota, to a Red Wing shoe store today. We got him a pair of good hiking boots and a pair of tennis shoes. He has always bought his shoes there. They are the best, and hopefully it will help when we walk. His old ones were making his ankles and knees hurt. We both feel so good taking our walks each day. It's our special time together.

Rick also sold his white tractor to Gabi and Austin. She's my great niece. They have a farm by Nimrod, Minnesota, and they needed a big tractor for a rock field. They took the

Oliver plow that went with it. We kinda hated to see it go, but we hardly use it at all. It's better if someone will get some use out of it. They came in the afternoon, but as you know, it all takes time to get started, hooked up, and pulled out. The tractor started perfectly, but the big tires needed air, and they checked the fluids, then on to the plow, which had been sitting for twenty to twenty-five years in the row of old equipment. First to hook up the pressure hoses to lift it. They were pretty worn and took quite a few tries to work. When they did work, they sprayed out fluid in a lot of places, but they got it to lift up and to stick a pin to hold it up there. It has two tires to roll on. One looked pretty good, the other pretty much exploded as they pulled it a few blocks to the shop to air up. So now they need to take the spare off the stand and replace the torn up one. We definitely feel like a typical farmer today.

Austin brought his brother with to help, thank goodness. You can tell they know what to do with each set back.

Gabi and I just pretty much watched as we were parts and tool runners. I love my Polaris days. They finally got it all hooked up and headed to Nimrod farm by 8:00 p.m. It took them about an hour before we heard they made it there okay.

Our dog Buddy has been itching his fur a lot. He now has sores on his back, and they are getting bigger. It's Thursday, so I figured I better call our Staples vet. They are so good there. They said, "Can you be here by two forty-five?" It gave us a half hour to get there as it's twenty miles. We were ready to go on our walk, but Buddy takes priority.

We got him there, and he did an exam. He has what's called hot spots. The vet said he has a very bad infection from a tick or insect bite. It had gone internally and was spreading. So Buddy had to stay at the clinic overnight because they had to put him out to clean and cleanse all his wounds after shaving his heavy fur off. So we left him in their care. It was a quiet night back at our house. Rick and I both missed him. He is such a honey of a dog. Next day we got him in the car, but on the way out, he jerked his leash while I was holding onto him. My back got pulled out, so I am pretty sore. It doesn't take much for my osteoporosis to act up when my bones get strained. So this weekend, I'm using heat and ice to feel comfortable. It usually only lasts a few days, thank goodness. Rick had to do all the mowing this weekend as bouncing around on the rider would not be good for me right now.

We had tornado weather tonight also. Due to this, we now have four deer stands out of commission. The mansion landed on the edge of the river down a steep bank. We think we can save parts from all of them and make at least one good one. I'm kinda thinking Ryan and my hunting days may be over. I love the hunt, so we will see by fall. I'm keeping busy with Buddy's prescriptions. He has to take antibiotics, two big red pills, for ten days. He also has prednisone to help dry up the lesions. We have *Bravecto* to treat to help to ward off the ticks and fleas. Also heartworm medicine. He is quite lethargic and drinking a lot of water. He is happy to be home though.

This week has been pretty low-key. I missed church on Sunday and breakfast with the girls on Monday. I don't feel I can drive safely when my back is sore. Tuesday, Rick and I went to get groceries and ate at the China buffet for lunch. He drove, so that helps me a lot. With ice and heat, it should get better soon. Rick has a procedure on Friday in St. Cloud. He needs a driver for on the way home. I should be good by then. It turned out I couldn't drive for him, so he took himself. It went real good, and he is on the mend. It's been a week, and he is doing good. Our Modern medicine is advanced now. We are lucky to live in the world with all the preventive procedures and breakthroughs they have made. He has another procedure in June to help prevent strokes and blood clots in his heart due to his A-fib. Then hopefully he'll be in good shape to go camping and make a bus trip. The pandemic has ramped up some, but we can still go without masks except if you fly somewhere. We are home for Memorial Day weekend and just doing small projects around the house and yard. The weather is pretty normal finally, so it's fun to just enjoy the great outdoors.

Monday, May 30, 2022. It's Memorial Day, and we are just staying home. We are going to go get groceries at Walmart after lunch. It's kinda a dreary day, and we had half-inch rain last night with thunderstorms. No damage this time. Supposed to storm about four or five this afternoon. We were leaving Walmart, and there was billowing black smoke coming from the road we go home on. Traffic was already backed up for blocks. Fire trucks and emergency vehicles were sounding from all directions. We were stuck in traffic for quite a while. The closer we got to County Road 4, the more smoke there was. People were all over the place trying to get close. We were just trying to get home. When we got to Ryan and Tena's house, the fire was in Minnesota Valley right behind their place. They were in the yard watching all the commotion. This is an irrigation business. First reports were that propane tanks had exploded and started the blaze. We managed to slowly get through the traffic and home. The police had shut down Highway 10 as the fire was a danger to vehicles there. We got home, put all our groceries away, and were just settled in for a nap.

All at once the sky turned a gray-greenish color. It got real still out and eerie. Then the alerts came for our area across our cell phones and cable TV. It didn't look good. There were tornado watches and severe thunderstorms. Around 4:30 p.m., Tena and the grand girls came out to seek shelter with us. They had been evacuated from their house by the fire. Ryan was across the road at Mason Brothers at his work. He had to go back in because of the threat of the fire so close to their business. There were other houses and group homes evacuated also.

The twins were in quite a panic, and Tena was worn to a frazzle. They sat in the pantry here with blankets because that's the inner room with no windows in our house. Our A-frame has many windows, so we have to stay away from outside walls. Everyone was on their cell phones watching the storm and alerts.

Ryan kept in touch to let us know how it was ten miles away in Wadena. We heard power lines were down, and power was out in areas. Now the storm has went from quiet to full-blown rain, hail, and wind. I had to keep busy, so I baked some good old brownies. At this point, all we can do is hope for the best and ride it out. It's now 5:15 p.m. and a lot worse. Like Tena said, at least we are all together.

Buddy, our dog, was so nervous, and they had brought Stinky out in its cat carrier to be with all of us. It's a pretty intense storm, but I always feel pretty safe here. By 5:30 p.m. it was getting light out to the southwest, so we knew most had passed. Tena and the girls headed back to town about sixish and could go to their house because the storm helped with putting the fire out. Thank goodness! We'll learn more of all the damage tomorrow. Eagle Bend, Forado, Hinkley, and Deer River were some of the town that had tornado damage. We were spared this time.

CHAPTER 46

Fostering Heroes

We had a pleasant surprise today. Two of our foster kids came to visit on this long Memorial Day weekend. Ryan and Tena came out with them. Ashley and Wayne are brother and sister, whom we had as foster children as they grew up at different times. It was so nice to see them catch up on some long overdue years. Wayne's wife, Carri, was with him. Ashley now has a little boy that's seventeen months old. He was a real cutie and came right to me. Abel is a sweet little guy. I made my day to see all of them. I am so proud of the people they have become. They fill my heart with so much love. It's a great feeling to know they still respect and care about us after all these years. We took a walk and went down by the river, saw the hunting shacks, and accessed the damage to the deer stands. They offered to help upright them when the time comes that we're ready to repair all of them or make a couple good ones. What a great day for all of us.

I want to interject here how it is in my eyes to foster others. The first step is a phone call from social services. They ask if we'd be willing to care for that child or children. We got all the details and usually have a day or two before we make a decision. We know the age, sex, and a few details of the situation. Our family talks it over and decides if we can handle the age and problems that may arise. We almost always said yes.

I would normally take a few of my earned days from work to settle them into our home. Our own kids would usually be in school while I picked up our new family member. When they would come home, everyone got to meet them. That was always exciting for all of us. Sometimes there were tears or anger as the reality of a new family and home set in.

Sometimes it went smoothly.

The first night is always the hardest. We would always try to stick to our routine to help smooth things. We would eat supper, have playtime or family fun, just watching TV or a movie, then bedtime by 8:00 p.m. on a school night. Six o' clock comes early to get four or five kids ready. The next day was going to school with them and finding their teacher and room. The nice part is a classroom's love to see a new student join them. I would then meet with a social worker to go over their foster plan before school got out. Just a few hours of my time but so necessary.

I also would go pick up essentials as most came with nothing but clothes on their back. I would go to Walmart to get clothes, PJs, socks and underwear, shoes, coat, or any necessity. Sometimes social workers had things at the office that were donated that would fit a child. One thing I remember from our foster parents' association lessons was they needed a small suitcase or backpack. Most were used to brown paper bags or trash bags to hold their belongings. That came across as being trash. They all loved having their own bag for visits or outings. How such a little thing could mean so much!

The first few days pass, and they now have gone over rules and expectations. We also would let them know of the consequences. We had basic rules like getting up when supposed to, eating together, and taking showers or baths as needed. You would not believe how hard some of these simple everyday things were for them. Schedules were not in their vocabulary. I found in our forty years of fostering that charts and doing incentives worked wonders for most. An example would be if you eat with us at supper thrice in a row, you get an ice cream treat. It didn't take them long to see we followed through with what we had told them.

There was always backsliding, mainly after they would have a visit with their family. But in a few days, they would bounce back to us. If there were court days, that could set some back for a week or more. That was always upsetting, and understandably so. There was always a honeymoon period of about a month. Then the true colors would come out.

I always felt they were torn children and scarred in so many ways. It's hard to comprehend. Some came with diagnosis of ADHD, autism, and OCD, which is obsessive compulsive disorder. Most had some form of bipolar disorder or depression. Labels never scared us though because knowing they now have food, shelter, and safety with love, it could change. So many cases it did. Love and care go a long way.

We had ages of two years old all the way up to seventeen years old. So of course, each child and age would bring different challenges. They would be in our home anywhere from a few days to several years.

Every step has been an adventure for them and for us. We always knew when they had turned a corner or matured when they started caring about themselves and others in our family along with their own biological family.

All the kids were so different and unique. I just hope we made a difference in their lives in a small or big way. Because of confidentiality and privacy, I purposely didn't use any specific child to write about. A few have been mentioned as they are still a big part of our life to this day.

When a foster child would leave, it was always so hard on our family and on them. It was bittersweet, though as many were adopted or went home for good.

I wouldn't change a day in the life of all these kids we cared for. I learned as much from them as I hope they did from us. They are heroes in my eyes. They have survived what was dealt them in their formative years, most of which was out of their control.

Many have made strides I couldn't have imagined. God

SHAROL MASON

bless all our foster children. Three of our foster kids wanted to share their foster life with me. They write from the heart, and it sounds like we helped them in their journey.

Wayne's Memories

My name is Wayne Vaughan, and this is how I came to be a foster child with Sharol and Ralph McQuiston. When I was around the age of four or five years, I was removed from my biological parents due to physical abuse. I was placed with the McQuiston family the second time I was taken away from my biological parents. I lived with them until I was nine and half years old. I was adopted by some of my relatives. I can remember showing up to the house and being very scared and very shy, not completely knowing what was going on and not trusting many people. After the homelife I was in, Sharol was the first person I met, and she showed me a room that was all mine. I didn't have to share my room. She had toys and new clothes for me that she went out and bought for me before I arrived. Sharol and Ralph came into my room the first night I was there and told me that room was my safe place and that no one would ever hurt me again. If I didn't want anyone in there, that was my choice, and they would respect that. It didn't take me very long to warm up to both Sharol and Ralph and the kids and grandkids that were always around. One of the best memories I had while I was a foster kid was that they never once treated me different than their own children and grandchildren. I was welcomed in with open arms. I learned so many different skills to be the proper gentleman.

One of my best memories is when Sharol would

SURVIVING LIFE AND
C🌐VID-19

294

take me and Forrest up to her brother's house to play. They had a Shetland pony up there, and I fell in love with horses because of that time we went up there. After Mom's craft fair that she would do, I remember one time while we were up at her brother's house, it was the middle of winter, Forrest and their two twin girls and I went outside to play in the snow. I know I got mad at one of the twins, and I whitewashed her, and she went inside crying, and I got into trouble, but after Mom sat me down and explained to me why that was not okay to do that to little girls, I learned to respect people more.

I can remember one night I was sound asleep, and I heard a weird noise outside of my bedroom window. So I looked out, and there was a horse trailer with another trailer behind it. Come to find out it was another relative of Mom's. He had two giant mules and the wagon that they pulled. We ended up putting them in a pen in the backyard. I was so excited that it took Mom forever to get me to calm down enough to go back to bed.

When I was about nine years old, I was having home visits with some of my biological family. I know after a few visits I told Mom that I didn't want to be around them. I didn't feel safe. She told my social work this information. I found out later that not only did Mom and Dad want to adopt me, but they were also my best friend's parents. Also other biological family that I didn't know about. After a few months, I was adopted by my biological aunt and uncle that had three boys of their own. I don't think I would have turned out to be the person I am today if it wasn't for Mom and Dad. They had a huge impact on my life, and I don't think that I will ever be able to repay them for that.

Response to Wayne

Ralph and I did try hard to teach you love and respect. I'm so glad you are part of our life. You were a joy to have and always learned from your mistakes. That's all a parent can expect. You have grown into such a good person and have made good boundaries in your life. I'm glad you felt you were treated just like our own. I love that you went into trucking and get to see our beautiful country. Keep Carri close and know you can come home anytime.

Love,
Mom

Janet's Memories

I came to know Sharol in my sophomore year of high school 1977. I had been in a previous foster home for three months, but they had to move out of state. I had an older sister who moved out and left by the time I was seven in 1968. I had hoped I could stay with her, but she was in Oregon. They (social services) would not let me stay with my grandparents because they were in a different county, so I am glad I had a family that accepted me and that I could graduate with my friends that I had been with for four years. I was lucky that I was in two great foster homes. I had heard horror stories of other foster children being in homes that were horrible and abusive. I had a great home with Sharol and Ralph, and we had fun as a family.

Sharol and her husband, Ralph, had two bio kids and one foster child, Robin, when I came to stay with them. Robin had gotten into trouble and ended up in their home. When I came, we had to share a room. My first real encounter after our meeting and tour of the house was a stern rule: "Do not smoke in the house and don't hide it if you do." I guess Robin was smoking and hid the lit cigarette under a pillow when Sharol came up in the room. The pillow started smoking and almost caught fire. I didn't smoke cigarettes, so I wasn't worried. Robin ran away two months later, and I had the room to myself for two years.

Sharol and Ralph's bio kids Amy and Joey were young when I lived there. Joey was three, and Amy was nine months. Sharol learned she could trust me with the kids. I felt like I was a free babysitter, but what teen doesn't. If I went somewhere, Sharol asked me to take Amy with me. We shared a birthday, and I loved her! I loved being a big sister. I had always wanted a younger sibling. She was so cute. At times people thought Amy was mine, and I was a teen mom. Looking back as an adult, Sharol trusted me with something special to her. That meant a lot to me. Also I am sure she wanted alone time with Joey. Joey was a lot of fun. It was hard for me to help him learn potty training when I was a sitter and he was a stander. Everyone sat down but his father. One time as I was going to the bathroom, he was beside me and had stood and urinated on the floor while watching me.

I was used to being alone, so I was pretty independent and really didn't understand what a family dynamic was. Sharol was six or seven years older than me, so I didn't see her as a parental figure. I think she tried to approach me as more of a friend than a parent. I don't think that worked for me, so I was a bit rebellious. She never explained her life but told me she understands being young and on her own. I went through a lot being labeled as a foster child.

People thought it was because I was a troublemaker and that was the reason I did not live with my parents. Sharol tried to help me with that anxiety. She said that you know what the truth is, so do not let it bother you. If I remember right, she stood up for me to one of her friends who was judgmental, and that helped me feel she had my back. I had some issues talking to my family. She was patient and let me share when and if I wanted to.

I have some good memories. A funny one is a time when we went camping in Bronson, Minnesota. Robin was still with us. Sharol and Ralph had other friends that either visited or camped with us. Robin and I were fifteen and older. The adults wanted to go off together, and Robin and I babysat all the kids while they were gone. When they came back, a park ranger was with them. They had been skinny-dipping and were caught. The park ranger escorted them back to get their IDs. It was like the first couple of months of living with them, so I thought, "Great role models." They didn't tell us about it, but one of the friends told us what had happened. That was my first camping trip, but I have continued to enjoy the outdoors and camping since then.

When I first lived there, her husband, Ralph, didn't talk to me for months. I thought he hated me. We later bonded over football of all things. He worked at an Arctic Cat, so we were able to ride demo snowmobiles that he kept there in the winter. He got in a bad accident and broke his leg while snowmobile riding.

Sharol and I bonded while riding snowmobiles. We had a great time. Anytime she asked me I was right behind her. One time we went down a ditch to get to the river. It was deeper and steeper than she realized. We slammed down hard, and I landed on top of her as she hit the handle bars and shield. She was worried about me, but I was fine. I worried about her because of my weight on top of her hitting the front. I thought she was hurt. She said she was fine, so we righted the machine and rode off. That was the only close call we had.

I remember while I was there I got my driving permit. Sharol let me drive, but Ralph never did. He didn't want me to take the driver's test with the Dodge Ram they had. I took my driver's test in Sharol's friend's car. Later, my dad gave me our old 1960 station wagon. Sharol and I took my car to Foston, Minnesota, I believe. We had a bad snowstorm on the way back. It was a white out, and I was driving. She didn't panic and just told me to pull over. It was hard when I could not see anything. When we pulled over and stopped, we waited for a while. When it all cleared, we saw a car about one inch in front of the car that was stopped. That was close. I was so glad she was with me. I could have panicked and hurt someone.

Sharol and I did a lot together, and she would include me with their friends. They were young adults and would have house parties. I would hang out, and as long as I stayed home, they would let me have a beer or two after I watched the kids and got them into bed. I always followed the rules and loved being a part of the friend group. Most of Sharol's friends were friendly and accepting of me. They were curious about my life but were understanding. We would sing and dance. It was a lot of fun.

I don't know how she knew when I had sex for the first time. She knew as soon as I got home. She was very concerned and made sure I was on the pill.

She knew the guy who I was dating was her age and went to school with her. I hated being on the pill. It made me sick, and I gained a lot of weight. I was basically a bitch, and I knew it. She didn't think I was pregnant because she knew weight gain was a possibility. Ralph accused me of being pregnant, and he was really hard on me. He was positive about it and was saying how hard it would be on me and them as a family taking care of me and a possible child. I was not pregnant because I was rarely sexually active after being on the pill. It really broke our relationship but not with Sharol. She trusted that I told her the truth. I was very lucky, and I did appreciate that she took care of me and did the right thing by taking me to doctors and planned parenthood.

Another memory I had is when I went to Iowa to visit my previous foster family. It was summer break, and Sharol and Ralph let me go for a few days. I don't remember why, but I called to ask to stay a bit longer, and Sharol felt like I wasn't coming back home. She voiced that to me, but I reassured her that I was coming back, but something came up, and Gloria and Mike wanted me for a weekend longer. I did come back, but I felt Sharol was afraid that I wouldn't. I hope she learned to trust me after that.

I felt accepted by family with Sharol and Ralph also by their families. I didn't have a family that was close after I was nine due to my parents' divorce and my mother being an only child. After we parted, I have never had a big family again, and I miss that.

When I did turn eighteen, I was adamant about being emancipated. It was granted, and I moved out before I graduated high school. I know that hurt Sharol's feelings. I was young and dumb, and I should have stayed. I felt that since I had lived on my own before and now that I was eighteen and legally an adult that I knew better as a young adult would feel. I did come back and visit even while in college until they moved away. They gave me a graduation gift that I still have and treasure. They knew I had bought things for when I was about to be on my own. The gift was a cedar chest that I could put all those things in. I did go off to college and visited. I also remember they paid for me to visit when they lived in Williston, North Dakota. After I had my daughter, I visited to have them meet my daughter in Wadena, Minnesota.

In conclusion, I was lucky to have a great foster home. I had love, attention, trust, and acceptance. I learned the family dynamic. I had everything I needed. Even though I was there for a short time, I learned a lot and took that forward in my life. I appreciate everything Sharol taught me, and I am grateful that she took me and other foster children into her life. She took a bad situation and changed it for the better for others like me.

I hope they appreciate her as well. She deserves it. She changed my life, and I am sure she continued that with other foster kids and the kids she encountered at the school she worked for twenty years plus. I love you, Sharol, and thank you.

Standard Release

I, Janet Krag-LeBlanc, give my permission to Sharol Mason to include my story or the use of likeness of the story in her book.

I represent and warrant that (i) I am the sole owner of the included intellectual property, and I release all proprietary rights to the material.

Signed:_____
Dated: November 15, 2022

Response to Janet

Robin was our first foster child. She was quite rebellious and ran away after a few months. Janet, our second foster child, moved in before she ran away, so they were foster sisters for a little while. They had to share a room, but they did okay with that. Janet was sixteen years old when she moved in in 1977 until her senior year in 1979. Joey was two and a half years old, and Amy was nine months old, and she and Janet share the same birthday. Janet loved her own room once Robin moved out. She did have a sister in Pendleton, Oregon, that was nine and a half years older than her. She could have moved there, but she would have to go through juvenile court for four to six months. She opted not to do that, and we were glad she did.

Her mother had abandoned her. She pretty much lived in a trailer by herself while Mom was at her boyfriend's house. Her mother drank quite a bit. Janet's dad lived in Detroit Lakes.

She love snowmobiling and going to the Vikings game and the Twins games with Ralph and me and with a few others that we stayed with. We would go to Orville and Susie's in Winona, and whoever wanted to go to the games would go. One cool memory I was reminded of was when Janet was just going to be turning eighteen but wasn't quite there. Ralph and Oroville went to the game They had signed up for a drawing for a purple logo Viking van. Wouldn't you know it, Janet won it, but due to her young age, Ralph would have to sign for her as her guardian. Due to her age and being a girl, he opted not to do that. I'm sure the tax and license and the paperwork had a lot to do with it. I wasn't there and learned about it later. I still don't understand why he didn't just take it and sign, and we could have given it to her when she turned eighteen. I don't know what he was thinking. Needless to say, Janet was never as mad as that day at Ralph. It took her many weeks to forgive him. If she has I'm not sure.

Janet, I loved hearing how you felt living with Ralph and me. You were just a typical teenager. We truly had a bond as a family and are so thankful for you being so willing to accept our little kids and chaos.

I do agree our best times we're camping, swimming, and snowmobiling. Also just family time. You just fit into it all. I am so glad we have kept in touch over the years and so proud of you as a mother and wife. You have become a very successful person even with all the obstacles in your young life. Believe me, not everyone turns out that way. I am so glad we are part of your life and hope in retirement we can get together and share more. With you being in another state, that will take some planning, but if there is a will, there's a way.

Love,
Your foster mom

Sweet, Sweet Sonja (Sonni)

In December of 2021, my foster mom, Sharol Mason, called me to let me know that my foster dad, Ralph McQuiston, was in the hospital in Wadena, Minnesota. He has cancer and only a couple days to live. His kids—Joey, Amy, and Ryan—are with him. Sharol said she would keep me updated on what is happening.

I left my house within twenty minutes of

that phone call. I live 190 miles from Wadena, Minnesota. It took me a little over three hours to get to the hospital. During my drive heading southeast, I was thinking of all the years and memories I have of Ralph and Sharol. I was so fortunate and blessed to meet this wonderful family so many years earlier.

Before I met my foster parents, Ralph and Sharol, I had what most would call and consider a normal life as a kid. I had a mom, a dad, four sisters, and three brothers. My mom passed away when I was twelve years old. She was a very sweet and loving mom. My father, in April of 1978, decided he didn't want us anymore. My older brother and sister were old enough to be on their own. My triplet sisters and I were now fourteen years old. My younger twin siblings were twelve years old, and our youngest brother was nine. We became ward of the state of Minnesota. Us triplets went to a home together, and the younger siblings went to another home. These were all temporary homes. We lived with this family from April until July 1978. At this time my uncle Loren and aunt Maggie went through the process where they were able to have us girls (triplets) come live with them. We were so excited to be with family again. We thought this would be a permanent home for us three girls.

Well, in February, seven months later, my aunt decided she did not want all three of us and only wanted one of us, and it wasn't me. So that February is when I met Sharol and Ralph McQuiston. The first time I met this couple and their two children was a Saturday afternoon. I went to visit for a few hours. The second time they had asked the social worker if I could spend a weekend to see if this transition would be a good fit for them and myself. The weekend went great, and after that they asked the worker if I could come live with them. The social worker brought me back to live with them.

Third is the charm!

This was my third home in nine months. I was fifteen years old now, and I really missed my triplet sisters. I had never really spent anytime away from them, and neither had they. We had shared the same bedroom and home until I had to move.

As I moved on, living with Sharol and Ralph, it didn't take me long to trust Sharol. That first day I will never forget where Sharol was standing in the kitchen, the smile, and sort of a giggle when she said, "Welcome, come on in." She still does that to this day. At the time she was doing daycare, and she introduced me to all her little kiddos she was taking care of. I learned real fast she was great with kids of all ages. She made time for all.

This past year, I have thought of this Bible verse many, many times. I think it fits with how I feel my foster mom has probably been her entire life.

Each of you should used whatever gift you have received to serve others.

—1 Peter 4:10

This verse means we need to use the things we do well to bless those around us.

I remember being in such a survival mode when I first moved in with them. But because of the way these two were, each in their special ways as parents and role models, I soon was able to feel part of a family again and be a normal teenage kid. Both Ralph and Sharol worked hard in different ways to care for not just their children but other people's children too. They both did this so well it was amazing to me. Ralph was only twenty-seven, and Sharol was twenty-four years old.

That first night before I went to bed, Sharol said to me, "I understand you are scared, and you miss your siblings especially your triplet sisters." She told me she had brothers and sisters and that I would get to meet them soon. She also said she was looking forward and couldn't wait to meet mine: I remember that I lay in bed that night thinking, "Well, maybe I will live here for awhile!"

We did many things as a family, like camping, family trips, and they included me on every family adventure. Joey was four years old. Amy was two years old, and Ryan was not yet conceived. He was born on April 24, 1980. They let me be the big sister to these three kids. They also let my sisters visit whenever, and so we got time together either at my house or theirs. We even had a few birthdays celebrated together.

In later years, Ralph even walked me down the aisle at my wedding, and Sharol did what every mom would do at her daughter's wedding. Oh, and yes, she cried too! I will never forget that time in my life. I am so grateful to have met and lived a part of my life with such a wonderful and giving family.

When I am asked how many siblings I have, I always say I have five sisters and five brothers. This is because even though I was only with them a few years, I became part of their family that February in 1979 and have remained in one another's lives by choice ever since.

I lived in many more homes after Sharol and Ralph had to move due to Arctic shutting down and both needing jobs. They moved to Williston, North

Dakota, for three years and then back to Wadena, Minnesota, where they still continued to be in my life. After I became an adult, I learned through time that Ralph and Sharol both had hard childhoods. I also never did find another home as wonderful as I did in Sharol and Ralph's family. Even though it was physically only a few years, I truly believe God's grace brought me to this home.

This was one hard goodbye. When I got to the hospital, Ralph was in bad shape. I sat with him all night long. I tried hard to help him feel comfortable. I sat there for hours thanking him for all he had done for me. He had made me feel safe. I told him how I remembered the fun things, like riding the wet bike, snowmobiling, and teaching me to drive. Oh, and I didn't forget that he showed me how to change oil on his brown Ford Bronco. Whether he could hear me or not, I shared a lot of special memories we had made through the years. I stayed two evenings with him and spent time with Joey, Amy, and Ryan at this difficult time.

After I left the hospital, I went to see my foster mom, Sharol, and she brought me lunch. and we talked for a long time. The next day, I drove back home, knowing this would be the last time I would see this man, who didn't have to care for another child but did. He shared his knowledge and home with so many children. On my way home, I continued to remember all forty-four years we had shared together. Ralph passed away on Tuesday, and I talked at his funeral about his caring nature.

Do nothing out of selfish ambition or vain conceit. Rather, in humility, value others above yourselves, not looking to your own interests but each of you to the interests of others.

—Philippians 2:3–4

I have told Sharol many times that she made such a huge difference in my life. I will never forget her kindness, patience, especially that first day I came into her life. I want to thank her for always looking at me with love and respect and for supporting me in many decisions along my life path.

I do read my Bible every night, which helps me journal about my life and keep things in perspective. I guess it helps me stay positive and loving with all the negativity that surrounds me at times. I don't know why it took Ralph's passing to realize that life is passing us by so quickly. Maybe this happens a lot to people in this way. I do know where my heart is, and nothing will ever change that. I love you and want to thank you one last time for opening my heart to all the great memories we've shared with hopefully lots more to come.

Looking back on all that has happened in my life, I do know without a doubt that God's plan for me, my foster parents Ralph and Sharol, Joey, Amy, Ryan, and all their families will always be my chosen family. I am so grateful to share and be a part of this wonderful family past, present, and forever.

My favorite Bible verses:

God brings good out of bad and we know that God causes all things to work together for good to those who love God, to those who are called according to his purpose.

—Romans 8:28

TAKE HEART MY DAUGHTER, YOUR FAITH HAS MADE YOU WELL.

—Matthew 9:22

Response to Sonni

Wow, I loved reading your memories and am very moved by how you felt we influenced your life. While in the moment doing foster care, I never thought about that, so it was good to hear. I do regret that you couldn't move with us to North Dakota. We did try and even went to the court judge, but he said, "The law is the law." There is no out-of-state exceptions. I have always felt it wasn't fair as you were so settled with us. I feel at the time I just followed my heart and just knew it was a calling. You were such an easy teenager compared to a few others we had. I do recall the first few days and weeks and knew you would be a part of our lives almost right away. It was so much fun when your sisters would come as it always boosted your spirit.

I also remember you as a hard worker and always willing to help out. You would babysit or help me with the kids on outings. When Ralph would be on night shift, you were great company. We sure did make some good memories snowmobiling, camping, wet-biking, going to parks, etc. You were a lot of help with the daycare also.

I am so glad over the years we have kept our bond going. It was so obvious when you spoke at Ralph's funeral and are keeping in touch with Joey, Amy, and Ryan all this time. I am so proud of who you have become and done so well with your own family. You sure got a sweet husband, and I am so glad about that. You have been there for your son and granddaughter through thick and thin. Someday you will see the rewards.

Keep on reading the Bible and pray for the ones who need that.

Love,
Your foster mom, Sharol

We took in more than a hundred children throughout our forty years doing care!

CHAPTER 47

Life Continues

June 1, 2022

A new start to another summer. It just doesn't seem like it because the temperature for the last eight months has been below average. We are still doing the wood stove to take the chill out of the house each morning. I sure hope the summer is warm for three months like it should be.

Rick has a heart procedure this coming week in St. Cloud Hospital. I am getting good at finding my way around there. He has had three other surgeries these past few months. Hopefully we're done with all this after this week. Four surgeries is enough along with E. coli infection stay.

I had a retirement party on Monday to go to. One of our gals from WDC school. It was so fun to see old coworkers and friends. Always a fun time.

Rick and I are heading to St. Cloud today for his heart implant. We got there by 8:15 a.m. and got checked in by 8:30 a.m. at the heart and vascular part of St. Cloud Hospital. It's quite the procedure in that it's amazing what our medical world can do. They showed us on a toylike heart model. The surgeon will go up through the vessel in his groin with a catheter. He will maneuver up till he comes to the heart. The camera down his esophagus guides the team to the left atrium, where an implant will be placed. We couldn't figure out how they got the implant to that point. Well, it is on the end of the catheter.

They showed us how they just push the end, and out it pops on the other end. It was so cool. I don't always write about Rick's adventures, but they always seem to affect us both. Well, all was going well, and we were just waiting as we were the third surgery this morning. The doctor came in and informed us he had got called to an emergency heart procedure to save the guy's life, and he was running two or so hours behind. We were glad he can save that life and just waited our turn. Finally he went in, and his heart team had said it would be about two hours.

I was so surprised when I got a call from his doctor on my cell phone a half hour into surgery. My heart fell to my knees, but he said, "Don't panic, everything's okay, but Rick's gag reflexes won't allow the camera down his throat. We will need to put him out completely."

I said, "Of course," and so they did. It was two hours later he got to recovery and woke up great but with a very sore throat from several tries. He doesn't remember any of it, which is so good. So the Watchman implant is in place and now needs to heal the tissue all around it. It takes up to six months for complete healing. Along that time line, he will have a lot of follow-ups with EKG, echocardiograms, and monitors to be sure there's no fluid or leaking. Generally there is no complications, but they need to keep watch on it. We are so thankful to the medical staff and God for all the successful surgeries they have done. He will spend one night in the hospital and go home tomorrow. He had a very restless night but managed okay. In the morning, I got up to the hospital around 8:30 a.m. as that's when they open for visitors. I stayed at my brother-in-law's, Maury, and Evy's house. I love my B&B there. He is doing so good even though he misses Evy like crazy, just like the rest of us.

He took me to her grave site, and we went out for ice cream. She has a beautiful headstone.

When I got to the hospital, he was kinda sleepy but woke up pretty good when they said he could go home. We didn't get out of there until noonish. We stopped at Perkins in Little Falls to eat lunch. Then on the road again.

My daughter Amy and Jon were coming to our house to

stay for the weekend. We have a graduation party for River (my grandson) this Saturday in Wadena. He is the last one to graduate from Joey and Kim's clan of seven kids. It's always a good time with the McQuiston relatives. Amy and Jon got to our place before we got home, but they unpacked and went to help set up the graduation party in town. Then we all went out for burgers at Little Round Still in town.

Rick settled in at home and was glad to have his own bed.

Saturday we all went to River's graduation party. We sat outside in seventy-five-degree weather and had great food and conversation. Got to catch up with all the relatives. Rick went with for a few hours but went home when he had had enough. I will catch a ride home with Amy and Jon later.

When I got home, I threw together some ice cream caramel rolls for breakfast. Amy and I visited awhile, but we all went to bed by 11:00 p.m. Got up in the morning, had eggs and rolls, and they took off for Wisconsin.

They have about five hours or more if they stop, etc. What a fun weekend. Tena and Ryan and the kids were at the party too, so I got to see all my kids together again.

It's Monday now, and I have PT again. It seems to be helping as my back is a lot better. Still not much lifting though. My therapist is great, and I have exercises to strengthen each day. This Wednesday I have her again but at 7:00 a.m. instead of 12:30 p.m. I like the early time, and today I went out for breakfast at 8:00 a.m. with an old friend. We went to the Boondocks Café. It was so good, and we got caught up too. Then at 10:00 a.m., I headed for Brainerd as my car has recalls on the headlight and hood latch. Long story short, that took longer than expected, but I went to McDonald's next door and had a Diet Pepsi, went for a walk, and kept checking back with them. It took two hours instead of a half hour as I was told. It's a good thing I have a lot of patience. I got back home after stopping at Aldie's to pick up a few things. Rick needed some medications, so I turned around and went to Wadena to pick them up. Of course, there's a big line at the pharmacy, so I decided I might as well get my second shingles shot while I'm waiting. So I got that, picked up the prescription, and got home again. What a day, and I thought retirement would be boring. Haha.

Well, I woke up Thursday, and I definitely had a reaction to the shot. I felt sick until Friday. I had a terrible headache, nausea, and just wanted to sleep. I was fine when I woke up Friday. Thank goodness.

So today I went out to Joey and Kim's camping place by Nimrod. I was checking out to see if they had bathrooms. Yes, they have an outdoor porta potty. They are having a gathering all weekend for their kids and any relatives that want to come. They plan on canoeing, kayaking, tubing, hiking, and swimming. Their site is one mile from the Crow Wing River. They have four-wheelers side by side and go to and from, or we can walk. Rick and I plan on going to spend time Saturday and have potluck supper with them. I will bring brownies for dessert. Wayne and Carrie will be there, and he is making mango and pineapple chicken wings in a great big smoker. He is one of my kids from way back. He grew up with my kids for some years. He is such a blessing to all of us. Rick and I ended up there for four or five hours. We went for a walk, had a great supper, and visited around the campfire. Just like old times.

They had the "Welcome to the Jungle" sign displayed.

Sunday we really got a warm spell. It is over one hundred degrees and going to be hot for a week or so. I went to church, and it was such a nice time. The sermon was praising our dads as it's Father's Day. The guys got a free tool and jar of peanuts. Then Rick and I decided to run to Amber and Vernon's and see how they're doing. They were gone again to the fair in Motley, Minnesota. When we went through Verndale, we saw there was a car show. So we took Buddy the dog home as he had gone for a ride with us, and then we went to the car show. It was so cool to see all those old cars from 1926 to the eighties!

We ate there as they had hamburgers and hot dog meals on the grill. Nice to not have to cook on such a hot day. We stayed out of the sun as much as we could. There was a nice wind also, which helped. It was nice to get home in our air-conditioning.

We are making brats on the grill for supper. I'm still not sure when to stop writing to end this book. I feel I will know when the time comes. I want the past, present, and future to somehow come together. A lot of my experiences throughout my journey are the same and repetitive, but toward the end, it's been easier to put a lot more detail day to day.

This week is the end of June 2022. Rick and I went to an open house for Isaiah and Tasha. They bought their first home and thirty of us went to have tacos and salads to welcome them in their new home. I saw my kids and had a great time.

I had gone to the Wadena fair and met up with Norma and others in our senior citizens group. We had a free meal and a live band to listen to. It was really nice. They played a lot of Johnny Cash and other oldies.

On Monday, the twenty-seventh, I met Tim and Donna, my brother and his wife, at four corners. It's over by Deer Creek, Minnesota, and I had gone for breakfast with my breakfast club in Henning, and I picked them up and drove all of us to Detroit Lakes, Minnesota, to see Alice and Theresa, our sisters. They live at Union Central in apartments of their own. It's senior apartments, and they are so nice and affordable. They have each other to do daily things together. We visited a while and got pictures of all of us. Then we went to the 59er restaurant for lunch. Of course, we had to check out the thrift stores and found some treasures.

Then we stopped for waffle ice cream cones on a patio

with more conversations. It was such a great day. The only thing that would have made it better would be if Audrey, Evelyn, and Ted could have been there. I'm sure they were watching from above.

Tuesday, Rick had some drainage from his stitches, so we went to Staples and took care of that. He's on an antibiotic, and the doctor removed the stitches.

Wednesday, we went to St. Cloud for a post-op from his UroLift, and all looked good. His urologist put him on a high dose of potassium for kidney stones. Maybe that will help with that issue or maybe even prevent stones?

We met Maury and Jackie at Perkins for coffee break after as his clinic is right by Perkins. So that's where I wait for Rick until he joins us. Then we stopped at KFC for the chicken buffet, but they don't do it anymore. So we went to Little Falls, Minnesota, and had a nice lunch. It's so fun to have those times together.

Rick has several more appointments this summer but all just follow-ups.

He is definitely on the mend.

I will end my book now as I had a dream about getting it published last night; that's my cue!

This summer will be pretty much like all the others. We mow our two acres every week. I do half, and he does the other half as we take turns on our zero-turn mower.

Our garden is beautiful again as we try to keep up with the weeds. Flower beds are in full bloom. We both love summer and will continue enjoying our reunions, camping, and farm shows. It's Fourth of July. Let's celebrate!

AFTERWORD

Well, this is bittersweet. I will update the COVID situation one last time. The cases have gone dramatically down. We had a cousin get it this week, but it's not much worse than a bad cold. My neighbor also has it this week. She is doing okay too. She went in right away with her symptoms, and they can administer an antiviral medication now. It helps ease the symptoms and with that rarely hospitalizations. It's called Paxlovid. I'm so glad that after two and a half years of this pandemic, we are turning the corner to eradicate it. It has really helped since most are getting immunized with the vaccine, social-distancing, staying home when sick, and using masks in high-risk areas. This virus has impacted all of us. It may be that people we know died. The fact we had to abide by rules and regulations with quarantines in place in homes, schools, hospitals, travel, churches, and many social situations. This may not be over, but it is now under control. I feel so bad for all the lives that were lost to such a devastating virus. I am thankful for having the time to concentrate on writing this book during this time. I don't know if I would have ever really finished without being grounded because of COVID-19.

I want to also thank my friends and family for supporting me in my endeavor and also to my brothers and sisters that filled in those years when we were separated as children. You all filled in the gaps that I feel my life was missing. Thanks to Rick, my patient husband, for giving me the space when I needed it to write from my heart and put my thoughts together without complaining. Thank you, Jackie, for offering to help type my rough copy. You have no idea how much it meant and the time it saved me.

This is one of our last pictures before Mom, Audrey, Evelyn, and Ted passed away

In conclusion, I still have a lot on our bucket list. Rick and I want to go to Europe and visit our foreign exchange students we had. We also want to go to Tennessee and Alaska again and take a riverboat cruise down the Mississippi River. We plan on many more bus trips, and who knows, maybe my next book will cover my next thirty years of travel and adventures.

This book to me has been so much fun to put my life in perspective. I never dreamed of anything other than what was dealt to me. I have always felt a positive vibe and would not change a thing. I always say, "If you love yourself, you can love everyone."

My hope is all who read this can take something from it and apply it to have a positive, loving life.

Until we meet again.

The End

SURVIVING LIFE AND
COVID-19

ABOUT THE AUTHOR

My name is Sharol Anne Curfman. When I married Ralph, my first husband, I became Sharol Anne McQuiston. Now I am Sharol Anne Mason as I married Rick, my second husband. My nickname throughout the years is S.A.M. when I was a waitress and signing paintings I created. Luckily my initials were the same in either case.

Rick and I live in rural Verndale, Minnesota, with a population of only 501 people.

I am 69 years old, retired from W.D.C. school as a certified paraprofessional of 34 years. In addition, I was licensed as a foster parent, respite provider, and a CNA.

In 2002, I needed to continue education which consisted of nine competencies and over one and half years of learning. Along with that I needed continuing education for the state for licensing requirements which included many days and hours of conferences and workshops. This led me to be quite knowledgeable in areas of ADHD, OC.D., F.A.S., autism, physical, mental, and emotional abuse and neglect.

In addition, I was trained in crisis prevention intervention, vulnerable adults, suicide, C.P.R., first aid, and medication dispensing. W.D.C. also required program, and workshop attendance for Title I, behaviors, and handicapped equipment knowledge. This was all so important to do my best in all my jobs over the years.

My hobbies include reading, writing, scrapbooking, diamond art, sewing, puzzles, and daily walks.

Lastly, my goals in the future are to travel, be kind and helpful and keep family and friends close to my heart each and every day.

SURVIVING LIFE AND
C VID-19